not

a

poster

child

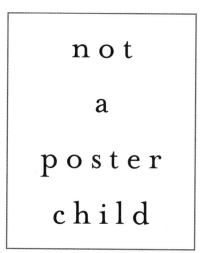

not

a

poster

child

living well with a disability

A Memoir

FRANCINE FALK-ALLEN

SWP

SHE WRITES PRESS

Published 2018
Printed in the United States of America
ISBN: 978-1-63152-391-5 pbk
ISBN: 978-1-63152-392-2 ebk
Library of Congress Control Number: 2018936550

Book design by Stacey Aaronson

For information, address:
She Writes Press
1563 Solano Ave #546
Berkeley, CA 94707

She Writes Press is a division of SparkPoint Studio, LLC.

For Richard

Table of Contents

introduction

*M*y life as a handicapped person has been in many ways a normal life, filled with the great joys, great sorrows, and the commonplace or mediocrity that all people enjoy or endure.

My purpose in writing this memoir is to convey what it is like to live a full life while handicapped with a paralyzed, short, atrophied foot and leg, and to get all my early memories of polio treatment written down before I begin to forget them. It takes guts to be handicapped. People will say unkind things. There will often be more that we cannot do than that which we can. I've spent a lifetime striving and struggling to be normal. We need folks to be patient while we adapt; independence is our fond desire but is sometimes unattainable. There are, however, solutions, and myriad ways to have a good time.

It is my deepest intention that this book will honor and represent millions of physically handicapped people. I realize that many have been far more physically limited than I, and do not mean to flaunt the ability I do have, or to convey a tone of self-pity. I also know that there are some with more severe limitations who have strived and accomplished far more than I did, whether in public service or in their personal lives. I am in awe of those folks. I have done as much as I could without exhausting my little body (and often have more than exhausted myself). I sometimes feel I should have been more focused. As Lily Tomlin said in her performance of Jane Wagner's *The Search for Signs of Intelligent Life in the Universe*, "I always wanted to be somebody. Now I see I should have been more specific."

The reality is, I was crippled by a merciless virus as a small child, and it changed what might have been. My choices and personality have been driven and created by awareness of my acute physical limitations as much as by what I desired. People have often—though not always—treated me differently than fully able people as a result of my disability; that's just how it is. My story is defined by those parameters.

It is impossible to write a memoir or reflection upon personal difficulty without thinking about oneself a great deal. Over the course of these six years of writing, I have had to take occasional breaks to avoid feeling too self-centered. I hope that whatever humor and sense of the absurd you may find here may make the writing tolerable if I have not succeeded in avoiding narcissism. Lots of people will find my stories "not funny," but if you are a fan of Monty Python, I ask you to remember the irony of the song, "Always Look on the Bright Side of Life"—sung while Brian was being crucified—as you read on.

For anyone whose life has been changed dramatically by disease, birth defects, war, injury, or aging, I salute your bravery and commitment to finding ability, meaning, and joy in your life despite your daunting challenges. This book is written for you and me, and with gratitude to the amazing rehabilitation people who have given us the gift of function.

Although everything in this book is true, some conversations are not verbatim, and a few names have been changed to protect privacy.

not a

poster

child

Francine, Easter, 1950, age 2 1/2

when I was a normie

*I*t's my birthday, and I'm three years old today! I'm running down the sidewalk on our street, West 109th, in our middle-class neighborhood in Los Angeles, near the edge of Gramercy Park. A northern leg of Westmont—later to become owned entirely by black and Hispanic folks. But today it's a very Anglo place to live, and kids are coming over to our house for my party.

In early December 1950, it's a little warm out in southern California. I'm wearing a full, very short, ruffled chiffon dress my mother made, and a round, flat, gathered paper hat set at a jaunty angle on my head. Mama is a remarkable seamstress, and her sister, my Aunt Marie, used to sew professionally, as a member of the garment workers' union.

I cannot tell you, sixty-some years later, why I am running, or why I'm out on the sidewalk without an adult. Possibly I escaped . . . something I will spend much of my life doing, until I hit forty or so. Maybe I'm running with a big birthday present I was excited to receive; I remember a box with a fat, overstuffed doll in it that I decided to call Ollie Dolly after the children's TV puppet show, *Kukla, Fran and Ollie*. Or maybe I'm just gleeful that it's my birthday. My mother will later tell me that when I was even smaller, I would steal cut lemons from the bottom of the fridge and scoot away in my Taylor Tot stroller, refusing to give up the lemon, although when I sucked on it, I puckered my entire face.

That day, high-tailing it down the sidewalk, is the last recollection I have of ever running, and I never want to forget it, which is part of why I am telling you my story now.

⤶

When I was perhaps in my thirties I told my mother about another early childhood memory: I was out in the backyard, alone, and eating a somewhat fresh banana skin out of the garbage can. I might have been quite hungry, but maybe I was just snacking or curious. Planes flew low overhead and scared me. I ran and hid under the stairs, stairs that were too steep and high for me to climb and get into the house. I put my hands over my ears. I was crying and afraid.

Decades later, Mom looked at me in disbelief as I recounted this story. "You were only two years old then!" she exclaimed, then turned to stare out the window and watch the smoke from her cigarette waft around her kitchen. We both took in the thought that she had left me down a long flight of stairs alone at two, expecting me to play in the backyard, and instead I ended up eating banana skins out of the stinky garbage can.

Throughout my childhood, Mother would proudly say, "You played so well by yourself as a toddler, you always did." When I shared with her the memory about the planes going over and being alone down in the back yard, I could tell she was stunned by the knowledge that I could remember back so far, and I suspect she wondered what else I could recall. I said nothing.

"We lived near the airport," she eventually continued, "and the planes flew low over our house when they took off."

My dad was a milkman, with his own small business, and my mother didn't work. We were renters. The people across the street, the Murrays, might have been owners. They had two little boys I played with all the time.

We dropped this adult conversation, but it was a moment of revelation for us both—for me, confirming a certain sense of distance my mother always conveyed. My mind had raced after hearing her response: *How could you leave a two-year-old alone in a backyard?* I wondered. *How could you let a toddler eat out of a garbage can? Is this what it meant to "play well by myself"? Did you know I was down there crying and afraid? Did you come down and get me?*

I didn't want to ask these questions of her.

～

At my third birthday party, there is a fantastic big black papier-mâché spider with black pipe cleaner legs that Mama made as a centerpiece for our large, dark, heavily ornate dining room table. The spider scares me, though it is comical; even in my shortness and inexperience, however, I can appreciate the ability it took to make it.

Accompanying the spider is a storybook doll we all know is Little Miss Muffet, my nickname. My parents started calling me "Miss Muffet" affectionately when I was a month old, and everyone will call me that or "Muffet" for all of my childhood, except at school. Eventually I will see the irony in my fear of real spiders, though my parents thought only to call me something cute.

The spider and the nursery rhyme theme are a hit with all, especially the mothers. Mama receives all the compliments graciously, tilting her head to one side; how wonderful that she's made something so amazing for her little girl. I don't think she realizes how frightening the spider is to me, and even if she did, she would only laugh and tell me it's not real.

This is the last hurrah before the virus comes. This is the

last day I can remember being a "normie," which is what the "crip" community, a handicapped veteran will tell me some forty years later, calls non-disabled people. It's a kind and affectionate way to say "fully abled, innocently unaware of the stuff we experience" and leave out the envy, regret, or wistfulness we might feel.

Mother, 1948, a few months after my birth

Me in the middle of neighbor kids, Los Angeles, 1950

2
—

taken from home

A few weeks after my third birthday, in early January of 1951, I was sick. My feet hurt. I was in my crib—I still slept in a crib, probably to keep me in bed when I should be—and on my knees, crying in the night, calling out over the crib bar, "Mommy, my shoes hurt!"

I recall sleeping in my shoes. My mother later said I never did, which perplexes me, though she is the one who told me (when I was in grammar school) that I did say these words, "My shoes hurt!" I'm guessing that my feet felt like I was wearing shoes that fit too tight. I knew the word "shoes" and I also knew the word "feet," so I must have been saying what I believed to be true. Perhaps I was delirious; I did run a temperature of 101 degrees for a week. After that, though, I appeared to be back to normal.

I was across the street at the Murrays' house in this same week, before or after the shoes incident, and I wouldn't play with the two little brothers, Stephen and Jeff. This was strange, as I was never lethargic; in fact, I was the kind of kid on whom you might have seen a harness. Mama hated napping with me because I wouldn't hold still.

Mrs. Murray called Mama on the phone: "Frances, Francine won't get up off the floor." Someone carried me home; Daddy always got home mid-afternoon, and Mama was a small woman with lower back problems who was unlikely to have picked me up at age three. It couldn't have been my teenage brother, Gene, because he was in a sanitarium with tuberculosis. Perhaps Mrs. Murray carried me.

⌣

I have a favorite photo of myself just prior to this: Six neighbor kids lined up against a wall in what looks to be a driveway, looking like The Little Rascals, the mischievous children of the popular 1940s short films, which I later watched almost daily when we got a television. One of the Murray boys—the older one, Stephen—is in the photo, blond and a foot taller than me. I'm guessing I had a crush on both him and his brother . . . I loved my daddy, and I loved boys, too.

In the photo, I'm in the middle of the group, and I've got jingle bells on my high-top toddlers' shoes (Mama tied them on so she would know where I was in the house, since I was inclined to get into stuff at every opportunity). My short dress adds to the "Little Rascals" image—I look a little like Darla from that series. I also look like I'm not sure there's enough room for me; someone, probably my dad, told us to stand close together so he could get us all in the Brownie viewfinder, and I'm looking up with my eyes and eyebrows, as if to say, "Am I doing this right?"

I knew the importance of being good and doing what adults said to do. I love how this picture shows the seriousness with which I took instructions, even at two and a half.

⌣

Because I wouldn't get up and play at the Murrays,' and because I cried in the night and said my shoes hurt, and I had been recently running a fever, I was taken to see Dr. Blackman, who delivered me in 1947 at Queen of the Angels Hospital in Los Angeles. I don't recall ever playing with the Murray kids again, though my mother did keep in touch with Mrs. Murray for many years.

In 1951, there'd been a polio threat for decades. Years later my mother told me, "They had the vaccine then, you had to ask for it from your doctor, but people were getting polio from the vaccine in those days, so many people, including us, did not get vaccinated."

This is not at all accurate, I learned when I was in my fifties, though I now understand why she might have gotten the time frame and facts mixed up. One batch of the vaccine made by Cutter Laboratories in April of 1955, four years after I came down with polio and a year after the first public trials, did cause some incidence of infection: 204 people contracted the disease, most of them experiencing paralysis, and 11 of them died. Normally, an incidence of one in 700,000 people would be expected from the inactivated virus vaccine, and those cases were sometimes found to be from exposure prior to vaccination. Theories proliferated as to the cause, but one thing was certain: some of the vials of vaccine at Cutter had contained live virus. This was probably because the virus was kept in storage too long, clumped, and the formaldehyde (which kills the live virus and keeps it inactive, allowing the recipient to create antibodies without getting the virus) could not penetrate these "clumps." Dr. Jonas Salk, the researcher who was the first to get the polio vaccine into trials and initiate the inoculation program that became instrumental in stopping the epidemic, later said that this period of infamy for the vaccine was the one time in his life when he felt suicidal.

After this debacle, the protocol for storage was vastly improved. More testing was required before the vaccine was released, and stricter tracking of the location of all vaccines was mandated by the government. (Though I do not love all aspects of government, here is one small but powerful instance of how useful record keeping can be when it is standardized across all states.)

By 1961, the rate of polio had dropped by 96 percent. The last known new case of it in the US occurred in 1999.

⌒

My mother had a way of distilling information into its most simplistic form and was a fearful person in general. As a child, though, I believed everything she told me. Now, having known her much better, I wonder if her line about fearing the vaccines was not an excuse—her feeling guilty that she and Daddy never asked our doctor about vaccinations, and then creating an explanation for her inquisitive daughter. Vaccines were not available when I contracted polio; they were not made public in the massive trial inoculation campaign until 1954. But it's most likely that she didn't remember the sequence of events, and when I asked about polio as a young child, she simply needed to tell me something about why I got it.

In all the time I lived with my mother, I recall her going to the doctor perhaps once. She either feared information or felt it was too expensive to go unless there was a dire circumstance—and the latter was certainly true. Economically, we lived a simple, slightly-below-middle-class life. I was taken to the doctor, later in my life, with strep throat and occasional other complaints, but never to the dentist; I was afraid of the potential pain and I think that my mother didn't want to deal with my protests, or the expense. When I was sixteen, my close friend's older male cousin commented discreetly to her that I would be pretty if I got those decayed front teeth fixed. After she told me this, I went to my mother and asked her to make an appointment with a dentist for me. I had one or two teeth removed and several filled, including the four front ones, with white enamel. I had been oblivious to this need.

Although I do not clearly remember my entire battery of polio symptoms at age three, what is typical with both paralytic and non-paralytic types is an onset involving nausea, headache, sore throat, back and neck stiffness, and pain. There are generally changes in reflexes and an elevated spinal fluid cell count. Poliomyelitis virus lives in the intestines and throat, but the usual gastrointestinal flu symptoms of bowel difficulties do not seem to be present. With paralytic polio, there is also weakness in one or more muscle groups. Spinal polio involves the trunk or extremities, more often the legs, and this is the type I had. The people who had bulbospinal polio are those who had acute respiratory difficulty and were put in iron lungs. (There were perhaps one or two dozen operative iron lungs still in the US in 2014, indicative of how few people were left sharing that equipment, surviving with this more life-threatening form of polio. Most polio patients with breathing difficulties, which can also begin to surface late in life, now use wheeled ventilators.)

There were so many backward attitudes about disease in the fifties. If someone had cancer, my mother spoke about it in hushed tones, almost as if it were the patient's fault. Polio had so many stigmas attached to it. Accounts I've read describe almost paranoiac thinking similar to that surrounding AIDS in the 1980s: You got it from the air, you got it from touching someone who didn't wash, you got it from associating with the wrong class of people, people who lived in filthy conditions and spat on the sidewalk. You got it from swimming pools. Throughout my life people have said to me, after asking me why I limped and hearing I'd had polio, "You got it from swimming pools. You must have gone in swimming pools." I never went in a swimming pool before I was at least nine. My mother didn't swim. Besides that, swimming pools are highly chlorinated, generally, and it's unlikely the virus could live in those conditions. An unchlorinated pool or pond, if there had been any in an area subject to the epidemic, would have been unwise recreation but still would probably not have incubated the virus due to dilution.

The myth about pools likely started because a public pool was a venue where many people congregated in close proximity, especially children, somewhat similar to when you catch a cold at a children's party or in a movie theater full of people. Polio is also a disease that typically catches on during warm weather. Many public pools also closed when there was a local epidemic, adding to the concept that they were a polio breeding site.

Polio is spread through direct contact with an infected person's secretions, most often their saliva or feces. And an infected person may have no symptoms.

‿

My next memory of this early time is vivid: I was in a very small room in a hospital (probably Queen of the Angels), hardly bigger than a large closet, and it was all white and that sickening color of pastel green tile—or perhaps it just became unpalatable to me. My parents later unwittingly chose it for our new kitchen, so I had to live with it for years. A friend in college later described it as "landlord green," and we speculated that it was for some reason a cheap and easily obtained color.

In the tiny, quarantined hospital room, having so recently gaily celebrated my third birthday, I was alone, day after day. I cried a lot. I was scared and had no understanding of why I'd been taken there, away from my mama and daddy, other than that I hadn't felt well. I'd been sick before, but had always been allowed to remain at home. I was wildly afraid, filled with despair and a sense of stark abandonment.

They came to visit me. I could see the strain of worry on Mama's face, and Daddy's, too. Their eyebrows were pointing up in the middle and my mother looked like she might cry or recently had. They were both dressed in what looked like bed sheets that tied behind the neck. I couldn't see their hands or their arms.

I was so glad to see them.

"Where is your purse?" I asked Mama. She always carried a big black purse, stuffed with God knew what—I wasn't allowed ever to look through it.

"It's here," she said. "My purse is here under the hospital gown, that's what's sticking out." It made her look like a pregnant kangaroo in a sheet, but she couldn't show me the purse because she wasn't supposed to take her hands out.

I sat up, reached my arms out over the top of the crib, and cried out, "Mama!" but she didn't reach for me. "Pick me up!" I implored. "Take me home! I want to go home!"

When neither of them reached for me, I started to cry. Mama always held me on her lap, every morning, sometimes reading me a story or singing to me, and Daddy held me on his lap each afternoon after work, when he read the paper.

"We can't touch you right now," Mama said.

I sobbed; I didn't understand. It seemed so cruel, though I knew they were following the rules of the ghastly hospital with its horrible white walls and green tile.

I believe this was their only visit after my admission; it was too upsetting for all of us and they knew that quarantine would be temporary.

I didn't know that, however. When would it ever be over? As it turned out, never, not really. This was the beginning of a life of ups and downs, falls and triumphs—a life that would make me tougher in spirit than I ever wanted to be.

By the time my parents visited me that day, the doctors

had told them what I could not have understood: "Your daughter has poliomyelitis. She is experiencing paralysis in her right leg, which is why she cannot stand up. Mr. and Mrs. Allen, your daughter will never walk again. She will be in a wheelchair for the rest of her life. We have to keep her quarantined for a couple of weeks; even you cannot touch her, and then we'll be moving her to a polio treatment center when she is no longer contagious." No wonder my mother was trying to keep from crying.

But the doctors didn't know me, and they didn't know my mother, and they were not anticipating that sometimes people get lucky, even in perverse ways.

The hotel that was turned into a rehab facility where I lived for six months during polio treatment. I was in the former ballroom with the big arched windows. Mother occasionally took me down to the beach behind the building.
Credit: Kaiser Foundation

making the best of imprisonment

$\mathscr{A}$fter two weeks in the hospital, I was moved to Kabet-Kaiser Institute, a rehabilitation center on the beach in Santa Monica. I lived there from late January 1951 through July of that year, six months in all. I was in a huge, daylight-filled room, called a ward, with thirty or forty other children who had polio. There were no children in iron lungs in my ward, so perhaps the bulbar-type patients who had so much difficulty breathing needed to be in an actual hospital or were at least on a different floor from us. (The iron lungs took up a lot of space and were very noisy; also, these patients needed a great deal of monitoring, to make sure the machine was operating and also to note if the patient started breathing independently—a rare milestone and almost miraculous sign of recovery.)

On the weekends, I got to escape to the apartment my parents rented in Santa Monica "for the duration." It was so small compared to our previous two-bedroom home with its backyard, planes flying overhead, and neighbor playmates. But I looked forward to those weekends like a laborer working away from home, which was in fact exactly who I was.

Previously the rehab facility had been the Edgewater Beach Hotel, and then the private Ambassador Club. Henry Kaiser had bought the place after seeing how successful Dr. Herman Kabet's rehab treatment for multiple sclerosis was. (One report says it was Kaiser's son who had MS and another that it was Henry Kaiser himself.) Kabet and Kaiser formed a rehabilitation foundation in 1946 along with Dr. Sidney Garfield (a founding physician of Kaiser Permanente, the health insurance and care company), the primary center being in Vallejo, California.

In my ward, each child was in a white crib, high up off the floor, with the crib bars spaced six inches apart, and up nearly all the time so that no one could get out and wander about, assuming you could move. So, unless you were so bold as to get up on your knees and look over, hanging on to the top rail, which I did as often as I could, you viewed your world through bars. Many of the children could not sit up and we all spent a huge amount of time prone. There must have been about six to ten cribs to a row, about four feet between cribs, and four or more rows of them. There were lockers for our few belongings along the far wall opposite the windows looking out on the street. I don't remember ever being moved to another area or visiting the other side of the room; I was in the same crib in the same row facing the same wall for the entire six months.

I've since seen pictures taken inside this Santa Monica facility, but there are no pictures of the children's room or ward with its multiple beds and lack of privacy. The pictures I saw were clearly of the adult ward, where, although the beds were also close together, there were small closets behind the heads of the beds, which provided a partition (around five or six feet tall) between them and the next row over, plus a small but roomier space for belongings. Thus, the adults had a modicum of privacy. This may have been partly a result of there being fewer adults than children with the virus.

The arrangement of the children's ward should have afforded me the opportunity to sit up and chat with kids nearby, at least those who were able to sit, and not just lie there staring at the two-story hotel ceilings with their elegant dark wood coffers, but I don't have a single friend from that time in my life, though I keep in touch with friends I've known since before kindergarten. My mother maintained no contact with any parents she may have met there, either, though she had a vast Christmas card list and corresponded with old neighbors such as the Murrays. That time must have been lonely for her as well, though my father was home in the late afternoons and evenings, and many of her brothers and sisters lived in the Los Angeles area. I can only guess that occasionally she may have visited with her siblings and old friends. She was essentially a loner anyway. But this new life was not the same as our old one, when we'd had neighbors nearby. My sister, who was twenty-two then, remembers visiting me at Kabet-Kaiser at least once, but she's the only person other than Mama who came around. This is not surprising given the imagined fear of contagion, despite all of us kids at the facility being past the phase of acute illness.

Clearly there was no consideration regarding creating real relationships at the rehab center, even though we were there for months and shared a most intimate experience. My recollection brings back not a single face, only a large group of anonymous afflicted children. There was never any fanfare about departures: you came in, you stayed, you left. (Perhaps among older children more bonds were forged.)

The floors at the facility were dark wood or linoleum, and the walls were white. There were a lot of windows, big ones, along the east side of the ward, but I don't remember what we viewed outside them. The pictures I've seen of the old hotel confirm this, as well as the fact that the windows that let in all that light looked out on a street, though I was never close enough to the panes to see anything but sky. I think they opened wide and the hospital personnel didn't want us to get curious and fall out.

On the other side of the building, out of our view, lay the beach and the Pacific Ocean. I have seen in old photos that there were also windows on that side, but they must have been either for offices or for the adults' rooms.

Photos from the Kaiser archive also revealed a promo picture taken with a famous singer of that era, Howard Keel. Several nurses, some with grim faces and some putting a smile of sorts on the situation, and at least one doctor, pose in the hospital, away from the scene of multiple beds full of sick children. Almost all of the dozen or so children of different ages and stages of treatment included in the photo look depressed and unwell, some in wheelchairs, some with crutches, some standing with Kenny sticks, some in pajamas, and some—the tiny girls in the front—dressed up in the style of ruffled short dresses I wore in that era. Some are smiling stiffly, I imagine having been told to smile for the camera; the rest, it seems, just couldn't get up the energy for photo-op cheer.

I don't know if the photo was intended to promote the great success of the rehab program—and it was very good, the only hope for most of us—or to promote Keel's involvement with volunteer work. But if it was to convey that these kids needed financial and emotional support for their recovery, the mood of the tableau was effective: sick kids lined up to demonstrate the sad difficulties of polio. I'm not in the photo, but I looked just like those other little girls in the front row.

❧

Days were the same, same, same, week after week. For the nursing staff, this made life manageable; for the children, possibly the predictability felt safe, but I don't remember looking forward to much of anything but the weekends.

Every morning, after being carried or wheeled to long, low children's tables over toward the windows in our big room, we had either oatmeal, a fried egg over easy or sunny side up, or scrambled eggs. For lunch, we often had soup and/or cottage cheese with canned fruit. We were required to eat what they gave us, whether we liked it or not. The dinners were totally unmemorable; it's possible I only remember the foods I disliked or came to detest. I don't recall eating any other foods but the ones I've listed here, though surely there must have been some variety. This was at least a nutritional menu: muscles affected by polio get their best chance for function on a high-protein but balanced diet. Polio patients, like athletes, often place far more strain on muscles, and protein helps maintain strength.

It took me decades after leaving the hospital to be able to stomach oatmeal, fried eggs (particularly the yolk), or cottage cheese without gagging, and soup often seemed a punishment. (Now I love preparing a hearty soup from scratch in the autumn and winter.) I could never find the words to express these preferences to my mother, and she felt I should "learn to eat these foods"—she even said, "You ate this in the hospital all the time!"

When a child is taken away from her family and leads her own life for a time, there are experiences that cannot be fully described or understood, as is the case for a soldier who's gone away to war. And even if I'd been able to find the vocabulary for my young memories, I am quite sure they would have been met with a "Tch" and tight, irritated, downturned lips from my mother. After all, she had withstood being the eldest of twelve children in the early twentieth century, moved out to support herself at fourteen, and her first husband had left her for someone else (a woman he married and stayed with the rest of his life). It was never too early to learn to be strong, if not stoic.

Every day in the hospital we withstood an injection of prostigmine, a muscle relaxant, for the spasms common to polio. A shot. Every day. At three years old. For approximately 180 consecutive days. Every time, it hurt, and every time, it scared me, and every time, I hated it. Don't believe it when people tell you that you become indifferent to repeated painful experiences. I became permanently needle-averse, and I still have to look away when I get a shot, get blood work, or see an injection administered in a movie, taking an involuntary inhalation through my teeth. It is possible, maybe even probable, that all of us had muscle spasms from the polio. But as an adult I came to think that the muscle relaxant may have partly been used to keep us calm and quiet. With dozens of potentially rowdy children to a room, it must have been a handy management tool for the hospital staff. Regardless of the drug's purpose, it was a nasty thing for a three-year-old to look forward to each day. I don't remember putting up a fuss about it, but I'll bet I did.

Another daily ritual was that of hot, wet wool blankets placed on our bodies. This was probably for pain or spasms and also to stimulate circulation, which can come to a near halt in a polio-affected limb. My polio leg has always been quite cold-sensitive, and what feels like normal-to-cool room temperatures to the rest of my body feels somewhat chilly to that leg. It always turns purple with red blotches in the winter, unless I rub it almost incessantly.

The blankets, referred to as "hot packs," were much too hot for a child at the start, but would subside gradually to a tolerable temperature and then drop to useless coolness. I'd lie there for what seemed like forever, clammy and cold in the end, until the packs were eventually removed. The heaviness felt like an additional way to keep me subdued; certainly I couldn't move beneath the weight. The aroma was just weird. If you know the smell of a wet wool blanket left by the heater to dry, you'll know this unusual, slightly unpleasant scent. Whenever it accosts my nose now—which, fortunately, is a rarity—I am instantly transported back to the hospital and the damp oppressiveness of the hot pack treatment.

We were allowed a few of our own toys, all of which were

kept in a cloth bag that was tied to each of our beds. These were the only diversions we had, whether they were dolls, coloring books, story books, or stuffed animals. I'm sure there were no xylophones or other noisy toys, or there would have been a cacophony.

One day, I dropped one of my toys, a little brown rubber dog, on the linoleum floor. "My doggie is on the floor!" I called out.

A nurse came quickly, partly to quiet the situation and partly because she thought I might have a physical problem. Well, to me it was a problem, for sure. I pointed my index finger at the toy on the floor, and the nurse—who seemed large to me, especially since my mother was so small—bent and picked it up. But instead of giving it to me, she dropped it in a large white canvas bag hanging on the wall across from my bed.

"No, it's my toy, it's not to throw away," I said. "It's MINE! I dropped it on the floor. I wanted you to get it for me." It was impossible for me to get out of my high-barred crib, but I thought she misunderstood and needed me to explain this to her.

The powerful authority, in her tight crisp white uniform and pointy hat, answered, "No, you can't have it anymore. Any toys dropped on the floor are put in that bag and we give them to orphan children." And she walked away. That was that.

I was stunned. This was an alarming disappointment, and it felt unfair. I began to cry.

This incident did teach me to never drop my playthings upon the floor, but I have to say, I cannot imagine a more pitiful group of little kids—though perhaps none of us were orphaned—than a ward full of children suffering from polio. I remember this sometimes when I see a Toys for Tots campaign and hope no mean nurses take the donated toys from some hapless kids. I wonder if unknowing kind people donated the toys we played with and sometimes let slip from our tiny fingers, to be distributed to children "less fortunate than us."

The next time my mother visited me, I asked her who "orphan children" were and pointed out that my toy was in that bag over there and was going to be given to them. When she explained that these were children with no mommy and daddy, I saw that their situation was quite sad and felt remorse not only for my error but for begrudging them my toy. This was my first memorable ethical or moral conflict: Was I a bad child? Was I a fortunate child?

I suppose it's possible that there was concern for germs from any toys that had fallen upon the floor, but then why display them so painfully nearby and tell us they were going to be given to more deserving children—children who would appreciate them enough to learn more control over their hands? Who evidently grew up faster than we did? I read an account of another polio girl who said that when she left the hospital in which she was rehabilitated, her toys were burned to prevent contamination. But this was *my* toy; I was the only one who had touched it.

Our temperatures were taken daily. I thought at one point that this might have been a method used to determine whose virus might still be active and to keep us isolated. However, since I was never moved, I assume that the other children were not moved either, except to eventually to be released, so probably the temp-taking was general monitoring. In any case, if any of us had had any type of infection, it would have been noticed immediately.

Originally, I was given an oral thermometer. I managed it as well as any well-behaved three-year-old might. The nurse would stick it in my mouth under my tongue, walk away, and come back in a few minutes to remove it, and usually I lay there until she returned—but one day I kneeled in the crib and looked out to watch the procedure as it was administered to other kids, and the thermometer dropped out of my mouth and fell to the floor. This was followed by the loud *clink* of the glass breaking, the fascinating splattering of the silver mercury, and a flurry of consternation as the nurse rushed back to admonish me and clean up the mess. Forever after, I got a rectal thermometer—a humiliating experience, especially in a roomful of other people, and one I'd not had since I was a baby. (This was, of course, just a short time before, but seemed long in my past, a third of my life ago.) I cried and begged not to have to endure this "baby" method, but was denied my requests for the rest of my long months of internment, verbally reminded of my transgression and why I'd lost my big-girl privilege, until I stopped asking. (My mother did provide me the dignity of oral temperature readings when I left the hospital.)

A few times a week, we children would have a short segment of fun in warm Jacuzzi baths. The littlest of us who were able to sit up were placed three at a time in long, porcelain-finished or ivory-colored baked-enamel metal bath tubs, probably six or seven feet long by two feet wide and maybe two feet deep. They were stand-alone tubs, close to floor level, with a rounded edge at the top, not the kind where you could sit on the edge easily, and of course we had to be lifted in.

We loved being together in the tubs, splashing away, and I know none of us thought of it as therapy. It was a little bit of social playtime, in contrast to our usual existence there, never touching any other kids, separated by our cribs. It was fun—an opportunity to be warm and wet and silly together. These were the too-rare good times.

Another big event, which happened once in the six months, was that we were taken down the hall in a convoy of wheelchairs to another room. It was darkened except for one end, which was well lit; I remember the floor having big dark green and white linoleum tiles. There were lots of white and dark green balloons all over the place, on the floor and all around—perhaps they'd released them from the ceiling to create a fun atmosphere. And guess who appeared? Clarabelle the Clown, of *Howdy Doody* TV fame! He went around the room honking his horns on his little communication box. You may remember that Clarabelle never spoke on TV, he just honked yes or no from the box at his waist. I remember nothing else about the hospital show except the subdued excitement of Clarabelle walking by me at somewhat close range, and the many balloons. Then it was over, and we were wheeled back to our cribs.

People who visit kids in hospitals are saints. Hopefully that's what that famous singer, Howard Keel, was up to, and not only something suggested by his publicist.

In a picture of the old Ambassador Club after it was turned into the rehab facility, I saw the spacious, high-ceilinged room with the large-checkered floor I'd remembered, though portrayed in black-and-white photography. In the photo it appeared to be an adult dining room, with tables of varying sizes laid with white tablecloths, either left as it was previously or set up newly for staff or patient meals. It was amazing to see that photo sixty years later and have my memory confirmed, adding credence to my other memories.

Me and my half-sister, LaVonne, around 1950.

4
—

next steps in rehab

At some point in my hospital detention, we began physical therapy. This was Dr. Kabet's remarkable restorative program. I don't know if there were prerequisite signs that preceded candidacy, or if everyone got a trial crack at it. I started with a physical therapist exercising me for flexibility and strength. Without this therapy, I might have lost what limited, three-year-old strength I had. It involved my pushing my foot against an adult's hand—powered from my newly weak knee and hip, since I'd lost all movement in my ankle—and having my limbs manipulated (for instance, having my legs moved as if I were on a bicycle).

My right leg was paralyzed below the knee (and still is), although the virus had affected me up to the musculature above my waist. My trunk on the right side is slightly smaller than the left, and I'm right-handed, so, you'd expect more muscle development on that side. I actually didn't realize this was the case until I was somewhat mature and noticed that my right breast was a bit smaller than the left, and that the marked smallness of my right hip was somewhat reflected in that side of my back and rib cage. I don't think anyone other than me would notice the trunk difference. The hip dissimilarity, however, is quite obvious. (As I grew, my hip and pelvis bones became elongated and deformed, in a natural attempt to compensate for the eventual two-inch length difference in my legs.)

It was believed then that any potential paralysis recovery would take place in the first year, which has since been shown to be essentially true in my case and in most others. Those who contracted polio as adults or near adults were usually able to generate more strength from their rehab, and often were eventually able to do much of what a normal person could do, with more initial strength in their mature limbs. However, they have often been the ones, later in life, who experience first and earliest what is termed post-polio effects or syndrome—a condition indicative of deterioration of motor neurons—having pushed their weakened muscles and especially motor neurons beyond what they could sustain for a lifetime. Polio survivors of the mid-1900s pushed themselves because the consequences were not known. Today, in countries where younger people have experienced polio, doctors can advise them to manage their energy more effectively over their lifetime. Everyone's neurons wear out eventually, to a greater or lesser degree, and for a polio patient, this often comes too soon.

༄

Defying the odds predicted at the onset of polio, eventually someone in charge at the Santa Monica facility decided that I could attempt to walk. I was outfitted with little half-crutches called "Kenny sticks," named after Sister Elizabeth Kenny, an Australian unaccredited nurse who devoted her life to rehabilitation of polio patients and other disabled people. (Nurses in Christian hospitals in Australia were apparently addressed as "Sister"; she was not a nun.) Easter Seals provided most of the funding and training for my therapy, which amounted in 1951 to approximately $1,000—around $9,500 in 2017 dollars. I don't know who paid for all the polio patients' treatment—whether it was a public program to address the epidemic, whether my parents paid to have me there, or if the foundation donated the service. Although many think the March of Dimes paid for all polio treatment, they did not; they paid primarily for the inoculation program and for some treatment. Their policy was to ask people to pay what they could afford, and to never turn away any polio patient. The Kabet-Kaiser Institute was not, as far as I have been able to verify through my research, funded by The March of Dimes, nor was my treatment.

⚘

The sticks did look like miniature crutches, with wing nuts allowing adjustment for the child's height. They were cut off about halfway up the forearm, with a cuff made of heavy, khaki-colored cotton braid that looked like it had a former life as army cot bracing. Perhaps this was early recycling. I put my tiny hands through the cuffs to grasp the wooden handles and held on tight, having been told that the nice physical therapists were going to teach me to walk again.

In the physical therapy room, the smooth floor was laid out with painted or colored paper shoeprints, not much bigger than my own small feet, making the area look as if some invisible elf had just been through the hospital. (Today I think with gratitude of the conscientious person who cut out all my footprints.) Next to the footprints were little disks representing the place to put my Kenny stick tips. The left prints and disks were red, and the right ones, the polio side, were light powder blue. My sticks each had a grosgrain ribbon bow tied on, red for left, blue for right. I was to put forward my left foot and my right stick, cross-coordinated.

I didn't have the concepts of left and right just yet, at three. I associated red with left and blue with right ever after, and probably because "left" meant strong to me, and was the foot I was taught to start out with consistently, I have always said "left and right" rather than "right and left," as seems to be the norm with most people, who are of course right-handed and right-oriented, as I mostly am as well. So, red shoeprint and blue crutch disk were parallel with each other, and then, set out in exactly my own tiny gait distance, blue shoeprint and red crutch circle for the next step. My arms made up for the strength that was lacking in my right leg, and if I wanted to stand in one spot without falling over, I could spread the sticks out to the side and their rubber tips would grab the floor slightly and help me stand up.

I learned to walk in this way, one foot forward with opposite crutch, other foot with other opposite crutch, repeat, repeat, repeat, until I became a little four-legged creature who could move on her own. Freedom. I've always enjoyed watching dogs and cats walk, how they coordinate their four legs. I thought they walked as I did with crutches, but upon closer scrutiny, I learned that's not true. A human using arm cuff crutches walks like no other animal. Some years ago, when one of the *Star Wars* movies came out, they had these monster metal robots with bendable legs in the back and straight sticks in the front, and the way they moved reminded me of how I walked with the Kenny sticks, and the way I walk now when I use my Lofstrand/ Canadian arm cuff crutches.

Also essential was some bracing on my right leg, which was somewhat atrophied in comparison to my other leg. This is a state that became more pronounced throughout my growing years as the normal leg continued to reach for adulthood while the polio leg lagged behind. (By age twenty, my right leg was two inches shorter than, but also half the dimension of, my left, more normal, stronger leg.) Along with high-topped "baby" shoes to support my ankles, I wore a heavy metal brace that attached to the right shoe and had a lever on either side of the knee that pulled straight up in order for me to bend my knee whenever I wished to sit. I pinched my little fingers repeatedly in those levers, but I needed the brace in order to stand. When I walked, it was with a normal, slightly bent knee on one side and the braced leg rigid.

Under the brace, I wore a thing the doctors and rehab people called my "twister-resistor." It was a gray cloth elasticized band about an inch and a half wide that had a thin red stripe down the middle. The band hooked onto the outside of my high-topped shoes near the toes, and crossed over to the inside of my calf and around the back of my leg to the outside of my thigh. (It may have attached to the top of the brace as well—I can't quite remember.) This helped to keep my foot and knee oriented forward instead of tending to flop outward in a duck or "*plié*" position.

In 1998, after my mother had died, I found a letter that she had written to my father when I was learning to walk again. He was in northern California, looking for a home delivery milk route to buy, while I was in the hospital in Santa Monica in 1951. I believe he was doing this so we could get out of plague-ridden Los Angeles. Mother wrote to him that she'd been watching me with the therapists in my walking lessons from behind a window with one-way glass. After the lesson, she told the therapists that she thought they were not being strict enough with me.

"We find that Francine is a very sensitive child," they told her. "She gets upset when she is reprimanded, and is discouraged by that type of instruction. However, when we encourage her, she is a model student and wants to do her best."

My mother found that to be an odd philosophy and was very surprised that it worked, given what a strong-willed child she thought me to be.

I wish that I could have known about this anecdote throughout my childhood, in order to remind her of this insight when her own strict Swiss-German-English upbringing was repeatedly visited upon me, the resulting effect being essentially to alienate me from my mother and to confuse for many years my perception of what a mother's love looked like. I wish I could have used the grown-up words, "Mama, that doesn't work with me. It just makes me more upset, especially when you spank me." Instead, all I could do was cry my heart out alone in my room and become resentful toward her.

Mama often told me that her dad would say that children should be seen and not heard, as an illustration of how much more liberal she was than her father, but also indicating that he may have been right. In the mornings, before I was school-aged, she held me on her lap, cigarette in hand, and sang to me and read me stories. She told me I'd call out in a singsong in the morning, "Maa-ma, come and wrap me up in the blue blaanket!"—an invitation to our morning cuddle. Mother loved babies on up through toddler age, but she felt older children needed to be shaped and disciplined or they'd become lawless, ill-mannered heathens. Judging from families I've seen in supermarkets, she may have been correct, but I'd rather have had a longer leash.

～

In my twenties, in the 1970s, I knew a lovely ceramicist who was a friend of a friend. I visited her shortly after my affectionate young cat, Shalimar, whom I'd saved in a rainstorm on Hallowe'en when she was only five weeks old, had died of leukemia. The next time I saw her, she gave me a stylized little porcelain figurine of Shalimar and me cuddled up together. On one of those visits, her little daughter had a tantrum about something that she was told not to do; my acquaintance was firm in her "no," and the child ran to her room in tears. The mother looked at my girlfriend and me and quipped, "Put another quarter in the therapy jar," and we went on with the conversation. I was impressed

NOT A POSTER CHILD   37

that she actually considered herself in any way responsible for her child's mental health or the development of her psyche. My mom made the very least transgression (like looking in her purse) seem like a major one. Her methodology did keep me in line, but the cost was our intimacy.

My mother came to the rehab facility each day to visit me for an hour or so, and sometimes she would take me out to the beach behind the old building. Once enjoyed by the Ambassador Club and Edgewater Beach Hotel patrons, it was now used by a very few members of the public who either did not know that the building was full of polio patients or were not deterred by fear of contagion as some might have been.

We would go down in the elevator and make our way around the building to the beach on the west. I would be in the Taylor Tot push cart. Mama would bend down and hand me a saltshaker, large in my tiny hands.

"Okay, when we get near a bird, shake the salt on its tail. It won't be able to fly, and we might be able to catch one."

Off we'd go, wheeling along the lawn or the edge of the sand where it was firm enough for the Taylor Tot, and Mama would run, pushing me from behind. We were racing!

We'd get near a bird, and it would take off.

"Oh, we missed that one. Let's try another one!"

"Okay! Look, more birds, there, Mama! Let's go!" I'd point with one hand and grip the saltshaker in the other.

We'd take off again and run after another bird. Of course, the birds flew away as soon as we got within six feet of them— our charging cart and the squealing little human in it were audible from yards away—but I never caught on to that and always was excited by this escape from institutional life.

I have to hand it to my mom; the bird catching game was pretty clever. Those jaunts were one of my few joys in those six months, along with the Jacuzzi baths, the one visit from Clarabelle, and the weekends spent at my parents' apartment.

I don't remember much about what we did on the weekends, except that then I got to see Daddy, with whom I was always quite close, and whom I missed dearly during my "work week." Mother told me later in life that after I was born, he paid more attention to me than he did to her, which I'm sure was very hard for her and must have added to the difficulties in our relationship. She said I'd follow him around in my diaper, during that short twenty-three months when I could walk, and he'd be in his BVDs or Fruit of the Looms, and our body types were so similar that I looked "like a little Bob" from the back. When he was attempting to fit our screen door in Los Angeles, he swore, "Ye gods!" and I swore back, "Ye gods, Daddy, the door doesn't fit!" My mother told him he'd better watch his language. (They'd have a fit if they heard me these days.)

I remember being in my crib at the apartment and him coming in to the tiny bedroom, leaning over the rail and talking to me, sometimes unable to resist teasing me. My mother said I would stick out my lower teeth at him like a little bulldog when he made me irritated, and he'd make the same face back at me, which would further incense me, and she'd chastise him for it.

I hated to go back to the hospital on Sunday nights.

❧

It took decades for me to fully appreciate the value of what those dedicated, innovative rehab people did with me in therapy, or the time and emotional commitment doing the therapy must have been for my mother. I was a three-year-old simply doing what I was told to do, and in my future childhood years, I just got up, put on the brace, grabbed my sticks, and was out the door, trying my best to be a normal kid. I didn't know then that I had initially been slated to spend my life sitting down, dependent on others to care for me, so gratitude for this gift of mobility didn't occur to me at the time. Appreciation of my "good fortune," that of being able to stand and walk, did not come until young adulthood.

But I also don't remember feeling particularly sorry for myself in my disability at age three, or even comparing myself to normal children. I felt very sad at being confined in the hospital for so long, not being able to play anymore (except in the bathtub or with my mama and the birds on the beach), and not seeing my parents, my old playmates, or anyone else I knew. I reached a somewhat depressed resignation, relieved by those interspersed moments of freedom. I may have cried out of loneliness, but I don't remember that. I just remember accepting the days of monotony and wishing every hour of every day that I could get out of there. After a few months, it seemed that there would never be any other life for me. I felt it was endless, and as if the fun part of life was over.

I do recall being a little angry about the entire situation, which is something you can see in a couple of post-hospital photos of me. I look resigned but not cheerful about it—a combination that may be somewhat ingrained in my personality. I know I haven't been horrible, and am certainly not irritated all the time, but anyone close to me has eventually seen me break down in tears over not being able to do things involving standing or walking, even some small, basic task, or has seen me angry and/or frustrated with my physical state. Though polio did not strike me as unfair when I was a child, the idea sure has crossed my mind more than a few times as an adult.

I've come to see that nearly everyone has many life experiences that are unfair. Mine were only more excessive than the average, and occurred earlier in life. I sometimes tell myself, sarcastically, that polio is the gift that keeps on giving.

~

When rehabilitation was deemed successful, I was finally released, with bows on my Kenny sticks, bows in my hair, and a brace on my leg. Yes, I was a strong-willed girl, and perhaps I would have been in a wheelchair all my life had I not had that determination and the assistance of some sympathetic people who saw my true nature.

A friend and I, July, 1951, the week I was released from the hospital, age 3 1/2.

In front of the lot my dad bought for our new home in Yuba City, late summer, 1951. Mother always turned me out impeccably, partly so that even though I was handicapped, I would look as pretty as other little girls.

5
—

back to childhood

*W*hile we lived in Santa Monica, my dad went traveling throughout California looking for a small town that had a milk delivery service for sale—someplace without disease epidemics and the other stresses of a large city, someplace safe where his little family could start a new life.

Here's how my parents met: In 1946, Bob was just home from the war and intent on marrying and settling down. Frances was recently divorced and living with her two teenage children in a bungalow apartment across the street from the bakery where she worked in L.A. So, she was often up very early to scoot across the street and start baking. (She was really good at it and passed a smidgeon of this talent on to me, though my work is more haphazard. The greatest compliment she ever paid me was that she really liked my pie crust and that it was "so tender and flaky," though I used butter and she used Crisco.)

Bob delivered milk to her home. Mother thought he was cute. (He was.) She was nice looking, more patrician than cute, even though she was very short. She told her baker boss that she'd really like to meet her milkman and didn't know what to do about it.

"Bake a couple of pies and put 'em out on the windowsill to cool just before he comes by in the morning," he said.

Always deferential to men, she asked, "What kind of pies should I bake?"

His quick answer: "Cherry!"

So she followed his advice. She must have gotten up a lot earlier than usual to pit all those cherries (I inherited her cherry pitter, so I know she at least sometimes used fresh fruit), make the crusts, and get two pies into the oven an hour before Bob Allen came by her window at 8:00 a.m. By the time he delivered the milk, there they were, aroma wafting through the open window as prescribed.

Bob walked up and said, "Boy, Mrs. Smith"—that was her married name—"those pies sure smell good!"

"Oh, would you like to come in and have a piece of pie and a cup of coffee?" she coyly answered.

A very few months later—on January 1, 1947—they were married, and I was born on December 8 of that year.

✐

Daddy was raised in Texas, and long after he died, on one of my many drives north through the Sacramento Valley from the San Francisco Bay Area, I suddenly had an "aha!" moment regarding my dad's choice of Yuba City. The climate was hot. The land was flat. In the distance, to the west, you could see "the world's smallest mountain range," or so it was nicknamed—the Sutter Buttes. The lazy Feather River ran through the "twin cities" of Marysville and Yuba City.

Holy smokes: it looked just like Texas. And in 1951, there was a milk route for sale there.

Growing up in Yuba City, none of us local kids could see why the two towns were referred to as twins; our town wanted to sprawl west out to its orchards, while Marysville was referred to as a cup, nearly surrounded by the river and its levee, and, being the older town, also had far more graceful houses—two-story gingerbreads—and tall trees. Yuba City had wealthy ranchers and the professionals who served them, and more high schoolers headed for Harvard and Stanford, while Yuba City mothers grew wary at the prospect of their daughter dating a Marysville boy. (They certainly were the first to take up the popularity of black clothing and Beatle boots, though our high school had the best rock and roll band, Drew Sallee and the Dead.)

To an outsider, though, the two towns did seem as one large one separated by only a river. Way off to the east of Marysville, you could make out the purple mountains of the Sierra Nevada.

↝

Upon my release from the hospital in 1951, my six months of polio captivity completed, we moved into a little Yuba City rental house on Percy Avenue, a bit too close to the undesirable part of town. This was only until the two-bedroom house my dad was helping build for us was finished.

Daddy studied mechanical engineering in high school, and it's possible he also took some college-level courses. His dad wrote to him in a letter I read that he was quite perturbed that Daddy didn't continue in school and that he kept the milk route instead, which he felt was a fool's errand and no career for an intelligent man. (The Allen clan, including myself, has a proclivity for engineering and accounting.) Daddy was also an ace mechanic who would comment, as a car drove by outside, on which cylinders weren't firing correctly. He served on a ship in the navy in WWII, then had a girlfriend or two before Mother. He loved being outdoors and cheerfully greeting a myriad of early-rising customers, whistling most of the time. He often stopped to help them plant fruit trees or share a cup of coffee. He had a coppery "farmer's tan"—arms, neck, and face—and the rest of him was Irish-Anglo colored, as I discovered when he used the bathroom. He was not a modest or prudish man.

While we were still on Percy, the next phase of therapy began: my mom worked my legs twice a day while I lay on my back. By this time, I was getting old enough (three-and-a-half and counting) to protest the routine, but she never let up. The doctors had prescribed a once-a-day program, but she insisted on doubling that, thinking if some was good, more was better. (Now we know that too much therapy can be detrimental, since it can wear out neurons that can never be regenerated.) I had several months to go before I hit the maximum benefit mark, so while Daddy delivered milk and built our house, we had our own work to do.

I know now that even though my mother and I had our strong differences and many emotional gaps during our long relationship, her diligence in my therapy immediately after my hospital release is largely responsible for my ability to walk for much of my life. She was determined that her child was not going to be severely handicapped—partly for my good, and partly for her own. I put up with the daily exercises, got to know my mommy and daddy again (it was particularly great to be with my dad every night after six months of weekends only, and be held on his lap once again while he read the paper), made friends with the Schwedhelm children next door, and enjoyed my return to a new normal. I remember playing with little cars, not just dolls—early girls' lib. I also likely wanted the cars and trucks because my dad had real cars and trucks.

We soon moved to our new five-room-plus-bath home on Brown Avenue, in a friendly, quiet, modest middle-class neighborhood with lots of kids. Our house was on a large, flat lot, grass in front and back (no stairs, although there were a few steps for me to struggle with). It had a fruitless mulberry tree that my dad had planted in the backyard, which decades later grew to sport a forty-foot-wide canopy. Soon after we established ourselves, my father installed an ornate iron gate through a chicken wire fence as an entrance into the fruit and vegetable garden. He planted a lawn around the mulberry and an elm surrounded by tall white Shasta daisies (which stink, in case you don't know that, but they looked good and were fun to color by adding food coloring to a vase of water and letting their stems carry it up to the flower), and an orange tree. In the family orchard at the back were two cherry trees (I often sat in one at the top of a ladder, with a child-sized bucket, picking the fruit: eat one, save one), as well as a peach, an apricot, an almond, a plum, and two pear trees. We grew full-sized watermelons and cantaloupes and so many tomatoes that my mother canned enough to last through the winter. Corn, string beans, cucumbers, eggplant, and even okra, a nod to my dad's southern roots, and plenty of other vegetables were also among my parents' crops.

When we moved to the new house, an older girl from up the block was sent by her mother to meet me. Her name was Daralyn (because they had anticipated a boy and meant to name him Darrel Lynn), and she has been my friend for nearly seven decades now. My mother did not want me to learn to ride a bicycle. (In high school I discovered that a girl with the exact same polio residuals I had rode a bike, a stunning revelation to me.) So Daralyn put me on the back bumper of her green big-tired Schwinn two-wheeler and pumped me all over the neighborhood. It has often been through the kindness of friends that I have been able to experience activities of life that I would have otherwise been destined to miss.

I had a series of beloved pets: Pluto the golden cocker spaniel, not brilliant but a good dog, named for the Disney character;

Gracie, a little tabby kitten named after George Burns's wife; and Pity Sing, a gorgeous, long-haired calico cat so named by Daralyn's mom because she was "such a pretty thing."

I made a determined attempt to have a normal childhood. I learned to skip in a step-step-LIFT, step-step-LIFT approximation of skipping that I later realized was very awkward looking, so I stopped trying to run, barring an emergency, by the time I reached thirteen. But in the early days, from ages three to six, I wore elastic support gizmos on my leg and foot and that heavy metal brace, and gimped along on those little crutches, trying to keep up with the other kids.

ॐ

I took naps every day until I was about six. I thought all children did. Around age seven, I realized other kids had stopped that before they entered kindergarten for the most part, other than falling asleep watching TV after a tiring day at school.

While waiting to nod off on my bed in the early afternoon, I would lie on my back with my legs in the air and let them gently sway around. I don't know what made me do that; it just felt good. Possibly it was related to the heaviness of my brace and the relief of having it off. It really pulled on my little leg, which was already so weak. Later, as an adult, a friend told me this "feet in the air" position is taught in bioenergetics: it's a way to get energy flowing. Makes sense to me that directing blood the other way in your legs would be advantageous for circulation. The blood flow in my smaller leg was so bad it was nearly nonexistent.

While lying there in bed, I would also try to wiggle the toes on my polio foot. I had the ability to move the littlest one in particular, up and down, while I stretched it a little out to the side, maybe as much as a quarter inch. If I did it too much it would start spasming and twitching on its own. I could bend my big toe just slightly, too. The others all mostly moved together if I tried to move any of them, and the movement was almost imperceptible. But I continued to check from time to time, to see if they still moved. (They have become less mobile over the years; these days, I can barely move any of them.)

Besides having almost no control over my toes, I also had— still have—what doctors call a "drop foot." Many polio, stroke, and neurologically damaged patients have a drop foot: it just hangs there, with no strength or ability to move up and down. I generally illustrate this by showing a limp wrist and flicking it up and down with my other hand and letting it fall. Between my toes and my drop foot, I've never been able to wear backless sandals or flip-flops. When I go to a spa they always want to give me a pair to wear, and can't understand why I want to wear my own. If they press, I just tell them: polio, can't wear those, they fall off my little right foot. This is inconceivable to young women, most of whom have never encountered a survivor of polio, if they've even heard of the disease. If they insist, I say, "It's as if my foot had a stroke." That is something they can at least imagine, even if they have never known a stroke patient.

❧

We really take walking for granted. I do, and I can barely do it. Babies are up and at it sometime between just under a year old and a year-and-a-half, which is considered late. I was talking in truncated sentences at eight months ("Baby go bye-bye!"), but I didn't get up and walk until I was about fourteen months. Then, only twenty-three months later, my normal walking life was over.

So, at about age four, my chief concern became walking without tripping, falling, or stubbing a toe. There was a Kaiser

Permanente ad that played a lot on the radio a couple of years ago promoting a great program called *Marché*. As the spiel went on, you learned that *marché* is French for "walking," and Allison Janney's voice went on to say, "You probably already know how to do that!" (Walk, she meant.) "Just get on out there and put one foot in front of the other." Easier said than done, in my case.

One winter afternoon after school, at age five or six, having newly abandoned my Kenny sticks, I tripped on nothing in particular in the garage, on my way from our new two-tone green 1953 DeSoto to the back door of the house, and landed chin-first on my ancient black metal rectangular lunchbox. Mama had to take me to the hospital for stitches. Three or four years later, I had a fall that produced an even worse cut, this time on my polio leg (my scar is one and a quarter inches long and nearly a quarter-inch wide). More Novocain, more stitches. A week or two of summer fun down the drain, no playing in the sprinklers or wading pools in the 100-degree days, and the later nastiness of stitches removal.

Lots of kids have stuff like this happen, so I'm not saying that it's because of polio that I went through all of this, but it certainly increased my chances of falling and injuring myself by some gargantuan percentage. I also began to see that if I did not want to totally tear myself up, I'd better start being more careful. Thus began a lifetime of being physically cautious—timid, even—burdened with the knowledge that if I slipped, I was going all the way down, every time.

～

My mother took me to someone's house when I was barely school age and told me to play with the little boy whose house it was while she talked to his mother. The boy was in his pajamas, even though it was well into the day. I am fairly sure I was there to get exposed to the chicken pox, which I contracted not long after that, as that's what parents thought was smart in those days. Our parents exposed us to diseases that were potentially dangerous or even lethal—chicken pox, measles, mumps—to "get it over with." Everyone got them and they were considered inevitable. My mother never socialized with other women unless invited or at church, so it was rare that she made a visit like this.

I felt this wave of attraction for my new friend—he didn't seem to mind that I was a girl, and was happy to explain to me the toy, puzzle, or game he played with while we stood at a big dining room table. I put my head on his shoulder while I listened to him. He looked at me with a slightly stunned expression, but went on with the explanation. It was my little secret romance. I just loved boys, probably because of my love and admiration for my daddy, and because my mother adored my dad more than any other person on the planet.

In kindergarten, I was attracted to a handsome kid named Darrel who had a slightly pompadour haircut and what we'd now call a James Dean aura. He moved away from our school district the next year. Despite this, and despite the fact that he wasn't showing much interest in any case, I thought about Darrel a lot. Really, do five-year-olds usually think about boys that much? I have no idea, but my recollection is that most of my friends were more interested simply in playing with children in general without getting in trouble. Girls mostly wanted to play with dolls and run, only one of which I could do, and boys were generally a bit of a pain in the butt—they were too rough and too goofy—but in my home, males were more important than females.

Occasionally, we'd go over to Vallejo, not far from San Francisco. This was a big trip for us, a drive of two hours or more on the two-lane valley highway of the early 1950s. We'd see a polio doctor there at Kaiser Foundation Rehabilitation

Center. The doctors in that big medical facility were the ones prescribing the changes for me in using or not using a brace, Kenny sticks, shoes, and other equipment, and monitoring my progress or stability. Driving those two hours was our only option: there was no doctor in Yuba City who was familiar with polio.

When I was six, Yuba City was one of many small towns participating in the spring 1954 polio vaccination trials. I was lined up in the dark hallway of the old brick school with maybe fifty other kids. No one had told us why we were standing there, so I asked my beloved kindergarten teacher, Mrs. Overstreet, thinking the wait must be for something fun.

"You are all going to the nurse's office to have a polio shot," she answered calmly.

"No!" I screamed. "I'm not going to have one! No!" I began sobbing, tears streaming down my cheeks, and started to flee back into the kindergarten room.

Mrs. Overstreet, stunned and unaware that I had the worst needle phobia possible, took me by the arm and said, "Francine, all the children in the school have to have one. It's just a shot; it won't be that bad."

I kept pulling away from her and screaming, now in a full meltdown frenzy and scared beyond measure. All the other children were now terrified as well, of course, thinking I knew something really monstrous about polio shots, since I was the only one who'd had polio.

Another teacher came to see what the problem was, and she and Mrs. Overstreet carried me kicking and screaming to the nurse's office down the hall and around the corner. I had the shot; it hurt, but no more than the shots I'd had daily in the hospital.

My parents were asked to get my future shots elsewhere.

⌒

The next time I was due for a polio vaccination, I was tricked into the expedition.

"Let's go," Daddy said. "I'm taking you someplace in the car."

"Where are we going, Daddy?" I asked.

"It's a surprise!"

I was now excited to go on this unusual outing alone with my dad, in the daytime. Every time I went someplace in the car with him, such as the Foster's Freeze, my mother was always with us. We drove about four miles in the DeSoto, over the Feather River bridge and into Marysville, and pulled up in front of an ivory-painted building that didn't really look like a place where fun could be had.

It was a doctor's office, of course, and I got my second shot that day. This time I did not have a fit, but I felt cheated about the "surprise." My dad, however, was good at minimizing this sort of thing.

"We couldn't tell you because you'd get upset, but see? It wasn't so bad!"

Apparently my mother had anticipated my potential tantrum and had insisted, "You have to take her. I'm not going to do it."

There were different strains of polio, so the vaccination process then required multiple injections at intervals of a few weeks or months. Even though I'd had the disease, there was no assurance at that time that I would not get a different strain.

I was subdued as we walked to the car from the clinic. Daddy opened the door on the passenger side, and I climbed in, holding on to the doorframe in order to steady myself—and WHAM! He slammed the DeSoto door on my tiny fingers. I'm guessing he was a little nervous too, over tricking his little girl and also getting a potentially upsetting event over with.

I cried out in pain and fear, "Open the door, Daddy!!!"

The look on his face was one of horror. Eyebrows up in the middle, just like that day in the hospital years before, and jaw dropped open, aghast. It took only a second for him to realize what had happened and swing the door open, whereupon I removed my hand from the frame and inspected it in awe.

Daddy took my little hand in his. "Does it hurt?"

It did, but not that bad, considering. The round padding all around the door and the slight gap in the doorframe had left almost enough room for little bitty fingers. He tested my fingers and saw that they were not broken. We were both relieved, and it certainly was a far more frightening, dramatic, and memorable incident than the measly shot.

My mother's first and my third vaccination was a droplet on a sugar cube, much later, in 1961. Much easier going down, although this was Dr. Albert Sabin's formula (who had been competing to get his vaccine out before Dr. Salk), and was live virus. Although very few people have gotten polio from this type of live vaccine, it has happened, and it is currently being discontinued worldwide, despite its ease of use.

not a poster child

*T*he March of Dimes was a campaign initiated to pay for polio vaccinations and patient care. Most victims of polio were small children, who were the most prone to severe aspects of the disease. Little children with smiling faces, braces, and Kenny sticks were portrayed on coin collection placards with a hundred slots for dimes, or on posters with a jar for money attached. These organizational promos implored donors to send in "even a dime"—the equivalent of ninety cents or so these days.

I saw these promos in stores, churches, gas stations, anywhere that people might be spending or receiving change. This is how the term "poster child" was born, though it has come to mean "a perfect example."

Once an older child at church stopped me in the hallway and said, "I saw your picture on the March of Dimes poster!"

I was so surprised. "I don't think so . . ."

"Yes, it was you!" she insisted. "She had brown hair just like yours!"

Then it happened again. Not long after, a kid at school said the same thing. And then a lady in a grocery store kindly bent down and said, "I saw your picture on the March of Dimes poster, dear."

At that point, no longer a skeptic, I thought that my picture was actually being used for the March of Dimes poster child, and I was a little excited to learn this. I looked forward to seeing myself the next time I saw a placard around town. There I'd be, Francine Allen, the poster child. But I soon saw that none of the posters had my picture, though the girl was about my age—around six—wore a brace, used Kenny sticks, and had hair similar to mine (although hers was not in the meticulous ringlets my mother created to draw attention away from my limp; I needed to look pretty, Mama's reasoning went, in order to make up for my defect—a concept I have never been able to drop).

I asked my mother if I was going to be the March of Dimes girl, and she assured me that I wasn't, and that there were no posters out there with my picture on them. I was a little disappointed, but what bothered me more was that people didn't recognize that it was not me, that any little girl with Kenny sticks and brown hair looked the same to them. It made me a little angry that that was my identity: The March of Dimes Poster Girl. Especially since I was experiencing none of the imagined benefits of being famous. It is possible that people thought, *What a brave little girl*, when they saw that poster, and that they also thought this about me. But I didn't think of that when I was six. I was just slightly perturbed that I didn't have a face to people—that I was identified by a limp, a brace, and crutches.

I was not a poster child—not in reality and not in terms of the smiley, optimistic, never-bothered attitude that is often wished for in disabled people. Others feel better if a crippled person reflects happy accomplishment. Certainly, that winsome courage is more appealing for the purpose of collecting donations! I was also not pathetic or helpless, though the poster was designed to elicit such thoughts about being a brave little crippled girl. (Please don't misunderstand: I am glad people did respond and fund polio vaccination and treatment. I just didn't like being thought of as pitiful.)

I was not always brave, though I had to be much of the time, and I was not always accepting of my plight, and I did not always bear it with a smile, though I was told in my twenties, "You were always such a happy-go-lucky kid around the neighborhood." It's true that when I was out, I was happy. Happy to be with other kids, happy to be able to swing higher than I should, happy to be on the park carousel while someone else ran and pushed it to dizzying speeds, happy to have Daralyn pumping me around town on her bike, happy to get an A in school.

Also happy not to be getting the spanking of my life with a Hi-Li paddle for something I did—or didn't do. "Stop crying or I'll give you something to cry about," Mama would say. (I learned not to ask for the Hi-Li paddle toy with the elastic and ball when we went to Sprouse-Reitz.) Sometimes I lay in bed and contemplated running away: What would I pack in my tiny toy suitcase? . . . My favorite doll, a pair of underpants, some shorts and a T-shirt, I decided. But where would I go? To Marilyn Mercer's house two blocks away? Her mother would turn me in.

I often lay there and cried and wished for a different life, a different mother. It was not my odd little leg so much as it was my other circumstances that bothered me. But eventually I'd accept that there was no escape, so the best thing to do was have fun and make friends, go to church and school, join Bluebirds, try to be normal, do whatever I could enjoy. I did all that at every opportunity, and cried when I felt overwhelmed.

❦

I've read in several books that it was not unusual for us polio kids to be spanked or beaten, even to the point of abuse, sometimes more than other kids in the family were. It was made clear to me early on that exceptions were not going to be made just because I was crippled, and I should learn to do things myself, on my own, without expecting any help or special treatment. I was taught to be as independent as possible. These attitudes or methods are a common thread recounted by other polio kids, but certainly not all parents were so strict. In my case, I was treated no worse than my much older half-siblings. My mother beat my brother with wooden coat hangers until they broke. (No wonder we rarely saw him after we moved north; the story was always that he couldn't travel because his lungs were damaged from the tuberculosis he'd contracted at sixteen.)

My transgressions ranged from talking back to spilling something to not doing what I was told soon enough, and I assume my sister and brother had the same parameters for behavior.

I know that my mother loved me. She was just afraid I would grow up not knowing right from wrong, according to her code, which she believed to be universal among good people. On a trip home I took to visit her as an adult, she let me in on a little secret: she said she cried every time she spanked me. Today, I wonder about the truth of this—and at the time I wondered why she kept doing it if it upset both of us so much.

My own assessment of my spankings, which echoes what other polio survivors—and normies, too—have said, is that the 1940s and 50s were an era in which "Spare the rod and spoil the child" was a common attitude among parents. My mother said this to me more than once, quoting her father. She was a great one for platitudes: "A penny saved is a penny earned," she liked to say, and I knew early on that this one came from Ben Franklin; he and my mom might have started a thrift savings bank. If, on the other hand, someone was cheap and not thinking of lasting value, she'd say, "He's penny-wise and pound-foolish." When I learned to darn socks—yes, we actually darned our socks—her favorite was, "A stitch in time saves nine." (I felt liberated when at long last I had enough income to throw away socks with holes in the toes.) "Waste not, want not," while Mama cut the toothpaste tubes open to get at the last of the stuff. "Idle hands are the Devil's workshop," if I said I was bored. "They robbed Peter to pay Paul," if someone used savings to pay a debt. "Don't cut off your nose to spite your face," if I said I wasn't going to play with so-and-so anymore. (It surprised me that such a gruesome phrase ever garnered any popularity.)

These were the sorts of words of wisdom my mother imparted with regularity, accompanied by the bobblehead movement she used for emphasis. Not too many heart-to-heart talks, but these admonitions echo in my mind whenever I have the temerity to make a mistake. I hear myself repeat them occasionally, and then either cringe or chuckle.

❧

My mother was concerned that I be taught that I could be the same and do the same as other children—something I've also learned was common in polio families—so I would need to try harder than others, not only physically but in school and all endeavors. This was good news/bad news. It was good to be encouraged, but it was a major problem to think I would one day be able to run or dance as an equal, or have the energy to engage in normal activities, or especially be seen as the same as everyone else. Mama seemed to think that if I tried hard enough, I might be able to build up my lost musculature—a medical impossibility. There was an underlying message that I needed to be an even better person than others in order to be accepted.

I believe my mother was embarrassed to have a handicapped child, a common feeling among polio kids' parents. I do not remember my dad ever conveying that sentiment; I was just his cuddly little girl who stuck by him in the backyard or sat on his lap while he read the paper. But when it came to Mama, if I made mistakes as a child, my parameters were narrower and my punishment came swifter, because I had something to make up for and there was no room for error. I needed to be perfect. And I was so very far from perfect.

More than once Mother said, "Sometimes I feel like going away and never coming back," with a meaningful look that communicated how hard I made her life. That frightened me: it raised thoughts of how I would live without a mother, and also made me feel despicable.

I did talk back to my mother at times—around second grade especially, as I was learning to stand up for myself—and I think I did not respect her as much as she thought I should, and perhaps not as much as she may have deserved. She had only wanted to be my father's wife.

Things my mother said and did eventually led me to understand that she feared I would be a burden, would be considered unattractive, would be rejected by men, would never marry, would live with her forever. One polio memoir I read told the story of how the young girl held the flat of her palm on her paralyzed thigh above her knee when she walked, to prevent her leg from buckling when it was tired. I used to do this as a child (and still do sometimes, especially now that I am experiencing new weakness in my atrophied leg). The girl's father chided her for this innovation and insisted she not do it—it looked strange and drew more attention to her limp, he said—even though not pressing her hand there sometimes made it more difficult for her to walk.

This kind of treatment—the thinking that I was too willful, when will was what I needed to develop more than other kids, or that I was not trying hard enough to walk normally—set up within me some self-doubt, but also a strength that was sometimes seen as defiance.

getting around the neighborhood

*A*fter I outgrew my brace, the polio doctor did not suggest that I continue to wear any kind of heavy support. What I did wear was an apparatus encircling my calf below my knee, a foam band with a layer of leather or other material on the outside, which was punched with metal brads through which a lacing could be tied. To this foam band, hollow stretchy rubber tubing was hooked at the top, like a long piece of half-cooked brown macaroni, about eight inches long. The other end hooked to the laces near the toe of my shoes. This helped hold my foot up, since without it, I was at great risk of tripping, with my foot just hanging there at the end of my leg. I also continued wearing a "twister-resistor" full-leg-length elastic band for a couple of years, which wrapped around my leg and trained my leg and foot to remember to point forward. (After I stopped wearing it, it was clear that my leg had a very short and unreliable memory. I had to think about each step I took and still must do so.) The elastic must have attached to my underpants leg with a safety pin or alligator clip.

High-topped lace-up shoes also gave my ankle some stability (although other children called them "baby shoes"), as without them I rolled my foot in, and walked almost on the inside of my ankle, a condition that worsened through childhood.

My left leg continued to grow at a normal pace and was further strengthened by the extra work it was doing. Standing on one leg—required for activities like hop scotch—was only possible on my left. I could never, and still cannot, leave my weight totally on my polio-affected leg for more than one second, or I begin to list to one side, and will fall if I don't put my weight down on my strong foot immediately or grab on to something stable.

My polio leg and foot grew as well, but so very slowly that soon my mother was buying two pairs of shoes in different sizes—sizes that diverged further and further through the years. By the time I reached high school, and had fortunately almost stopped growing and become a definite short person, my feet were more than four sizes apart, one in children's sizes and one in women's sizes, making it difficult to buy a matched set.

✎

Daralyn's brother had a Flexie Flyer. It was a wooden slatted sled about three feet long with six-inch rubber wheels and black rubber steering handles that controlled the front wheels. The boys, and some girls, would lie on their stomachs, bend their knees, feet in the air, and take off down the sidewalk.

I had to try it. Anything with wheels had its appeal, and unlike pedaling on a bicycle, it looked like something I could do.

Daralyn and I asked her brother if we could play with it one day.

"Okay," he said, "but you better not break it."

Daralyn rode on it first, giving me a reminder demo; it was her brother's, after all.

My turn: I lay down on the sled, eye level about eight inches above the sidewalk, and pushed myself off with my strong leg, rolling away at a pretty fast clip. I could steer with the handles into our flat driveway and stop myself with the handle brakes, sort of, or run up against the edge of the lawn or onto the lawn itself in order to stop.

I went back and forth a few times, up and down the block. Then, like nearly all the other kids had done before me, I lost control, rolled off one of our neighborhood rollaway curbs, and smashed my face on the asphalt street—an unpleasant surprise, since I thought I was doing so well.

I got the forehead goose egg and the swollen, bruised, and scraped upper lip that were the stigmata of enjoying this particular vehicle. *Owie.* Plus, I looked like an idiot for a week with that big puffed-up lip. But that didn't deter me: I had to try it again a few times after I healed up. The next time I hit the pavement, and sported the same messed-up face, my mother barred me from ever cruising on a Flexie Flyer again.

"You could knock one of your teeth out on that thing," she said. "Don't let me ever catch you on it again."

I knew better than to defy her.

❧

Though I never rode a stand-alone two-wheeler bike, a friend would let me borrow her little sister's bike, which had training wheels on it, so I could ride a block or two around the neighborhood with the other kids. But the weakness of my "lazy leg," as my mother called it, would have made it difficult for me to go any farther than that. I did love the feel of cruising—so much easier and faster than walking! Sometimes I actually dreamed I was riding a bike up the street, with two strong legs and no balance wheels. I would awaken remembering what the shade trees looked like overhead and truly feel as if I'd been riding a bike— exhilarated by that easy, rolling freedom.

Ultimately, my only consistent means of transportation throughout my young life were: a tricycle, which I gave up in third grade; the back bumper of Daralyn's Schwinn (till she got a skinny-fendered purple ten-speed when I was about twelve); someone's car; and my feet. If you grew up in a suburb in the United States, especially one as flat as they are in California's Central Valley, and did not grow up in severe poverty, you probably had a bike, along with every other kid you knew. That's how kids got to most of the places they went. Since I was unable to ride, I spent a lot of bikeless time at home alone in the afternoons while other kids were off someplace I couldn't go. This partial isolation set me up with two personality traits: I sought the company of my peers at almost any cost as a young person (in high school, I'd go to the weekly teen dances with strep throat if I could get away with it), and I learned to find things to do on my own—reading, drawing, watching movies, singing by myself in the backyard! All these pastimes became almost thrilling to me. This eventually had me evolve into the solitude-loving but basically friendly recluse I am today. And, of course, it may have been genetic: my dad had a similar nature.

❦

Shoes, of course, were expensive, since we had to buy two pairs each time, and then there was the cost of the orthopedic buildup on the heel and sole. This work, done at the local shoe repair, only partially compensated for the length difference in my legs— but a little bar across the sole of the smaller shoe did help my foot rock forward after I slapped it down on the floor or sidewalk (I have no control over bringing my heel down first and rolling up to the ball of my foot, another aspect of a drop foot).

Since we were a family of lower-middle-class income, I was taught to care for and repeatedly repair my shoes. As I grew older, this allowed me to have a few pairs at once—important to a young girl concerned with her appearance!

Generally, oxfords were my mother's shoe of choice for me, but I did have loafers eventually (beloved Cordovan red with tassels in the fourth grade). I have always owned one or another pair of Mary Janes, which will stay on my foot—not the case with many other shoes, since I have no toe-grabbing ability. At one point I also had one pair of black patent flats a friend had handed down to me which I insisted on wearing; both shoes were the same size, so I used a wide rubber band to keep the right one on my small foot. (Once I dreamed I went to church naked, wearing only these shoes with the obvious rubber band. Waking, I thought, *Well, I don't know which is worse, being at church naked or wearing a shoe with a rubber band.*)

The older I got, the more I wanted flats and dressier shoes, which often were not particularly comfortable and did not offer much support to my paralyzed foot and ankle. But vanity drove me, and I tried to wear shoes as much like those that other girls were wearing as was possible, though I could never wear a heel that was more than an inch and a half high, including the lift, or I'd turn my ankle.

In high school, I learned about an organization called the National Odd Shoe Exchange, or NOSE, which for a small fee set a person up with a membership and one or two partners with exactly opposite-sized feet and similar tastes. For a few years I had a happy exchange of shoes with a girl up in North Dakota, but in college we lost track of each other, and then NOSE gradually seemed to have a breakdown in its administration. I tried several times during my life to find another exchange partner, but they never did provide one. They still exist, and I send them the extra shoes I buy—the ones I can't wear for the opposite feet—and I imagine they sit in a warehouse until someone requests something in those sizes.

But shoes were among the more superficial and solvable problems in my childhood.

Me and Daralyn, Easter, 1956.

8

—

the crippled kid meets sticks and stones

Children I knew in the neighborhood accepted my limitations and we played together almost normally. I couldn't run, so it was quite unrealistic to engage me in games like baseball, which at that time girls only played in PE class, but there were lots of games of Red Light/Green Light, Mother May I, and Swing the Statue on our front lawn, as well as Hide and Go Seek around the neighborhood. If kids were riding bikes that day, I went home and read Nancy Drew or Judy Bolton books or watched TV, unless Daralyn was there to pump me. She biked me farther than my mother would have wanted us to go, and I loved it. I was cheeriest when I wasn't home, for the most part.

I loved to play with dolls, knowing this was practice for the family I expected to have someday. I see now that I also used these helpless pretend children to release my frustrations. I remember biting one of my dolls on her hard plastic arm until my teeth hurt. I created make-believe doll-sized apartment buildings out of my child-scaled table and chairs, complete with taped-on pieces of paper sporting drawn elevator buttons. Living in an apartment seemed like the most glamorous life imaginable. I played Monopoly, Finance, and Clue with my friends, and watched tons of television.

TV was fast becoming a babysitter for working moms, or even moms who wanted a break. For me, it was also a rest stop: I was required to take an hour's nap midday up until I was six or seven, since I fatigued so easily, so a half-hour on the couch after school was not laziness but necessity. If I pushed too hard, my little leg would buckle under me like a marathon runner at race's end. And on Saturday mornings, of course, every pajamaed kid in town was in front of the TV. Early childhood favorites were *Ding Dong School* with Miss Frances, *Winky Dink and You* (vinyl sheet on the TV screen so we could draw parts of the cartoon with crayon), *My Friend Flicka*, and *Fury*, the last two being horse-with-kid-owner shows. I also loved Howdy Doody the puppet; having met Clarabelle the clown in the hospital confirmed my devotion, plus I loved the emcee, Buffalo Bob, especially since Bob was my daddy's name. *Red Ryder* with Little Beaver, his Indian boy sidekick and sneaky informer, were another personal favorite. At one point I started making-believe that Little Beaver lived over my bedroom with his thirteen friends (expressing my longing for siblings), and I required anyone entering my room to walk around the imaginary staircase. People snickered or smiled. I knew they were patronizing me and didn't like it, but understood: pretend was pretend, even if for me it was pretend-real.

Then there was—be still, my beating heart—*The Cisco Kid*. Cisco and Pancho, Cisco handsome and Hispanic, Pancho paunchy and meant to be the stereotype of a friendly Mexican. "Oh, Cisco!"; "Oh, Pancho!" they'd say at the end, and ride off into the chaparral. I wanted to be *some* kind of kid with a capital K, but really, I knew I was known as The Crippled Girl or The Crippled Kid.

In the evenings, there was *Your Hit Parade*, with Gisele MacKenzie, Snooky Lanson, Dorothy Collins, and Tommy Lionetti, and eventually there was *The Ed Sullivan Show*. There was so much life out there, so much to being an entertainer! I knew all the songs and sang them, sometimes while dancing about the living room. Yes, I could dance, albeit in the lame way you'd imagine a little girl with a paralyzed leg and foot would dance. (Often I've said, "I can't do that," to invitations to do something requiring strength in my foot or legs. And then some well-meaning person has implored, "Oh, just try!" and then said quietly, "Oh—I see," after I've made the effort.)

In early school days, my off-balance skip was my substitute for running, and it sufficed for getting up and down the block quickly when the sidewalk was hot and we were all going barefoot. At school, the children were not always as understanding as in my own neighborhood, and by first or second grade I had been tagged with the moniker "Hopalong Cassidy" by one boy in particular, Steven, though occasionally others would toss it in my face as well.

He started picking on me as early as kindergarten. One sunny day I was leaning against the ivory stucco wall in the playground during recess, probably resting. He approached until he was standing right in front of me. He stepped closer, until he was pinning me up against the wall with his big stomach, giving me an intimate view of his green plaid flannel shirt.

Frightened, I squirmed as he stared down into my eyes, savoring his power over me.

"Stop it!" I said. "Move! I'll tell Mrs. Overstreet!"

He wasn't cowed by this threat. He just continued to stare into my eyes. I had no idea what he intended to do, other than keep me pinned to the wall. My heart was racing in terror, but my thought was that he couldn't hurt me very much right there in front of everyone in the kindergarten play yard . . . could he? And recess did have an end.

After an eternity of a few minutes, the bell rang and he had to let me go—but the vulnerable feeling stayed with me. It was clear to me I had been lucky this time, and thus learned at the tender age of five-and-a-half that I needed to stay clear of bullies, since I was small and could not run.

⤳

A year later, I was still enduring Steven's taunts, but he hadn't had an opportunity to physically bully me again. Then one afternoon after school, my friend Karen and I were waiting near the brick steps outside the kindergarten/first grade door for our mothers to pick us up, and Steven happened to come out just after we did.

He began his taunts: "You're Hopalong Cassidy! Hopalong Cassidy!"

"Leave me alone!" I said crossly. I was never afraid to talk back—which is, unfortunately, just the type of behavior that eggs a bully on.

Once again, he was standing close in front of me, taking an intimidating posture. But this time, suddenly, he punched me hard in the solar plexus.

It knocked the wind out of me and I could not get a breath in or out, let alone speak. The three of us were stunned, shocked, mouths agape; I am certain that Steven never thought he could cause such a dramatic result.

Karen ran into the school, and seconds later Mrs. Malloy, our plump and gentle first grade teacher, came out and found me gasping for breath, Steven standing there glued to the same spot, eyes wide, paralyzed by the effect of his violence, too young to know to flee the scene of the crime.

Mrs. Malloy grabbed him by the arm and gave him a look that could kill, then turned to me. "Are you all right, Francine?"

I was still in shock but nodded yes. I managed to whisper in disbelief, "He punched me in the stomach!"

Mrs. Malloy hauled him up the steps by the arm, and now he was the one who was clearly afraid. Karen and I knew they were off down the long, dark hall to Principal Nason's office—bad luck for Steven, because Mr. Nason happened to live just around the corner from us and knew our family and my condition.

In those days, corporal punishment was still legal in grammar school, and we assumed that Steven had gotten the licking of his life with a wooden paddle—the licking my mother was always threatening to give me. Mr. Nason never said a word to me about it, but Steven gave me a wide berth for the rest of grammar school. My mother's advice on hearing the story was to stay clear of him . . . as if I had not already tried.

My belief is that many things like this happen to children that they are not able to fully articulate. I didn't have the vocabulary to say, "Kids at school are bullying me and scaring me"—plus, by the time I got home and was playing with other children and having a good time, an incident like this would not have been at the front of my mind. I might have told Mama, "Kids at school are calling me names," but she would have responded with, "Don't pay any attention to them"—which, I feel, is a form of discounting a child's experience. I know that occasionally I was asked what I did at school, but never, "Are the children nice to you? Do you have fun playing with them?" I don't think my mother understood that I was being bullied, or perhaps she did and didn't want to dwell on it.

Mrs. Malloy, though, knew the truth of the situation.

I realize now that poor Steven was probably bullied at home by his older brother or parents. It was a case of kicking the dog, finding someone who was below you on the totem pole who could not fight back or run from the "fat kid." I would guess that kids called Steven "Fatty." But in my early school days, I could not know or understand any of that, and was just glad my hero the principal had laid down the law for my nemesis (though I did feel sorry that Steven got the awful paddling). After that I was relatively safe at school—for a while.

My mom said I always enjoyed the fifteen-minute opera shows because I loved the costumes (I have only a vague recollection of this). I suspect that actually I loved the drama and the music. I always loved to sing, and I took a couple of years of piano lessons, practicing on two different neighbors' pianos, since ours had been sold in Los Angeles—my dad hadn't wanted to pay the fifty dollars to move it north. My mother the singer regretted that forever after.

In grammar school, I encouraged the neighbor kids to join me in organizing and practicing for shows that we never actually presented. We'd make up songs and sing them on our big front porch, put on makeup, create ridiculous skits that no one ever saw. It was great fun, and I could not imagine anything better than being an actress or a singer. I saw this as my eventual future, and if you'd told me then that it would never happen, I would not have believed you. It didn't cross my mind that having a gimpy leg was a detriment to becoming a glamorous movie star or a professional singer.

A girl I didn't know approached me in the first grade schoolyard one sunny California day. She stood in front of me and looked into my face, then looked down at my little leg and stared at it. I had no idea where this encounter was going.

She made eye contact again and stated, simply, "You're crippled."

"I know," I said. I mean, what else was there to say? I already knew I was defective and thought it was pretty odd that she thought she needed to tell me. Did she think I was crippled and also stupid? I stared back at her; she looked down at my leg again, then, bored with the discussion, walked away.

This scenario, or one similar to it, has taken place many times over the course of my life. When I was younger, sometimes the child would say nothing and just inspect me. Sometimes these encounters made me angry, and sometimes just stunned, embarrassed, and sad. At first, I said, "So what?" But I learned not to ask that, because it sometimes unleashed a list of other observations, such as, "You can't walk right. This is how you walk," followed by a demo I always felt was exaggerated (though I realize now that it wasn't); or, "You can't run. You can't catch me," followed by the taunter grabbing one of my belongings and running with it.

Sometimes, though, if I said, "So what?" they'd just answer, "Nothing," shrug, and walk away, much like the first little girl. I always saw that as a small victory: one more person had learned that he or she didn't scare me, that they couldn't upset me, that I was mentally fit, so there was something right about me. But there were also times when I waited to cry until I was home alone.

❧

It falls to those of us who are different to find a way to suggest appropriate behavior to innocent blurters, especially kids. I was not always good at it. In fact, I see that in a lot of instances I was pissed off inside and wrote the person off as a jerk, when in fact he or she was simply ignorant. I know I have been sarcastic to a lot of people in my lifetime, and I guard against it now, but it took me decades to be calm about other people's bad manners in this respect. By the time I was in my thirties, although I still had significant anger about a lot of things, I did begin to see that people often said or did things without thinking first, and realized that it wasn't worth it to be upset over a lack of knowledge or awareness. (TMI alert: I still get angry, since I cannot squat, when women pee on the toilet seat, which I estimate at least 30 percent of American women do. Ick. I had an encounter a couple of years ago at a movie theater with a well-heeled, attractive blonde who had just done this; she was at first apologetic for using the DP stall, but I told her quietly, that's okay, just please don't pee on the seat because I can't squat, and she spun on that heel and gave me her back. I called her a bad name under my breath and turned away myself. Not proud of my behavior, but, next time I'll just make the request and leave it at that. My appeal: Take a seat, ladies. Use a seat cover if you like. You're not going to get a disease. And please don't use your foot to flush. Many handicapped people cannot use their foot; they generally must use their hand, and the bottom of your shoe is the most germ-laden thing in the bathroom.)

My next most memorable altercation after Steven the Bully took place in second grade when a friendly Italian girl, Eva, started calling me "Baby." I was shorter than nearly everyone else in the class, if not the whole grade, and still wore those high-topped "baby" shoes. Eva liked to lean in toward me with a smile and say, "Ba-by! You're a ba-by!" and laugh.

She knew she got to me with her name-calling. She may have thought we were having fun together, because she didn't seem to be a mean girl otherwise. Maybe she had brothers who teased her at home.

"I'm not a baby!" I would protest. "Don't call me that!" I'd get upset; be angry with her; limp off in a huff. Nothing seemed to deter her. Boy, she made me mad. I hated being teased. I took myself so seriously and had worked so hard to be grown up, to look nice, to do the right things to be respected as a big girl.

Finally, one fateful day, Eva pushed me to my limit. "Ba-by!" she said with a big smile, right up close to my face—and I hauled off and slugged her in the nose with my little right fist.

Her nose promptly began to bleed profusely. I gasped. We were both shocked. We looked at each other with the same expression: *What do we do now?*

"Let's hide in the bathroom," Eva said.

"Okay," I said, glad that she wasn't going to report me. I think she saw before I did that she was also going to get into trouble for taunting the crippled girl if the entire story were told, but I was sure I was the one that would be sent to the principal's office this time.

We sneaked into the restroom just as the bell rang for the end of recess.

"Here's some toilet paper," I suggested, handing her a few sheets. The tissue didn't do much good, but at least it kept the blood from dripping down her face.

"I'm sorry!" I said.

"It was my fault too, Francine," Eva said. "I'm really sorry."

We stood there in the cold bathroom looking at each other, unsure what we were going to do. The bleeding showed no sign of stopping.

Mrs. Palmer, our nice-but-no-nonsense older teacher, missed us both immediately after the other second-graders had filed into the classroom. The first place she looked was in the bathroom.

"You girls are late for class!" she admonished us. "Didn't you hear the bell ring?"

"But Eva has a bloody nose!" I said, leaving out the details.

"Oh, my goodness," she said. "You can stay here with her, Francine, until it stops. I have to get back to the classroom.

Here, Eva, lie down on the bench." (There was a wooden bench installed in there, with metal plumbing pipe legs.)

Mrs. Palmer pulled a paper towel from the wall dispenser, tore off a little piece of it, wet it under the cold faucet, and folded it up into a rectangle about an inch-and-a-half long and a quarter-inch wide. "Now, Eva, open your mouth a little bit. I'm going to put this under your upper lip." She did so, and said, "Okay, you two girls come back to class when her nose stops bleeding."

When Mrs. Palmer's footsteps had gone down the hall and into our classroom, we both started to giggle.

"Thank you for not telling on me," I said.

"It's okay; you didn't tell on me, either," Eva said.

Then we had a silent truce. I liked her more at that moment and saw that she had not meant to be mean, she was just a tease and had taken it a bit too far.

Eva said in a few minutes, "Did it stop?"

"Yes, I think it stopped. I wonder why that works?" (Why putting a wet paper towel under an upper lip could possibly stop a nosebleed is still a puzzle to me.)

She sat up carefully. "Well, I guess we have to go back to class now."

We smiled at each other.

I, like Steven the Bully, had had no idea that I could cause such harm, let alone produce all that blood! Movies in the '50s were a bit sterilized, and cowboys and other men were always punching each other. Who knew a nose would bleed like that? Eva was totally clear that she had pushed me to violence and defensiveness, and I was clear that I had caused worse damage than her taunting. We were not "best friends forever" after that, but we did invite each other to a couple of birthday parties, and neither of us, to my knowledge, ever told anyone what had really happened. It felt like a pact between sisters.

I don't remember, prior to pubescence, being particularly aware of what people thought about my gimpy leg and lopsided walk, other than what I've mentioned before: being imitated, heckled, or picked on by children because there was no likelihood that I'd be able to run away or fight back—which, I'd privately proved to myself and my friend Eva, was a false assumption. Having learned that punching someone in the nose was not a good option, I turned to chanting, "Sticks and stones will break my bones but words will never hurt me"—but they did. The words did hurt. I didn't want to be The Crippled Kid; I just wanted to be like everyone else.

Me and Daddy, December, 1947

Reading the paper, December, 1953

9
—

daddy

*I*n the fall of 1954, after we had taken a multi-state western
United States trip in our new 1953 two-tone green DeSoto—
the only trip outside of California that my family ever took
together—my dad set about procuring two big new white International Harvester milk trucks. He, one of his route drivers,
and Grandpa Weber, my mom's dad, went to pick them up out
in St. Louis, Missouri. Given the new DeSoto, the vacation,
and the new trucks, things must have been going well for
Daddy's milk delivery service.

The three men took the train east in September, and on
Sunday the 22nd, Daddy called and talked to Mama in the evening. He told her they were going to leave at five-thirty the next
morning, before dawn, with the two trucks; Daddy's employee
would drive one and Grandpa would drive the other while my
dad rode with him.

When Mama got off the phone, she said, "I feel like I should
call them back and tell them not to leave so early. Your
grandpa's going to drive." I had an inkling what this meant:
Grandpa was notorious for falling asleep in a chair fifteen minutes into any TV show.

Monday morning, the 23rd, was a warm and sunny September day—typical, except that there was a very early knock at our
front door as I was getting ready for first grade.

I answered the door for Mama while she did the breakfast dishes and found a man standing on our front porch—a policeman, except he was dressed in beige, so I know now that he must have been a sheriff.

He took off his hat as I looked at him with wary curiosity through the screen door.

"Is your mother here?"

I knew something was really wrong; I thought perhaps something had happened to a neighbor.

"Yes . . ." I turned. "Mama? There's a policeman here . . ."

She came out of the kitchen and as soon as she saw the sheriff through the screen door, she cried out, "Oh, no!" and her face contorted, close to tears.

"May I come in, Mrs. Allen?" He opened the screen door and respectfully entered our living room. Then he said, gently and quietly, "Mrs. Allen, I am so sorry. Your husband was killed in an accident outside Downs, Kansas, early this morning, around 5:30 a.m. Kansas time. Your father, Mr. Weber, was driving."

Mama collapsed into a chair and wept profusely while I tried to take in this information. I just didn't have a context for death at that point. I knew what it meant on TV, and had witnessed the traumatic and grisly death of my kitten, Gracie, when my dad ran over her with the DeSoto, but I was vague on what the entire meaning was when someone you knew died. Someone who lived with you and cuddled you and was a milkman. I did understand that my daddy was dead, but what now? I felt frozen in time, and frightened that Mama was so devastated. My mother's grief took precedence and I tried to comfort her, my hand on her shoulder, as she sobbed in the rose-colored chair in our living room—the same chair Daddy had sat in with her perched on the arm when he'd commented to her eight years before, "When we get married . . ." That had been his shy proposal.

"Your father fell asleep at the wheel and the milk truck they were driving went off the road and into a ravine," the sheriff explained. "Mr. Allen went through the windshield and was killed instantly. He was sleeping in the back of the truck and we believe he never woke up; he likely died in his sleep."

Through her sobs, my mother managed to ask, "Is Daddy okay?"

"Yes, he has a broken knee and some minor chest damage and is in the hospital there. Would you like me to go and get a neighbor?"

She answered yes and told him to go across the street to Inez Rice's house; she came immediately and stayed with my mother for a few hours.

I had a picture in my mind of Daddy's truck going off the road and down and his body going through the windshield. I saw this over and over. I did not know what a ravine was and asked about that later, when my mother was more composed. One thing I didn't quite believe was that he hadn't woken up. *If he hit the windshield*, I thought, *that probably woke him up*. But none of us wanted to think he went through the agony of knowing that in moments he was about to die, or that he was conscious of the pain when his chest was crushed.

৹

Mama blamed herself ever after for not calling Daddy back the night before and asking him to make a later start. He was only forty-one years old. A few years later, I would think, *Why in the world did Daddy let Grandpa drive, given his habit of falling asleep?*

Prior to this haunting question, I had considered my dad a genius.

৹

It seemed like dozens of relatives came to stay with us, but I'm sure only my sister, her husband, and their toddler daughter actually slept at the house. Many of Mama's ten siblings came— the ones from Los Angeles, at least—along with their spouses and children. The church brought casseroles and other food, particularly on the day of the funeral. My mother, in her devastation, allowed this—others coming into her home, taking over, and handling the food. She liked to cook, but she clearly could not have managed this on her own.

I was enjoying getting to spend time with my teenage boy cousins. I had a big crush on Lynn, who was too old to consider me anything other than the poor little crippled cousin whose dad had died. But he and my cousin Donald and uncle Ralph, my mother's teenage brother, actually taught me to play poker, and I was pretty good at it for a nearly-seven-year-old. We sat in our small, dusty-rose-colored living room and dealt the cards on my little Disney-themed card table, using match sticks for ante. Math and logic came easily, and I understood the hierarchy of the face cards and the numbers. (I still like five-card draw, even on video poker.) I can only guess that these older boys were tolerating me because they had to, but I don't remember them being unkind at all. The women and men were in the kitchen, cooking food and doing dishes and talking about whatever it was adults discussed when there'd been a death. Probably stories of days gone by and sibling updates. I don't remember hushed tones or crying, but it was a relief for me to have the distracting card game and be treated like a big kid.

The funeral was crowded with relatives I knew and people I didn't recognize. My dad was their brother-in-law, their uncle, my half-sister's stepfather, their milkman who helped plant their fruit trees and came in for coffee, their friend. I don't remember a single word of the service—I'm sure the complexity was over my head—but I knew the mood was quiet and unhappy. "Somber" was a word I'd learn later.

The scent of the few standing funereal flower arrangements was overpowering: gladiolus, which Mama loved, roses, carnations, mums, a cacophony of floral aromas. Were we taking them all home, Mama? No, we weren't. (They'd stay at the gravesite.) Several had ribbon banners hung diagonally across them. The one that caught my eye had gold paper letters that said, "D A D D Y." Was that from me, Mama? Yes, it was. (Florists' shops still smell like a funeral to me. So glad to be able to order online.)

⌇

My mom wanted me to go and see my dad in the casket so I would know he really was dead, because she thought I didn't understand—thought I believed he was coming home with my grandfather on the train.

I never thought that; I knew Daddy was not alive, just like Gracie the kitten. I knew he was coming home dead, in a box. I'd heard the adults talking at our house. Still, against advice from relatives and friends, who wanted to protect me from this hard, inescapable reality, Mama had me sit next to her in the front row. She took me right up to the casket and held me up to peer down at my daddy through the black net over the open section of the coffin, like a bridal veil but with an opposing purpose. He looked surprisingly good. Mama held me in her arms and said, with a catch in her voice, "He looks like he's sleeping, doesn't he? He even has a little bit of a smile on his face, as if he's playing possum."

"Playing possum" was something my dad did at the end of his naps in the afternoon, after arriving home from his milk route. I'd approach the couch and say, "Daddy, are you awake?"

and he'd smile and lie there with his eyes closed. I'd get the joke and say, "You're not asleep, you're awake!" and push on his chest until he opened his eyes and threw his arms around me, laughing. "He was playing possum!" Mama would say.

But I knew this was not the case here. I was just glad that he looked so peaceful, as Mama said. Knowing he'd been in a terrible accident with his new trucks, and that his chest had been crushed, I had been afraid of what he'd look like—that he would look all beat up and have terror on his face. But then, I reasoned, he had been sleeping when the truck went off the bridge. I'd heard all this when it was discussed. All the words.

Why did Mama think I hadn't heard all that? Did she think I wasn't paying attention? Because I was a child? I just didn't have the words to describe what I was thinking and feeling. I was shocked and afraid. And a little insulted that Mama thought I was so dumb. I didn't tell her; I didn't know the word "insulted"—and besides, she was so upset. That scared me too. I felt her grief was so deep and all-encompassing. I knew this was because her love for him was as deep. I knew this, though no one had said it. Though it seemed I was the one who needed sheltering, I was protecting my mama. I felt that her loss was more important than mine. She never knew this and I never thought to bring it up as an adult.

He looked truly beautiful lying there in the polished wood coffin—smooth maple or maybe even mahogany, like good furniture.

"They did a nice job with him, he looks really good," Mama said.

I could see that he had makeup on. I heard later that it was to cover his bruises and scrapes, as was the dark net veil.

I don't regret seeing him; this is my last memory of my father: a handsome, peaceful, half-smiling face, some remainder of his affectionate, teasing humor still there.

My mother, sister, and I—and possibly my father's sisters—rode in a black limousine to the funeral and the cemetery. This seemed highly luxurious to me and I thought it was nice of them to treat us so well, not knowing that no one in deep grief is fully capable of making that drive.

At the gravesite, I was expecting the twenty-one-gun salute that Mama had explained would happen because my dad was a World War II Naval veteran. She didn't want me to be frightened; I had never liked loud noises and would cover my ears for firecrackers. I assumed they would fire twenty-one guns, one at a time, and thought that would take a pretty long time, but knew it was in honor of my dad. Instead, the gunshots were actually three rifles shot seven times. I thought maybe they were doing the shortened version because we lived so far out in the country and they couldn't get enough soldiers with guns, or perhaps my dad was a lesser war hero. It still seemed to go on forever, and was so startling every time they fired a shot. I had never heard a gun fired before, other than on TV Westerns, and was unprepared for the volume and the shock. My ears rang afterward and I thought that as tributes went, I liked the flowers better than all those awful guns.

They lowered the casket into the ground and all the adults cried. Finally, we left the flowers standing around the grave and solemnly made our way the seven miles back to our house, where we were surrounded by casseroles and the effort at jovial company of siblings, cousins, aunts, and uncles.

After the relatives departed, it was back to the business of trying to live a normal life, but my mother was never the same. She lived most of her life in grief, and it was pointed out to me by an intuitive friend, long after she died, that the way I later grieved loss as an adult was with a depth that seemed to be in honor of my mother, beyond the sadness measured in my own adult life. (I came to see in my forties that I had lived feeling that if I were not sad, I was dishonoring my mother's grief and my father's death. In 1984, when she was married to my second stepfather, my favorite of the two, my mother told me that it was the first Christmas she had not been sad "in thirty years," and gave me a meaningful look.)

Every morning that I lived with Mama, she sat with her cup of guilty coffee and chain-smoked guilty Salem cigarettes (she was a devout Mormon), staring out the window, thinking of the past. I believe she did this for all of her widowed life, even through her third and fourth marriages—up until my last stepdad's understanding of the depth of her love for my dad, as a widower himself, finally broke the spell. She then lived a few years of long-deserved relative happiness before her death from lung cancer in 1993.

my country, 'tis of thee

*A*s a handicapped seven-year-old with a depressed mother, I was numbly adapting to fatherlessness, which I experienced as a vague, lonely, gaping hole in my life. He was not there anymore when I came home from school. Daddy was not there at dinner, or on the weekends. No one whistled in the house or stole candy from the kitchen cupboard, rattling the bag so I'd chase him and our dog, Pluto, would chase me. No one was in the living room hugging Mama. There was no more sitting in his warm lap with white terrycloth bathrobe arms around me while he read the paper; no more the scent of his tanned male skin. Neither was there the considerable presence of his slightly husky body in his underwear, walking around the house during hot weather, Mama chiding him to put some clothes on or close the blinds. The joy was gone from our little family; losing him had decimated us.

Most days after school I'd let myself into the empty house, since Mama was now managing the milk delivery business and its two or three drivers. I'd be upset that no one was there, and that Mama didn't arrange to be home when I got there. A couple of times I sobbed and beat my fists on my dad's big easy chair, crying out, "Why don't you come *home?*" I meant my mother, but now I see that unconsciously I meant my father as well.

Those tearful times, when I'd see her car turn into the drive,

I'd run and hide. I wasn't playing; I wanted her to feel concern that I was not there, to go through the same ugly sense of endless time being alone with no one to care for me. I didn't know she already felt that, day in and day out. She found my hiding annoying, and always knew I was either there or at a neighbor's house anyway. She depended on me to take care of myself, watch TV, find something to do. She may not have seen the pain I was going through, or that my attempts to manipulate her emotions were a cry for help, an act of desperation on the part of a little girl. Or, she did see these things, and felt the best thing was to pretend none of it was happening and just keep daily life moving along. In those days, therapy was only for crazy people. I was a latchkey kid, except that no one in our neighborhood locked their houses in the 1950s, so I did not have the status of owning a key to our house (and never did).

～

On December 8, 1955, my eighth birthday, I was sick with German measles, a three-week malady, complete with high fever and dreams while awake. I kept experiencing myself walking down a corridor of a hospital with its floor of large green-and-white linoleum tiles—a fever-induced conglomeration of the hospital where I was quarantined and the Santa Monica rehab facility. The floor would in some places suddenly be made of only newspaper, and I would start to fall through, be quite frightened, and then come to my senses.

I told my mother what was happening to me, and she said, "Oh, you're just delirious," a new word for my second-grade vocabulary. It was very clear to me what it meant. It's interesting to me now that the sickness brought forth two of my worst fears: being in the hospital and falling. What the newspaper floor was about I don't know, except that it represented flimsiness and conveyed a lack of support; I knew that wet newspaper tore easily, having used it for papier-mâché.

I recovered before Christmas, but didn't have much time to enjoy it: all of Marysville and Yuba City were on high alert throughout Christmas week due to unrelenting rains, and around midnight on the 23rd/24th Mama woke me and told me we had to evacuate, because the over-full Feather River's levee was starting to give way.

We spent a not very merry Christmas at the Sutter High School gym, seven miles away, where we slept on the floor with a lot of people we didn't know, mostly from the Yuba City farm labor camp for migrant workers. I think Mama thought this was when I stopped believing in Santa, but in truth, I had recognized her handwriting on tags the Christmas before, the first one where Daddy wasn't there. I hadn't told her so she would not be disappointed.

I had received a little red diary with a lock and key the previous Christmas, and I wrote in it regularly. My diary entry for December 25, 1955, reads: "Today we had a flood, for the first time in my life, when I was 8." I had developed the philosophy already that life was going to be punctuated by a series of huge mishaps. I thought everyone's childhood, everyone's life, was full of heartbreaking trouble. No wonder I was drawn to dramatic movies. No wonder when kids got mad at me, I was afraid it was the end of the friendship, or maybe the end of life as I knew it. No wonder I cried easily at harsh words—not that most little girls wouldn't.

⁓

The drivers from our milk delivery business did not know where we were for two days and worried that we might have perished. No cell phones in those days, of course. One of the drivers lived in Sutter, and his wife came looking for us at the gymnasium, aghast that my mother was too proud to ask to stay with them. I had not known we had friends in Sutter and was equally surprised. After that we slept in their sons' bedroom for a couple of weeks.

Mama went back to the house daily and returned morose each late afternoon. This was not an experience a single mom could easily face, especially while still grieving. She was starting the cleanup, and I kept asking to come back home as well. She told me over and over, "You can't: it's too dirty, the house looks terrible, and there's nothing for you to do. Besides, it will make you cry to see it."

Finally, two weeks into the process, she brought me back to the house with her. I then could see what "three feet of water in the neighborhood and a foot in the house" meant. I did cry when I entered the house my father helped build and saw the devastation, though it was already partially remedied by my mother's efforts. I'm sure she had wept more than once, there alone. There was dried silt three-eighths of an inch thick on all the formerly beautiful hardwood floors. Surveying the rest of the house, this seemed to be the thing we could actually do something about. We got down on our hands and knees and proceeded to scrape off the river mud with metal kitchen spatulas, day after day. There was some talk of the silt being a potentially dangerous health hazard, but what else could we do? I remember doing the entire dining room, but maybe it just seemed like I did. At least Mama and I were doing something together.

All our furniture was essentially ruined, though the upholstered chairs were eventually recovered. The hide-a-bed sofa had to be replaced. I helped glue the moldings back on Mama's inexpensive but precious walnut dining room set, the one that had displayed the spider and Miss Muffet doll just five years earlier. The walls had water marks and dirt a foot up from the floor. All of my toys and belongings that had been at floor level were ruined except for those that could be washed. If they could be salvaged, I helped wash them. Mama had packed my favorite dolls—my little family—into the car, so those were not harmed.

I never bit them again.

~

I'd felt stable and unchanged for the most part at school since my dad's death, though perhaps a little depressed. (After the flood, everyone was depressed anyway.) I liked my second-grade teacher, Mrs. Palmer—the same considerate and practical lady who taught Eva and me to use a paper towel for nosebleeds. I also loved music class. Once a week, Miss Allen—a rotund, strange (in our childhood estimation), manly-looking woman with short, kinky, graying black hair—came in to teach us to read music and sing.

I always looked forward to this class immensely. Then, one afternoon, we were singing "My Country, 'Tis of Thee" and got to the line, "land where our fathers died," and I looked around the room, immediately thought, *I'm the only one in here without a daddy*, and started to cry. This was the first time I had had a deep awareness that I was fatherless, and specifically that I was never going to see my own daddy again. For the first time, I was overcome with grief at my loss, though a year or more had passed since my dad's death.

Mrs. Palmer got up from her desk, came and took my hand, and led me to the cloak room at the back of the classroom—the place where kids were taken for a good talking-to, reprimand, or sometimes a slap; the place where the speech therapist gave lessons to the kids with lisps. It was only coincidentally where we kept our coats, rubber boots and hats, and a few school supplies.

I had never been "taken to the cloak room" before and didn't think this boded well, but I knew Mrs. Palmer was always my friend. She squatted down so that her face was at the very low height of my own and quietly said, "Now Francine, what's the matter?"

"We got to that line, 'land where our fathers died,' and my daddy really *did* die!" I blurted out. "Everybody else has a daddy but me!" I started to cry again, tears and sobbing just spilling out of me, the knowledge really sinking in that I would never see my dear, sweet, affectionate, funny, teasing daddy again. Never. That other children had fathers and I never would. That that part of my life was over, and I had only the painful, bittersweet memories of his scent, his arms, his laughter, his handsome face.

"Oh, you're just being melodramatic," Mrs. Palmer said.

I somehow instantly got the meaning of this new word. It was condescending, and my crying over my dad's death was considered to be acting in some way, like on TV, not genuine, and inappropriate. I was so surprised, I didn't know how to react.

"Now just calm down, stay here in the cloak room, and when the recess bell rings, go outside and play with the other kids." With that, Mrs. Palmer left me there alone, stunned.

I'd been trying to be as adult as I could about my situation, trying *not* to be "melodramatic," and I felt betrayed that Mrs. Palmer was not the warm adult friend I'd thought she was. My behavior must be shameful and childish, I thought, and I should not be acting like a child. After all, I had learned not to be childish already, in all those months in the hospital.

I was confused about how to deal with these conflicting feelings. But I did as I was told: I calmed down and went outside to play, embarrassed to now be a "cloak room kid." I had not really felt sorry for myself before this, but I certainly felt pathetic now.

I have since forgiven Mrs. Palmer. People are uncomfortable

with pain and sadness. They often want it to just go away, and are quick to suggest that others with acute pain or sadness just pretend things are okay and find some semblance of order and normalcy. This, I believe, assuages the feelings of the person who's uncomfortable, and who may feel helpless to offer any words or actions of relief in the face of grief. There is an undeniable pathos in a handicapped child mourning the sudden death of her father. People also knew the financial hardship this was going to visit upon my mother.

Possibly Mrs. Palmer told my mother about that incident, but no one ever mentioned my breakdown again, and I kept my tears inside for decades.

～

I cried about the loss of my father again when I was in my forties and doing therapy about my relationships with men and my attraction to those who tended to be unavailable—like my father, though his "abandoning" me was due to a tragedy he could not have foreseen. In therapy, I took the opportunity to cleanse my heart of my loss and look at how it had affected my life. I could finally reclaim my full complement of emotions and no longer pretend I was tough. Nearly four decades after my father's death, I finally allowed myself to grieve, to let in the real pain I'd been told was invalid. (The invalid girl has an invalid emotion. Too ironic.)

As an adult, with the help of counseling, I imagined that little girl I had been, saw her crying on her dad's chair and in the cloak room, and invited her into my lap, held her close, allowed her tears. I told her I would never abandon her or judge her. That it was going to be all right now, she no longer had to pretend to be a grown-up. She was part of me, the adult me who saw how difficult it must have been, and she was safe now. But in 1956, I was eight, small for my age, precocious, and once again being forced by circumstance to learn to be a little adult.

⟋

After the flood, we ate more macaroni and cheese and hamburger and had fried chicken only on Sunday nights. I am sure that Mama could not run Daddy's business as successfully as he had, especially since she could not drive a truck or do deliveries. She sometimes took me along when she went to the homes of past-due customers. I see now that this was so that they would see she was raising a handicapped child alone.

Step by step, month by month, we gradually fashioned our lives into a new normal in 1956.

carol (francine) the christian girl

*W*e belonged to the right church for that time. The Mormon hierarchy provided food and other needed goods, shipped in from Salt Lake City, where the tithings of the pious had purchased a tremendous warehouse of groceries and supplies. I'll say this for the Mormons: they plan ahead and they take care of their own. We were eating Deseret Brand canned and dry goods for months. The Red Cross was also in town providing relief, and either they or the church came and sanded our floors and refinished them and repainted the house, inside and out, in the same white, pink, rose, and ivory colors my mother had originally chosen.

I don't remember ever attending church until we got firmly planted in our own home on Brown Avenue in Yuba City, when I was almost four. There, our church was just three blocks away, so Mother and I walked on many Sundays, though we were often running late so usually we'd hop in the DeSoto and drive over. (Daddy didn't come; he was a Methodist, but never attended church anyway.)

The first memory I have of Sunday school is of being in a class with other kids when I was five. The teacher was "Sister" Naomi Henry, who had short, sandy red hair, freckles, and a compassionate smile. Mormons called all adults by "Sister" or "Brother," as in "Sister Hansen" or "Brother Matthews" instead of "Mr." or "Mrs."

"We're going to go around the room and learn everyone's names," Sister Henry said.

"First or middle name?" I asked when she got to me.

She smiled—this was not what she expected from a five-year-old—and said, "First name."

"Carol," I told her. And this was true; but no one ever called me Carol. I always felt a little guilty, like I was pulling the wool over people's eyes at church, when they called me Carol. In a way, though, this was appropriate, since in the long run this was not where I belonged. I did feel that when they called me Carol, they were addressing the Christian polio girl, and when people called me Francine, they were addressing the whole polio girl. So my relationship with the church was a little schizy from the get-go.

One Sunday, Sister Henry told us, "Today I would like each of you to make up a story and draw pictures on the blackboard to go with your story."

We were near the Christmas season, so I had that in mind when it was my turn.

I walked to the blackboard, fairly nervous about the daunting assignment, and picked up the chalk.

"Once there were some trees in the woods," I began. "Most of the trees were tall and straight and perfect." I drew some symmetrical fir or pine tree outlines. Everyone was patient while I took my time. "It was Christmas time, so people came to chop down the trees and take them home." I drew a smaller tree that leaned to one side and had a misshapen trunk. "But there was one little tree that was lopsided and crooked, and no one was picking it to take home. It was sad that all the other trees were going to someone's house for Christmas. Then one day, right before Christmas, finally someone loved it and took it home to decorate with lights and ornaments!"

I drew a few ornaments on the tree. And then I sat down, pleased that I'd been able to think up a story.

Sister Henry's face was tender with understanding when I finished speaking. Her look told me that I'd described myself unintentionally, and I was a little embarrassed. She said, "Thank you, Carol, that was a very nice story."

I always gravitated to underdog stories where the least likely but most sincere characters somehow won out, and that's all I'd done—make up a story like you'd see on *Lassie*, on TV. I hadn't known where I was going with it until I started drawing on the blackboard.

ے

Here's what I loved about church: First, dressing up. I loved to look nice, like the other girls. Second, seeing my church friends. Third, gazing at the picture of "Jesus" at the front of the chapel. (I was at the church for Daralyn's mom's funeral reception in 2016, and they had taken the picture down; I've been musing on why this might be.) This was Jesus with the light brown hair who looked like some of the hippie guys I eventually hung out with in the 1960s and 70s. In the painting, he was gazing up toward his Heavenly Father. He was so handsome. How could you not love him?

The fourth thing I loved was the music, the singing. There was sometimes a performance of Handel's "Messiah" at Christmas, which I loved. Talk about your alleluias.

What I didn't love about church was sitting still with Mother. But the music led me to a greater appreciation of classical and especially choral music. Music was definitely feeding my soul early on and was inspiring to Christian Polio Girl. All those voices raised up to God! When a large group of people sings one beautiful song with harmony and dynamics, it truly is uplifting, making it easy to believe in divinity. Singing is also a heart-opening and physically exhilarating experience and creates a feeling of unity with the other singers. If the church had done nothing but sing and left out the sermons, I might have stuck with them a whole lot longer.

⌁

At some point in my childhood, I asked that question most people who believe in God eventually ask: "Why does God let bad things happen?" For instance, if there is a God, why did he let the Nazis kill all those Jewish people?

We watched a lot of movies about World War II and Nazi Germany in the fifties. My grandfather was of Swiss-German descent and his second wife, my step-grandmother, was German. I asked Mother while watching one of those movies, "Were we for the Germans or the Americans in the war?"

"For the Americans!" she said with some alarm. "Why do you ask that?" (She was keeping a secret about my step-grandma—who, I later found out, had been a Nazi sympathizer—and wondered if I'd heard something about her past.)

"Because Grandpa and Grandma are German," I said.

Mother kept her silence.

Of course, along with why the Holocaust had been "allowed" by God, my underlying personal question was, *Why did God let me and all those other children get polio? Did I do something wrong when I was little? Were my parents and I being punished?* I really had a hard time believing this was God's will. Why would He punish an innocent three-year-old?

When I inquired, or when other kids asked the same theosophical questions, the pat answers we received from adults were myriad and cliché: "God tests those He loves most"; "Everything happens for a reason"; "God moves in mysterious ways, his wondrous works to perform"; "God gives us free will; many people abuse that free will, are tempted by the Devil, and give in to him, and that is why there is evil amongst humans." That last one made the most sense to my simplistic, childish thinking. God good, Devil bad. Side with one or the other.

But of course, that simplicity did not continue to suffice for my inquiring mind.

Occasionally, after Daddy died, we watched Oral Roberts, the evangelist, on television. (My dad would not have watched a show like that; he would have preferred to watch wrestling and chuckle.) Mr. Roberts would give a sermon and then people would line up to be healed. Someone with a wheelchair, a crutch, a limp, or some apparent illness would approach the stage slowly and sit in a chair. Oral Roberts would lay his hands on the person's head and pray, and then firmly press on the head a few times with dramatic emphasis and ask God to *"Heal* this man of his infirmities, O God, *heal* him, we pray in the name of Jesus Christ, our Lord, Amen!!!"

I always thought, *Gosh, doesn't that hurt their neck?* But afterward, the person would get up and walk away and leave his crutches on stage, and everyone would applaud and shout.

I turned to my mother once and said, "Can we go to see him? Maybe he could heal me."

"No-o-o," she answered, in her "for heaven's sake" voice.

I don't think we watched the show much after that. Whether Mother believed in faith healing or not (I soon saw it as a hoax), she didn't want me to get my hopes up about that sort of thing.

My first truly spiritual experience happened at Camp Fire Girls' camp nearly two years after the flood, in 1957, when I was nine. I had occasionally spent the night at friends' houses before this, but other than my hospital stint, I had never been away from home as long as a week—and of course, my mother had come to see me every day in the hospital. I never even had a babysitter. So this was a big thing, to go away to the Sierra Nevada mountains of California, a three-hour drive up into the hills, with Daralyn and her mom—especially since Daralyn was in a tent with older girls and I was in the nine-year-olds' tent, where I didn't know anyone at first.

Mother was happy to be home alone for a week and eat Chinese and Mexican food, which I eschewed until later learning that ethnic foods were cool.

At Camp Me Wa Hi ("by the water in the hills" in Pidgin American Indian that someone had made up), I had free time in between sessions one day, and I wandered a short way from the tent into the surrounding woods—far enough to be alone, but close enough to still hear the voices of girls and know I was not lost. I found a little stand of ferns, willowy shrubbery, and saplings, with an area underneath the greenery where the ground was partially clear, and sat down under the low, leafy canopy. It felt like my own little protected fairy haven. I looked up through the fronds and waving twigs to the sky and trees above. The light through the spring green leaves transfixed me with their exquisite translucence. What color! What light! What a miracle was this natural world.

And then a new thought: *I am here totally alone. No one knows where I am. No one in the world.* I was having my first experience of being solitary, and it was happening in this place of beauty. I was hooked. It was exhilarating. My soul felt unencumbered. From that day forward, I sought out solitary places of nature and beauty.

12
—

just another schoolgirl
(who discovers water)

*T*he last couple of years of grammar school were fun and easier: kids knew me, and being among the oldest kids in my class gave me some confidence. I knew I was bright, and I got invited to most of the birthday parties, though there were some girls that were clearly in a more advanced social sphere, partly because they'd learned social expectations that I didn't quite have down yet, and sometimes because their families were also more sophisticated and/or had money.

I have always had to allow myself a little extra time to get from one point to another, and have always erred on the side of pretending I am normal and can do things as quickly as anyone else, but most of my teachers cut me no slack. The advice I received from all adults was that I needed to stop what I was doing before other people, cut my fun or tasks short, leave something out: makeup, hair styling, and so on.

It's a lot to ask, especially of a child or teenage girl; I was often late—and being late for class could result in time spent in detention after school, or, as happened in the second grade, writing "I will not be late for school" one hundred times (Mrs. Palmer's room, again, though that time was Mama's fault—she consistently was not ready to leave on time in the morning).

My poor, depressed mother spent eons staring out the window and chain-smoking after my dad died. She didn't have to be anyplace on time, and I paid the price for our tardiness. It has always been a source of tension for me, estimating how long things are going to take (even though, in an ironic twist of fate, I eventually became a cost estimator in a factory, and did precise time and motion studies).

Despite my physical slowness, however, I always enjoyed being active. When I wasn't watching afternoon or Saturday morning TV during those years, or voraciously reading, I was mostly outside in good weather. I'd do my awkward skip up the block to Daralyn's (before I was old enough to become self-conscious about the way it looked) or over to the next block to see my friends Marilyn, Joyce, and Carolyn, or to the next-door neighbors', Retha and Missy, or Ellen's across the street. Out and about, all the time. My mom would call around the neighborhood to fetch me home at dinner. This suited my independent nature. With my dad gone and my mom working till late afternoon, there was no longer anyone home in the afternoon, and I preferred being at someone else's house to being home alone with a TV movie after school, unless I was too fatigued to play.

Kickball was the sport we played in grammar school, and I had as my fourth grade Phys Ed teacher Mrs. Cooey, who thought I should run despite my paralysis. We all referred to her as Mrs. Cootie, and she truly was a weird, crotchety bug. I could not kick with my strong leg, because I had to stand on that one. If I stood on the polio leg for my max of one second, and kicked with the strong foot, I'd either fall over or only be able to tap it with a short little kick—plus, I'd miss the ball most of the time— so instead I gave it the best I had with my "lazy leg," as Mother called it. Sometimes I could kick it straight, sometimes it went sideways.

The ball would only make it to the infield. I did begin to see that kicking it away from first base was an advantage. But Mrs. Cooey made me run the bases, which was a fool's fantasy. I got lots of skinned knees from slipping on the gravelly blacktop as I did my gimpy step-step-skip; plus, I never once made it to first base. As a result, not surprisingly, no one ever wanted me for their team. I was the last one standing when the captains selected teams. If a close girlfriend was the captain, I'd sometimes get a mercy pick. I soon began to think, *I wouldn't want me on the team, either!*

One morning, my homeroom teacher, Mrs. McDowell, came striding out from the old one-story brick and ivory stucco school building with its Spanish tile roof and marched over to the kickball area with a determined vengeance that impressed us all mightily. We wondered what was about to happen. I thought it likely that some girl was in trouble and had been found out for some infraction.

Mrs. McDowell was known as a sweet but firm and strong teacher. She sometimes rubbed my cold little leg with her caring, rough hands when it turned purple in the winter, so I considered her an adult friend.

She was not, it turned out, after one of us. She marched right up to Mrs. Cooey, arms swinging at her sides, and said, "What are you doing? You can't make her run those bases! She could get hurt out here! Can you imagine what might happen to her if she has a bad fall!?" And then to me, "Francine, you just kick. You do the best you can, and have someone else run for you. You can still play the game, but you don't have to run." With a fiery parting look for Mrs. Cooey, she turned on her heel and strode back to monitor the rest of the playground.

Wow. Somebody standing up for me. I had never seen one authority figure challenge another before, least of all in my defense. I knew better than to say anything to my PE teacher, but I may have given her a look that said, *Okay, now we have a new understanding, you old bat.* The other girls were stunned, and I vaguely remember a little amazed gossip going around later on. From then on, though I was never in the first draft, of course, I was not so ostracized in the team-picking process, since I could kick the ball enough to enable a good runner (someone like my friend Kathryn) to make it to first base, maybe second if the outfielder fumbled. In this way, though I was never enthusiastic about kickball, at least I could play it and be one of the team members instead of sitting and reading a book and waiting for PE or recess to be over.

As for Mrs. Cooey, I believe now that she had a bad back. She was fat and walked as if her waist was in a brace, as if her upper body was separate from her lower, a disconnected rotation going on there. Maybe she had some lifelong injury; maybe she thought that if she'd only been pushed to do sports, she would not be as stiff as she ended up being.

Or maybe she was just a mean old bat.

﹏

Four square was a game I could play somewhat competitively. There was a cool but intense atmosphere surrounding this lunchtime sport. There were perhaps six fields painted on the playground blacktop. Each field was divided into four smaller squares, one kid to each square. It was like tennis, in a way, though played in a micro area without a net, and with a big bouncy ball about ten inches in diameter, which made a really satisfying, reverberating *thwongggg!* when it hit the ground. The server bounced it and slapped it lightly into someone else's square, and it was hit in turn into various squares. If you could not hit the ball or if it was hit in an outside corner or a spot where you could not reach it, you were out. If you hit it outside the lines or in your own square, out you went; end of the line, for (hopefully) a short wait before your re-entry.

Generally, the round started out pretty easy and friendly and then heated up. It was fun to keep it going but if you did that for too long, the other kids didn't get in to play. If you tried to put people out right at the beginning, you were considered a poor sport with too much attitude. In those days we would have called it just plain mean. I played with kids I knew and liked, and it may be that they were exceptionally kind to me, knowing that I could not run to get the ball in a far corner. Whatever the case was, I loved four square. I could stand up more easily for a half hour back then, and I was in line for that game almost every day. And when I missed or made a wrong hit and my ball was out, I got right back in line.

Dodgeball was a different story. What a masochistic game. Stand in line and people throw that same innocent four square ball *at* you . . . and you're supposed to get out of the way? Forget it. I got hit all the time, and it hurt. That was a game for boys or tomboys, as far as I was concerned.

ᐟᐟᐟ

Around age ten to twelve, I went to visit my much older sister, LaVonne, in San Francisco, whom I looked up to as a fascinating role model. (Her dad was my mom's first husband, and she was nearly nineteen when I was born.) We would occasionally make the three-hour trip to the city from Yuba City, though Mother (no longer "Mama") hated to drive. Luckily for me, I was allowed at last to take the Greyhound bus and stay a week or two with my sister and her family.

While I was there, LaVonne took me shopping one day for a coat, which my mother had neglected to pack for me, though she knew San Francisco was much colder than Yuba City, even in the summer. My sister was a little disgusted that Mother had not thought of this, saying, "Tch! Mother didn't pack a *coat* for you?" pursing her lips and shaking her head. But she was also not very surprised: our mother could be a little spacey, despite her pragmatism and domesticity.

We were walking along the sidewalk and I was enjoying the foreign atmosphere of a city, looking forward to riding a cable car or going to the huge Sprouse-Reitz for an ice cream soda, when my sister commented, "I gave that lady a dirty look. I always give people a dirty look when they stare at you."

I felt pride at this display of love from my big sister. But I had not realized that anyone was staring at me; in fact, I never noticed that happening, other than when kids at school were so obvious about it. Now I was embarrassed that I had not known this. People were staring at me because of how I walked. On the streets of San Francisco. Probably everywhere I went. Possibly it had been happening a lot, and I didn't even know it. I felt so foolish.

I did not wish that my sister hadn't said anything; she didn't know that I was unaware of this phenomenon. I felt that she loved me and was sticking up for me, and I was glad to have a champion in the world, even for the simple gesture of occasionally giving somebody a dirty look. I also felt like I needed to do several rather contradictory things: buck up, pretend I didn't care, act proud of who I was even though I was ashamed of my crippled walk—my weird, unfeminine walk—and try and learn to walk differently, to bend my left knee a little to make that leg seem shorter or not walk in front of people at all unless I had to.

That last option was going to prove almost impossible, especially as a lifelong approach, though I mastered it in many circumstances, particularly those involving meeting boys outside of school. If you stand on the sidelines, or spend the party sitting down, or stay in the car at the drive-in, no one can see how you walk. I did always jump at the chance to dance later on, if asked. But I began to beg off doing things in PE at school more and more. I didn't want to be stared at or have those thoughts stimulated: *She can't do this, she looks really weird, gimpy, stupid, crippled; our team will lose if she plays with us.* I didn't want people to call me a "spaz." And I sure didn't want people to know that sometimes, in fact, one or another of my toes *was* a little spastic, since I didn't always have control over what little nerve action existed down there. I was just glad the toe moved at all, in its paralyzed environment.

◈

Thank God for swimming pools, where, although the entirety of my weak, skinny, drop-foot limb was laid bare when I wore a swimsuit, once I was in the water, I was free and able—almost equal.

I had encountered my first full-sized deep-water swimming pool as a little girl when I went to Daralyn's next-door neighbors' house. I had a very frightening experience there: the Russells insisted that I don a life jacket, and between me and Daralyn, we managed to buckle it on me upside down. When I went away from the edge of the pool and ducked under the water, I got stuck upside down, and for a few moments, till Daralyn or someone else righted me, I was quite sure I was about to drown.

Despite this supposed near-death experience, in the very hot Yuba City summers (we're talking days that sometimes hit 117 degrees, and months of over 100-degree temps), we'd hear the Russells and their guests next door and sing things at the top of our lungs like, "I wanna go swimmin' with bow leg-ged women and dive . . . between . . . their legs!" We hoped this wanton display would entice them to call us over for a swim. It never did.

In 1957, however—at age nine, at Camp Fire Girls camp, surrounded by pine trees and girlfriends—I tentatively decided that I was going to learn to swim. My mom didn't swim and was afraid of the water, so this was not something she encouraged, even though it was known to be excellent exercise for polio survivors.

I got some swimming instruction from my counselors, but was really shy about looking foolish and also about the potential of drowning, so I didn't participate much in the classes. I did watch, however. And I practiced. And I got the hang of it: Take a big breath, put your face in the water, breathe out through your nose, turn your head to the side so your mouth comes up above the surface, gulp some air, blow it out into the water, and repeat. Coordinate this with arm strokes to pull yourself forward, and kick your legs. (Kicking was not so easy, but it was doable.) And keep your legs straight—that creates more forward thrust. Wow.

I know the counselors must have been watching me; there were lifeguards on duty all the time. But I felt like I was teaching myself to swim. Now and then some considerate women's swim instructor would coach and encourage me.

What liberation! Movement without the drag of a leg that didn't fully participate. My arms handling part of the propulsion. Being in water was almost like flying—at least, how I imagined it to be. And it was in some ways easier than walking, since water acts as a support.

By the end of the summer, with practice at pools at home when I could finagle it (the Covas across the street put a pool in, and I was welcome to use it whenever I wished), I was swimming nearly as well as other kids. Without the serious leg power, I'd never be competitive or play water polo, but who cared? It was something physical that I could do, and fairly well, for a gimpy kid. There was grace involved, and effort, and coordination of arms and legs and breath. Plus, swimming was a cool and sociable thing to do in our valley town.

The only drawback, as I moved into puberty and then became a teenager, was that my polio leg was pretty dismal looking—embarrassing at the public pool. At pools during high school, now I was being stared at even more, because in clothing, with a foam calf prosthetic and stockings and shoes, there was a slightly less disturbing crip thing going on, so it was more of a spectacle for my friends to see my bare, naked leg.

I just had to get in the water and then you couldn't see it. Or, if we were sunbathing or talking, I'd sit on the side with my strong leg crossed over my little one. (I still do this at times.)

I realize that it may be easy to think, *What the heck, why care about what all those other teenagers thought? In a few years, you might not even know them anymore. Be proud of who you are.* Possibly there are polio women who really didn't care what they looked like or what others thought when they were teenagers. But I really wanted to be accepted, and to be seen as pretty. I wanted to be the same as everyone else. I had a somewhat severe physical deformity, and it made me want to blend in all the more.

Now, I don't care much. People stare, and I look at them and either smile or just make eye contact and look away, depending on how I feel. But as a kid, it was very hard. I was mortified about my disability, particularly in that time when boys were looking at girls as potential dates and discussing their physical attributes. I did my best to hide or mask my leg and gait, but that really was impossible. And this added to my pretense of acting like I didn't care about things like that. (That was part of why I embraced hippiedom a couple of years later: there was at least a semblance of looks not being so important.)

⤖

Much later, in middle age, I once had a dream about a Duck God.

I dreamed that he was flying around in the sky with a human head (though sometimes with a bill) and sometimes a human body, sometimes a duck's body. He was silver, as if he had a skin of slightly matte Mylar, all over. Those of us on the ground, in some dream city, could see him flying around up there, looking down on us. He had a mercurial aura, very fast and very intriguing, and no ill will—important in a god.

Then the Duck God flew down toward me and looked at me from a few feet away. He invited me wordlessly to fly with him, and I did—and I realized that the sky was not air, it was water; it was like gel. It was wonderful, smooth, cool, silvery aqua, and soft. I was flying through an air space that felt like water.

Much like swimming.

Sixth grade, age twelve, bewildered and close to puberty.

13

—

the (even more) awkward years

*W*hen I was somewhere in the range of eleven to thirteen, Mother was going to night school at the junior college, taking a variety of courses such as political science and typing and whatever she thought would improve her and get her out of the house. I was surprised that she did this but thought it was a smart and youthful endeavor, especially for her.

One evening at dinner, after our meal was on the kitchen table, she said, "There's a young woman at the junior college who has a false leg, and you can hardly tell. She doesn't even limp."

"Mom, how did you know she had a false leg if you can't tell?"

"I asked her. I thought it looked like it might be a false leg."

(I'd never seen a false leg, and this "can't tell/but I can tell" dichotomy was confusing to me.)

"So, I asked her if she had a false leg, and she said, 'Yes, it's a prosthesis.' I asked what had happened to her and she said she had been in an accident and had to have her leg amputated."

"My gosh!" I said. "How horrible." I waited to see what else Mother had to say, a little embarrassed that she had approached this handicapped woman with intimate questions and a little afraid I was about to hear more details about her stump or whatever else my nosy mother had pried out of the poor woman.

But Mother said, "She is beautiful, and you couldn't tell she was missing a leg unless you knew what to look for; she could walk normally."

I silently mused over this: *Yes, but what is it like when she is not wearing the false leg, the prosthesis?* She'd have to hop on one leg or use a crutch, all the time. Pretty tiring and difficult, more so than what I had going on. And there must have been something that was a pretty big clue that the leg was not real. But I took it that Mother was trying to encourage me that you could be attractive and handicapped, which was definitely a worry for me, and probably more of a worry for her. I am also sure, based on the types of encouragement I was given and indirect comments she made, that she thought I might be dependent upon her all of my life and might never attract a husband, and this was why she showed such concern that I go to college and learn to support myself.

⁓

Not long after this, Mother had another story, again at our kitchen table.

"I talked with Lila Holdaway the other day." I was not a huge fan of this garrulous woman from the church with a deep southern accent; I felt she was a little too inquisitive and, by our quiet, homey standards, too outgoing. But she had invited us to her home not long before, for her daughter's baby shower. I had been the only child in attendance, all dressed up and on awkward good behavior, which felt weird and not much fun, but I'd liked the cake and the games. I had never had a babysitter, and I was old enough to stay home alone anyway, but I think Mother had wanted me to see what a baby shower was.

Mother continued without my encouragement, "Lila asked me, 'Wah don'tchoo just get 'er polio leg cut aahf, and get 'er a PLA-stic leg? Then both 'er legs would be the same.'"

I looked at Mother incredulously for a moment and then burst into laughter. "She thinks I should *get my leg cut off!?*" More laughter at the naiveté of this sincere woman. "That's crazy! Does she think I'd be better off with just one leg? At least I can stand up!"

Mother didn't answer me but sat there quietly smoking, wrist bent, cigarette held to the side at shoulder level, eyes becoming slightly distant, as they did when she had a private thought, doing the ear-toward-shoulder, side-to-side, bobble-head movement she did when she'd come up with something she thought was noteworthy or right. (I would much later think this head gesture looked like the East Indian gesture for "yes.")

I had thought we were sharing a bonding moment about the misunderstanding people have about handicaps. Over the years, however, I have realized that my mother was tentatively suggesting something she thought might be a solution for the embarrassment and stigma of having a limpy, off-balance, un-attractive, unfeminine gait. My own mother was suggesting I have my leg amputated, and thought better of pushing the idea after hearing my reaction.

If I had realized this at the time, I would have gone to my room and sobbed for a week, and probably avoided speaking to her for at least a month. It would have been even worse had she added the idea that I might never marry.

Even today there is risk of infection with amputations and they are generally only done when the limb is a threat to the person's life. I have known people who have had amputations and they'd all prefer to have been able to keep the limb. Seems obvious, huh? But today, I realize how naïve my mother was and also how much she worried about how things looked to others. She just wanted a normal life for her handicapped girl. She didn't understand that being an amputee would have made me even less a normie.

"Point your toe straight," Mother always told me, because I threw my polio foot out to the side—typical of people with a weak, paralyzed leg. This unconscious gait, with my knee also slightly pointed outward, was a bad habit, training the muscles to operate in a way that would be detrimental and potentially influencing improper bone growth. Throwing my foot outward also dramatically emphasized my "crippled kid" aspect.

I hated being constantly corrected, and remember especially the times Mother would say this when we either walked the three blocks to church or walked in after driving because we were, as usual, running too late to walk the distance. But she impressed it upon me, and I did learn to be aware of pointing my foot forward much of the time, which made it less likely I'd hit my foot on something. So I'm grateful for her persistent gait corrections now. Even today, when I discover I'm unconsciously throwing my foot out, especially when I'm tired, I hear her voice saying, "Point your toe straight," and make an effort to do just that.

Much later on, it would become clear that when I did correctly position my right foot, I then threw my left, strong foot out to the side, making a semi-circular motion to allow for its extra two inches in length. (Imagine if you had no shoe on one side and a two-inch heel on the other foot. Then imagine having to do that for decades.) I was not aware of this trajectory until I accidentally kicked a box of oil paints in college with my longer-legged strong foot and dislocated and broke my little toe. I immediately saw what the problem was: I didn't know where my strong foot had been going. This was at age twenty-one, a bit of a long time coming, but something I immediately incorporated into my walking awareness. Probably when I'd been throwing the polio foot out to the side, this made it easier for the left foot to travel forward in a straight line. I tried to start walking with the strong knee a little bent, as I'd learned to do in San Francisco earlier in life to mask my limp a little. It's hard to keep that up, though.

Every change we make in the functioning of our bodies will affect some other part. Evolution has favored balanced parts. For an unbalanced polio patient, there are more than the normal changes and adaptations throughout life; they are constant.

❧

In middle and high school in the 50s and 60s, it was common for girls to wear the ring of a boy around their necks on a long chain, to signify you were "going steady." I wore Stanley DeMille's for a couple of weeks in sixth grade and that was the longest serious—and I use this word facetiously—romance I had until I was in high school.

Going steady could mean that you actually went out on dates with that person, and no one else, or it could mean, at the sixth-grade level, that the two kids in question had simply identified that they liked each other more than any other person of the opposite sex for a week or two. If you were going steady in middle school, you had someone to sit with at the ball games, or maybe walk you home holding hands, or pass you notes in class that made your heart beat more quickly, and maybe you'd kiss once in a while.

Girls that developed early physically and were also popular may have been doing more than that, but I didn't hear about any hanky-panky till I was in high school. I was kind of an ugly duckling at this stage; my sixth grade Gray Avenue School picture shows a girl who looks as if she's lost in a world she doesn't understand. I'm wearing a white blouse, Peter Pan collar, blue scarf tied at the neck. My wan smile reveals a space between my front teeth, which were at angles other than right. "You'd better start pushing your front teeth out with your thumb," Mother said, "because we can't afford braces." I had not noticed my teeth were crooked until then and now had another thing to feel self-conscious about.

My hair, in the picture, is a variation on a tight pageboy, with curled bangs high off my forehead, achieved with rubber curlers. This was the first hairstyle I created on my own, and it looks like something a young girl with scant fashion sense would come up with. I really cared that I was included and The Same, but I wanted to have some sort of unique look, and it wasn't working.

୧୨

One day in sixth grade, I entered the girls' restroom just after the bell rang indicating five minutes to get to class. There would be barely enough time for me to use the facilities and get to my homeroom.

Two other sets of girlish feet came in as soon as I closed the stall door and occupied the stall next to me. *Why were they both in there together,* I wondered? *Maybe one is helping the other with a bra strap or zipper,* I guessed.

The voice of a friend from church, Michelle, piped up, "I think Francine just wants people to pity her."

"Yeah," answered my other friend, Clare, "she just wants pity. She just feels sorry for herself."

"Let's get to class," Michelle said.

They left together; I don't even think either of them used the toilet.

I was stunned. I didn't know whether to cry or go to class. I could feel that my face was hot with embarrassment. Did they know I was in the next stall? It seemed obvious that they'd wanted me to hear this exchange. I would never know, but my intuition told me they'd seen me go into the bathroom and had been planning this.

And then, running through my mind: *Do I really feel sorry for myself? Do I really want pity? My gosh, of course not, I want to be the same as everyone else.* I did expect that people would have some sensitivity that I was limited physically. Anyone might think this was unfortunate—but "pity"? Wasn't pity for people who needed a great deal of help, money, some sort of aid? Who were desperate? Was wanting people to cut me some slack regarding my physical speed and strength feeling sorry for myself? Was I really projecting that I wanted people's pity? I was distraught and humiliated.

I'd thought these girls were my friends and liked me. Were they doing me a favor, trying to enlighten me about what other kids thought? Were they doing this to get back at me? Because of what? Because I was smart and got top grades?

It was a bit much for a twelve-year-old to process. I can't remember if I discussed it with my mother, but I know what her response would have been: "Don't pay attention to them." Mother was not as dependent upon friendships as I was, and just didn't know what kind of advice to give me much of the time, so she kept her advice brief or put it in platitudes. But I couldn't ignore what other kids did or said at that time.

The issue nagged at me all through that school year and was often present for me through the ensuing years when I spoke with these two girls. And of course, I was not mature enough to ask them about it; I was mortified that I had even heard the conversation.

I have seen one of them a couple of times as an adult and have been genuinely happy to see her each time, and she has seemingly felt the same. She has always been a sweet, intelligent person, and my reconciliation with the long-ago event is that she was likely influenced by the other catty young girl. One wants to rationalize these experiences. I didn't think about the sixth grade at all when I saw her—it didn't occur to me until days later. I imagine she must have forgotten it long before I did. But this overheard bathroom conversation led me to a turning point: *My gosh, I cannot act in a way that would stimulate that impression of courting pity. I have to be strong.* My already strong personality (according to my mother, defined by my expressing my thoughts freely) was pushed up a notch, and I committed myself to appearing much tougher than I really was. I was convinced that I needed to try even harder to prove that I was not different, that I was the same as everyone else— which, of course, was the recommended and accredited school- of-hard-knocks polio approach insisted upon by many polio kids' parents. This was preposterous, and set me on a course of years of convincing myself that I did not care about things that in fact I cared about deeply.

❦

On another fateful day at school in the sixth grade, I'd walked back to class from lunch recess, and my polio leg suddenly ached so much that I could not stand. It continued to hurt after I sat down at my big rose-pink metal desk by the windows, and it was terrifying for me. This was the first time I had had pain in that leg since the initial onset nearly ten years before. I began to cry, right in class—humiliating, but I couldn't help it.

My teacher, Mrs. Hyatt, approached my desk and leaned in close. She pushed her black-framed glasses up on her nose with her middle finger, a habit she had when considering something. She was pretty, despite the space between her front teeth, which gave me hope—especially since she was married.

"Francine," she whispered, "what's the matter?"

"My leg hurts," I whispered back.

"Let's go to the nurse's office, then."

"I can't; it hurts too much to walk." By now I was completely embarrassed that students in the room were watching us.

She left the room quietly and returned in a couple of minutes with Mr. Long, a big, strong, seventh grade coach. He came straight to my desk and picked me up right out of the chair, as if I were a tiny damsel in distress. "Let's get you to the nurse's office," he said. I grabbed my lunch pail, and he carried me out of the room.

As soon as we were in the hallway, I started to sob.

"What happened?" Mr. Long asked. "Did you fall?"

"No," I said, "this has never happened before. It's my polio leg. It just hurts really bad." It was a deep ache, but I didn't know how to describe it then.

We arrived at the nurse's office and he laid me down on the one bed there. "Don't worry, now," he said. "Someone will call your mother."

The nurse in her white uniform was a bit alarmed. "Now, what seems to be the trouble?" she asked me.

"I don't know," I again answered. "My leg just hurts, a lot. My polio leg. I can't walk on it."

"Oh, perhaps it's just growing pains."

Growing pains!? Well, it would be good news if this leg were about to start growing.

I didn't know it, but I *was* about to grow two more inches and reach my thirteen-year-old height of five feet. My little leg, however, didn't ever catch up.

The nurse got Mother on the phone.

"Mrs. Allen? We have Francine here in the nurse's office, and she's complaining of pain in her polio leg. No, she's lying down here. No, she says she can't walk on it."

I suspect Mother had suggested that I walk home after school.

"Well, can you come and pick her up?"

Mother came to the school about twenty minutes later. She was annoyed and angry, thinking I could have walked the three blocks home, and insisted that I walk to the DeSoto, parked out on the street one hundred feet away. I found that the pain had subsided somewhat; it was now a duller ache. I limped to the car.

After we got past the main door of the school, she said, "I don't appreciate your pulling this. I had to leave work to come pick you up. You can walk!"

"I can now, but I couldn't before. It really hurt, Mother. The nurse said it might be growing pains. Is there such a thing as 'growing pains'?"

"No, I don't think so. She was probably just saying that."

She had been a child who would do charades to stay out of school, whereas I considered a sick day at home a huge loss of social and scholastic time. She was probably worried about what caused this pain, but my sense was that she thought I should have toughed it out, or that I was exaggerating.

Mother had little patience for body issues—mine, anyway.

We were sitting at the kitchen table one Saturday afternoon, and she said, "I'm going to get you a training bra."

"*What!? Why!?*"

"Your breasts are starting to develop."

I was mortified. My face grew hot, and I glanced down at my chest. People must be able to see that I was getting breasts and I had not even noticed. I still thought of myself as a little girl.

"I don't want one."

"I want you to get one; besides, it will help protect your nipples so your clothing doesn't rub against them."

Nipples. My mother just said, "nipples." So, were my nipples developing too, and could people also see those? I wasn't going to look down at them again. *Okay,* I thought, *maybe I better get a bra to cover these things up.*

"I'll get you one, and you can try it," she said. "The training bras have stretchy cups so they stretch as you grow. See, look at this ad in the paper."

There it was, a photo of a young girl with barely developed breasts in a white bra with stretchy cups. You couldn't see her nipples.

"Okay," I said. "But if I don't like it, I'm not going to wear it."

I actually did like it, once I got used to the somewhat tight feeling around my rib cage, because now that I knew I had breasts and also the more embarrassing nipples, I felt like I had something between me, my undershirts and sweaters, and the gawking world. The boys sometimes snapped the back of my bra through my blouses, which I found to be a disconcerting acknowledgement of my maturing body. I think it was probably a compliment that they noticed, but I was mortified by their behavior—until I saw that they did this to many of the girls, who tittered and said the boys were stupid. I tried to adopt this attitude.

࿐

When I was twelve and a half, I went to San Francisco in the summer to spend a week with my sister, LaVonne, and her family. I started my period while I was there and went through nearly a box of Kleenex before LaVonne called from work to see how the day was going. She treated my news matter-of-factly—simply told me where she kept her menstrual products—

and I was relieved that a big deal was not made of it. When I shyly told my mother over the phone what had transpired, she was silent.

Back home again, at one of our kitchen table talks (mealtime was about the only time we were seated face-to-face), Mother and I discussed Kotex and accompanying belts. Suddenly, she commented indignantly, "I didn't start my period until I was fourteen!" with an accusatory look at me, and the accompanying bobblehead movement.

I stared back at her. I didn't know what to say. As if I'd had a choice! I felt, after that, that she thought I was oversexed, and I was embarrassed about my "early" development, which was actually right in line with the other sixth graders.

When I had a day or two of debilitating, doubled-over cramps with heavy periods in high school and needed to stay in bed, Mother thought I was lying about it, as she had never had cramps. My body type and inner functions seem to have taken after the Allen/Owen side, not so much the Weber/Smith side. Mother thought whatever happened to me that she hadn't experienced herself was either a sham or abnormal. This did not help our already tense relationship, exacerbated by my thoughts that my mother was frustratingly simple-minded and outdated in her thinking.

⚭

At summer church camp that year, I won a cardboard award plaque for "Miss Primp." This was likely instigated by my old friend from the sixth-grade bathroom, Michelle, and her mother, a counselor. I was again embarrassed, because it was true: I was so careful about my appearance—my pony tail, my clothing, all of it—even at girls' summer camp.

Michelle had a natural, pixie-like beauty, despite her tomboy walk and athleticism, and was attractive to boys. When one of the girls I liked at camp, who was meeting me for the first time, ribbed me about being Miss Primp, I took it more good-naturedly—I just explained that I felt I needed to look the best possible to make up for my weird walk and skinny, paralyzed leg.

"Are you kidding?" she said. "That's some wiggle you've got there." She followed this up with a hand gesture that described the rolling wave of my fanny as seen from the back as if it were something especially attractive. Prior to that comment, no one had ever said anything like this to me.

The following school year, seventh grade, I did manage to ditch the old hairstyle and instead wore a long fringe of bangs with my chestnut hair pulled back just on top, with the rest falling to my shoulders. With a tiny bit of lipstick, I felt like I was beginning to look as nice as other girls.

how i spent my summer

A round 1961, I somehow got invited to be on the March of Dimes telethon being shot at the northern California KCRA-TV station. So, I guess somebody did decide I was sort of a poster child. There was no registry of polio kids, so I'm not sure how they found me. Was the March of Dimes trolling for crippled kids at Kaiser in Vallejo? Did my mom see an ad and like the idea of me being on TV?

By the time the event rolled around I was kind of expecting acknowledgment of some sort and was excited about being on television. I donned my good yellow angora sweater and a pastel wool plaid skirt—it was the nicest thing I had to wear for an occasion like this—and we drove the fifty miles to Sacramento.

Once there, we spent a couple of hours waiting backstage for me to be called on. There was no cool and comfy dressing room where we could lounge and watch a monitor. Finally, they cued me onstage and I limped out. By that time, I was perspiring like crazy; I was shiny-faced and my bangs were limp, separated, and hanging in my eyes. My fluffy sweater was acting as a personal sauna, worsened by the intensely bright and hot lights on stage.

Hoss Cartwright of the "Bonanza" TV show (Dan Blocker) took my small hand in his huge paw and interviewed me, if you could call it that. He mostly put his big, perspiry arm around me and—with no cowboy accent at all—said nice things into the camera about how people should contribute. He was very sweet, but his large head was also dripping with sweat—he was suffering even more than I was under those lights. I appreciated that he was spending hours doing this to raise money for polio treatment and vaccination. The man was a saint.

By 1961, people already were beginning to think polio was "over with." (It wasn't; the epidemic had peaked, but it would be another forty years before the US would see its last new case.) I was petrified in the harsh glare, afraid I'd say something dumb, embarrassed at being so hot and shiny, and although occasionally a clever child, I hardly said a word that day. After a minute or two, Hoss patted me on the back and sent me backstage.

When it was over, Mother and I went out to the car and drove home without fanfare, as if nothing had happened.

"Well," she said, "that was a waste of time."

I agreed with her. I was tired and just wanted to get home and take off my hot clothes. So much for meeting celebrities. And at school, only one person had seen me; the telethons were so long that no one could bear to watch the entire show.

Still, two minutes of poster child fame, eh?

❧

I was thirteen when Mother took me to a clinic to see an orthopedic surgeon from Sacramento named Robert Mearns in the spring after the TV appearance. Two decades later I would learn that he had an impeccable reputation among orthopedists, but at the time all I knew was that he was in our town at a clinic, taking appointments with kids who had had polio or other foot and limb maladies.

Dr. Mearns told us that because I had almost reached my full height, which at that point was about four feet ten, it would be smart to consider one or both of a couple of potential surgeries. Possibly some charity or government agency was offering to pay; it's doubtful that Mother had the money for something that pricey. If she did foot the bill, this would have been a most expensive gift.

"One option is to remove one bone on the outside of your polio foot and fuse two others together," Dr. Mearns said—this is how I remember his words, anyway—"to stabilize your foot so you won't roll it inward."

"Rolling" the ankle meant that it pushed in and down as I walked, which could eventually cause the joint to begin to touch the ground. The correction was a triple arthrodesis (triple, I know now, because it is the fusion of the talocalcaneal, talonavicular, and calcaneocuboid joints in the foot). Whether any bone was actually removed, I do not know.

No one mentioned to us before the operation that it might not be a permanent fix. Later in life the correction can start to weaken, causing the ankle to once again "roll" inside, though possibly not as severely. (This started to happen to me about fifty years later. Luckily I got the stable forty years most people get out of this procedure plus an extra ten.)

The ankle roll was already making my awkward gait even more difficult for any distance at all, though I was somewhat oblivious to this. I was a pre-teen and most of my awareness was going into making good grades or hoping I was as pretty and popular as other girls, plus some real sadness, confusion, and sense of loss at having to give up dolls. (One of my friends had recently—disdainfully—commented, "I don't want to play with *dolls*," when she'd come to visit. I think she already had actual breasts at twelve. My first thought was, *Okay, what else is there to do?* but I hadn't said it, suddenly aware that, again, it was time to grow up from a childhood that had not felt childish since I was three.)

The other potential operation suggested was to put a stop in my Achilles tendon. Stabilizing the Achilles would essentially put an end to my drop foot. The downside was that I would have to decide at thirteen on one lifetime heel height, since my foot would be frozen in one position.

My foot is essentially a weak hinged platform at the bottom of my leg. This allows me to stand and maybe walk, but not run. This condition, as I mentioned earlier, greatly increases the potential for tripping (and falling), as the big toe, which in my case is also paralyzed and hangs even lower than the plane of my foot, has a tendency to catch on even tiny things, unless I wear some type of ankle brace, laced boots, or orthotic to support the toe and ankle. I also have sprained that toe, but only five or ten times—a surprisingly low number, considering the risk. If you've ever caught a sandal on a stepping stone and gone flying, you have an inkling of one frequent hazard befalling those of us with a drop foot.

At the time the second operation was suggested, I had dreams of wearing high heels and prom dresses and doing all the things grown-up ladies did in high heels. No one mentioned that this was less likely than a visit from the White Rabbit.

Mother gave me the option to choose which operations I wanted. So I nixed the Achilles operation. I was fearful of having a foot that did not move up and down. I also thought (naively) that maybe someday it was not going to be a drop foot anymore, and I might, yes, wear high heels. I did agree to the ankle stabilization (the triple arthrodesis), however, and plans were made to do the surgery in the summer between seventh and eighth grades, in Mercy Hospital in Sacramento.

This was the same summer I informed Mother with gravity that now that I was a teenager, she must never call me by the nickname "Miss Muffet" or "Muffet" again. When she began to form my given name, "Fran-cine," in her mouth, it was difficult for her and sounded like two words. Forever after, she spoke it that way—"Fran-cine." Never quickly, always deliberately, always reminding me, though not purposely, that I asked her to call me by my real name. That I had forged a calm exit plan from the humiliation of my nickname, just as I would plan, a few years later, an exit from my childhood home.

～

The worst aspects for me, facing this surgery, were fear of the expected pain afterward, how serious it sounded, and the rehabilitation process. I also wondered if it would actually improve my condition. The whole prospect of having my body cut into, a bone broken away, and those other two bones somehow knitted together (with a steel pin, it turned out, which much later set off the early airport security alarms) was deeply frightening. Losing consciousness with anesthesia also frightened me, since I had fallen and knocked myself out twice before. I was convinced that it was necessary, so I followed through with the plan—but I was panicked by the time they took me into the yucky green operating room and began administering the anesthesia.

I awoke to horrible pain and nausea, which I had not been advised to expect, in a darkened room. The nurses were slow to respond to my need when I called out, "I'm going to throw up!" (And it was *green* in the stainless steel tray they provided.) When I was wracked with sobs of deeply aching pain, they tut-tutted me and acted as if I were not being stalwart enough. There were one or two other young surgery patients in the same room with me, which had four beds in it, and the nurses seemed more concerned with those kids' sleep than my pain.

"Don't cry!" they admonished me. "You'll wake the other children. You need to be quiet."

When, at last, Dr. Mearns came on his rounds, he immediately recommended painkillers for me, and chastened the nurses in whispering tones across the room from my bed.

"She's in a lot of pain," he said. "This was a serious operation. You should have tended to this. If she complains of pain, give her something for it, and it will help her sleep."

I have a great deal of respect for nurses now, but in the first thirteen years of my life I did not have good experiences with them. Luckily, they listened to the doctor, and the drugs did help. Still, even with the painkillers, my foot was throbbing, and I could not get into a position where I was not in acute pain. Additionally, when I first looked at the cast, there was an alarming deep red spot on the outside at the surgery spot.

When he next came to see me, Dr. Mearns—one of the most considerate and gentle doctors I have ever had, well understanding my fears and pain and the emotional angst of a thirteen-year-old—told me that the red spot was normal, there would be some seepage of blood for a while. The operation, he said, had been successful.

⌣

I'd had a choice, because I was thirteen, of being in the children's or the adult ward at the hospital. In mulling this over, with no clear idea what this choice really meant, I had opted for the children's ward; I thought it would be more fun, and that being with adults would present a stodgy, quiet option.

Big mistake.

It was only after I'd spent one day in the hospital that they told me and Mother that only parents could visit in the children's ward, no one else. Not even my sister, who was now thirty-two, could come to visit me.

"Not even my *sister?*" I said, incredulous.

On the third day of my stay, a nurse came to my bed and said, "Someone's here to see you, so we're going to take you down the hall." This was a bit of excitement for me. She helped me through the awkward process of getting out of the bed and standing on one foot, the other foot painfully throbbing in its heavy cast, then sitting down in a wheelchair.

I was wheeled down the hall to the end of the children's ward, where LaVonne was holding the exterior door open and standing outside the hospital on a landing.

"Boy, am I ever angry!" she exclaimed. "They wouldn't let me come in to see you! I told them you only have one parent and your father is dead. I said, 'I'm an adult relative, so why can't I take the place of her other parent?' But they said, 'No, that's the rule.' I would have brought the girls"—my two nieces—"in to see you too, if I could have. I gave those people a piece of my mind! Finally, someone said I could stand out here for a minute and they'd go get you so I could see you."

I really appreciated her righteous anger. We had a few moments when I could tell her that it hurt and I hated it there, and then she had to leave before they caught her prolonging the illegal visit.

This visitor restriction created a very lonely situation for the week or more that I was hospitalized, but at least my big sister had made the effort and once again stood up for me.

❧

After my stint in the hospital came training in using crutches—the underarm type, as I could not put any weight on the cast. Anyone who has broken a foot may know the trials of bathing with a plastic bag, keeping the cast covered and the foot up out of water. No showers during this time. (Now, of course, there are often removable casts, but generally not for surgery like this, when there is risk of damaging the work before it heals.)

I went back to eighth grade on crutches. I had to deal with and manage slippery floors, scary moments, and my good angora sweater pilling under the arms. I had aching hands, shoulders, and armpit muscles, and an armpit rash on my sensitive skin, newly de-fuzzed with Nair depilatory—Mother was nearly hairless and shaved nothing, and didn't think I should either. On the plus side, I had no PE classes, which had always been either humiliating or tiring for me anyway. My treasured social life was impaired a bit, but I could concentrate on my studies and make good grades.

Back at school, one of my girlfriends, Gail Armstrong, asked, "Was the operation a success?"

This seemed like such a grown-up question and I wasn't sure how to answer, since we actually didn't know yet.

"The doctor said it was," I told her, "but it's going to be three months before we know for sure."

～

The cast removal was a hopeful event. Prior to the operation, we had been told that wearing the cast would only last three months, which was why we'd scheduled the surgery for summer. Just one summer lost, I'd thought. I loved summers for being the only magic, lazy time of the year other than Christmas. As a kid, this seemed a pretty big sacrifice.

We drove down to Sacramento to Dr. Mearns's office and waited in the cool lab room, me shivering in a hospital gown.

When Dr. Mearns came in, he said, "Are you ready to get this thing off?"

"Yes," I said, "but how do you do that?"

"I'm going to cut it off with a special saw." He took from a drawer a little cord-powered, drill-like device with a small round blade at the end.

"A *saw*?" I said with alarm. "But what if you cut my leg?!"

"This only goes through plaster," he assured me. "If it hits anything else, it stops."

I was still apprehensive, but he began to cut with the high-pitched, screaming saw, first down one side of the cast and then the other, while I sat rigid with fear. When I didn't get cut right away, I relaxed a little.

As the cast opened up, a horrible, sickly sweet, rotten odor began to emit from it—and what was inside was as disgusting-looking as it was smelly. I had not expected the stench and the pale look of soft, dead skin. Thick pieces were peeling off my foot, especially, and up my leg—less so near the top, where it had had more air.

"Eeewww," I said with dismay.

"That's normal after the skin has not been exposed to air for three months," Dr. Mearns said. "It will recover."

I was no longer in pain or swollen, though I had not put weight on the foot yet, and I'd thought this was it: I was moving on to walking again. However, we weren't done.

"It's healing well," Dr. Mearns said. "I'm pleased with the progress. But because of the poor circulation in your leg, you'll need to keep wearing a cast for another couple of months."

A couple more months? I was deflated and disheartened by the unexpected extension.

⌇

When the second cast came off in early winter, I still needed to use the crutches.

"Okay," Dr. Mearns said, "it's going to be sore, but you can start putting weight on it and then practice walking."

I slipped off the examining table in his lab room, standing on my strong leg and tentatively putting my little foot down. But as soon as I actually put weight on it, a searing, sharp pain shot through my foot.

"Owwww!" I cried out. "I can't do it!"

"I know it hurts," said the gentle doctor. "But see how your ankle is straight now and doesn't roll in? That's exactly what we wanted. It won't get better and stop hurting unless you walk on it. You don't have to do it all at once. Just walk on it, with your crutches, a little every day."

ى

I did start trying to walk at home, but it hurt so much that I often broke down crying. My little foot was too sore to even put a shoe on it, so I wore a soft cotton knee sock over a supportive Ace bandage, which I had to learn to wrap. Even donning the sock was painful at first. I felt as if I'd never walk again without crutches or pain, and thus would never walk independently again at all. I was going on fourteen and felt as if my life as I had known it was pretty much over. Here was the upset about a dim future I hadn't had the maturity to experience when I was three.

I didn't put weight on my foot at school; when I was standing still, I kept all my weight on my strong leg, my hands, and crutches. A couple of weeks into the process, once I was less in pain, I tried to walk without the crutches at home, and my foot was so weak that my knee buckled and I stumbled. My leg seemed to have lost body memory of how it felt to walk!

I sobbed deeply and frequently throughout this sojourn. I lost my balance easily because my foot, ankle, and gimpy little leg had dramatically weakened further from lack of use.

But in a little over a month I was off the crutches entirely. Six months on crutches and another month or two of physical therapy had meant no swimming in the over-100-degree weather with a hot, itchy cast and missing lots of school events. I had continued to sing in the girls' chorus, however, and was even able to attend the vocal competitions in Chico, far enough north that we traveled in buses. I participated in those regionals for two or three years with my school, even on crutches. And now I had a stable ankle, even though I still had a drop foot.

I continued to limp badly and would forever, but I no longer rolled my ankle toward the floor, which made it somewhat easier to walk. I could now walk perhaps a half-mile to a mile, in fact—with fatigue, of course, but that was better than staying home while the other kids went wherever it was that we just had to go as young teenagers.

The year before all this, Daralyn had turned fifteen and gotten her much lighter ten-speed purple bike. I was getting too heavy for a back bumper anyway. Our best bet now was to use the little bus that shuttled back and forth between Marysville and Yuba City. It only went east and west, so all neighborhoods located to the north and south became accessible to me only if I could get my mother, or someone else's, to take me by car.

In another kind of transporting, I discovered Motown R&B around this time, which inspired me to want to dance and get out and about. I was blooming, morphing from the homely, uncertain girl I'd been into someone who at least emulated loveliness, with my light pink lipstick and soft, shoulder-length hair.

high hopes for high school

A year later, I went into high school expecting a lot of dating, parties, and making new friends. Only part of that ensued.

Being the crippled girl had not mattered much in grammar school, and also not too much in middle school—but it did begin to matter when we were all going to dances and choosing people to date who had the potential of being our life partners, a reality that I did not see coming as I entered ninth grade. I was one of three or four handicapped girls in our school; at least three of us were polio survivors, and two of us had similarly obvious limps and paralysis. With two thousand kids in our school, we comprised a pretty small subset.

In high school, the boys I'd known all my life were friendly to me, always—except if they thought I was flirting with them or interested in going out with them. This was something I had not bargained for, me with my romantic and slightly grasping heart and maybe too-flirtatious or clingy demeanor. My memories may be different than the boys' are; I imagine they were more concerned with seeming to be cool and getting up the courage to ask girls out. Maybe some were interested in me and I was not friendly enough to them, aspiring as I was for some handsome preppy guy at first. Still, most boys were looking at girls who didn't limp.

One summer day, just prior to the start of our freshman

year, I was lounging and chatting with a few girlfriends on the athletic field behind the high school.

"My older brother told me you have to be really careful with sex—that even if a boy gets his penis near you and doesn't put it inside, you could still get pregnant," Theresa said.

"Eewww!" I said. "Why would anyone let a boy put his penis near you?" The films I had seen in middle school had never explicitly illustrated or explained sex between men and women. They'd used pictures of bulls and cows, but they'd never came out and said that women willingly allowed human penises into their vaginas. I thought only dirty-minded people did that, and most women wouldn't consent to it.

"Pregnancy is caused by God when two people love each other and get married," I said.

The other three girls started laughing uncontrollably.

"Francine!" Mary said when she caught her breath. "You think that?"

"Yes. Only animals do that."

"No, people do that. You can't get pregnant unless the sperm get into your vagina. And my sister said it feels really good when a boy touches you between your legs, and it's hard to say no."

My face colored. "Oh. But *my* parents . . . ? Oh." I was so embarrassed to have been so naïve.

Another thing that was a big surprise was that the older girls just hated us. I had expected that the sophomores would be adoptive big sisters, taking us under their wings. I was sad to learn that this was not to be—that, in fact, they thought we were competition and therefore scorned us. In gym, the sophomore girls treated us like the people who had come to take over their rightful job— which was apparently to dominate the attention of the sophomore, junior, and senior boys. Freshmen girls were basically the new pickings. Some girls in my class saw this and took advantage of it, but I did not see myself as someone with any kind of advantage.

The junior and senior girls thought the same of us, but were more confident in their ability to attract boys and keep them around, hoping by senior year to be on the verge of getting an engagement ring.

Hold it! An engagement ring at eighteen? you may be thinking. *Isn't that a little young?*

Yes, it's incredibly young—but we didn't know that. We thought we needed to land a fiancé by then or we'd end up out there in the nowhere land of college, far from home, looking for someone no one knew, who might not fit into our valley town society. (From an evolutionary standpoint, this would have been a good thing.) There was status in finding a boy who was a few years older and going to high school or college somewhere other than Yuba City, but the primary goal was getting a boyfriend.

⤶

Our church had a feature they referred to as "visiting teachers," and they came to our home once a month for an hour. I was never totally clear what they were actually teaching, because, God knows, we clearly got a great deal of instruction at church. They always sent a woman to our house—probably because Mother was a widow, and they deemed it inappropriate to send a man around to visit her alone.

On one of these occasions, the three of us were discussing my lukewarm attitude toward attending high school student seminary classes, which were held at 7:30 a.m., before school, Monday through Friday. I'd gone for the first year of high school, and really didn't want to continue.

Mrs. Bishop peered at me. "You'll be continuing with seminary classes, won't you, Carol?" (They still called me Carol at church; I'd never corrected them.)

"Well, I have to get up too early, by six, after I'm up late studying the night before, so I'm not going to go this year." Not many kids, and certainly none of the church kids I knew, were in the advanced academic classes I was taking. Those who were not in the "double x" program or did not have a child enrolled in them could not possibly have understood the amount and intensity of homework—at a minimum, five hours each night and another day's worth on the weekends, for all of high school. Plus, of course, I would never miss a teen dance (every Saturday night), a party if I were invited, or an occasional movie, if Mom would pay for it.

"Why do you need to get up so early?" Mrs. Bishop asked. "Surely you could get up at seven and get there on time; you live so close."

Half an hour? I was already thinking this was getting a little invasive; the polite thing would have been to leave it at my first excuse. The church, however, was quite concerned that its teenagers were going to "fall away" from it (and in my case, they had reason to be concerned).

Mrs. Bishop didn't know that I had to stop and rest after each of the three blocks I walked to school, or how it fatigued me to carry a pile of books. (No book bags or backpacks in those days.) Many days, Mother took me in the car, but even then, there was the issue of her always being late as well. To our church lady, though, it was a walk of only a couple of minutes.

"I need time to take a shower, eat breakfast, and do my hair and makeup," I told her, thinking, *and put on the prosthesis I wear with double stockings over it so my leg can try to masquerade as normal.* This was similar to but more than the process every other high school girl was putting herself through each morning, for heaven's sake.

"Oh, Carol, I think you're trying to look too nice," Mrs. Bishop said.

Internally, I closed my eyes and shook my head to process

her comment. It was at that time beyond my understanding that anyone, ever, could look too nice.

"I have something to make up for, so I like to look my best," I told her. I thought it should be obvious that a handicapped kid—a handicapped girl in particular—would have to make a greater effort. How else would the boys overlook her ugly ungainly limp, missing arm, or whatever she did not have that all the other potential girlfriends did? In my mind, even being the smartest or funniest girl would not make up for a physical defect in the highly competitive world of seeking the attention of innocently clueless high school boys.

⸙

By this point I had begun to question much of what they were telling us at church. As a child, I had believed that there was a God—a nice male spirit, perhaps a bit strict—and that Jesus Christ was his son, and that Jesus had been born of an earthly virgin mother and his heavenly father, God. Knowing nothing about sex as a child, and thinking my mother was a virgin too, this story was not at all a stretch for me. I accepted the Bible, and the Book of Mormon, as literally true.

As I matured, I had begun to ask Mother questions like, "But how could God create the earth in only six days?" The trees in our backyard, after all, had taken years to mature.

Mother was surprisingly broad-minded about a narrow range of religious tenets, given her solid belief in her religion. Her answer was that the six days were simply symbolic. To God, she said, thousands of years were like a day, because He was eternal.

This made sense to me, and because I had been thus prepped that Adam and Eve might be just symbols for the beginning of humanity and not two actual people named Adam and Eve who literally lived in a garden, I had no conflict when I was taught evolution in school . . . though it's possible that Mother still believed that part of the Bible was literal. She was a little complicated in that regard, which may have contributed to her angst about whether she might not go to heaven (she smoked and drank coffee, which were seen as detrimental to the gift of the body and something a Mormon was not supposed to do).

I didn't like having questions about the church. I was torn because, among other things, I knew nice people who smoked. I also began to know some Buddhists, and Jewish people, and other folks who did not go to church, and I just couldn't believe that God was not going to accept all these folks into heaven. It just didn't seem very . . . *Christian* to me. Also, if everyone who died was going to have to wait in something like Purgatory until every single person on earth died and accepted Jesus as their Lord . . . well that just seemed like an unrealistic, inefficient plan. Especially when I learned that the population of the earth was expanding, keeping Judgment Day farther and farther away. *What are we all going to do up there while we're waiting for everybody else to die?* I wondered. I had a strong hunch that God was not going to have movies or other entertainment available, and no one in my 1950s circle had been talking about an afterlife of eternal bliss.

The older I got, the more questions I had.

ᴖ

The foam calf prosthesis I wore was a big deal, by the way.

It was made by taking a casting of my left, strong calf, and then reversing it to make a pretend right calf out of soft, flesh-colored foam. A casting was taken of my smaller leg so the inside of the fake calf fit quite snugly, though in the winter, when my leg shrank, it tended to slide down, and I'd have to slip into the girls' room or sit in the back of class to pull or shimmy the thing back up in place.

For the first one I had, I was called in to the prosthetic place in Sacramento to try it on and get advice about it.

When we got there, the orthotist handed it to me with pride.

"This is wrong," I said right away. "It's another left calf, not a right."

"Oh, no," he said, "put it on, you'll see."

I held it next to my left leg—two left legs side by side—and looked at him.

"Please, try it on," he implored.

"Okay, but I'm not going to wear it."

I put it on. I was indisputably right. I stood there in front of him and my mother and just glared at them, as if to say, "Look!"

They saw it; it looked like I had two left legs. (This brings to mind the film *Best in Show*, wherein Eugene Levy plays a dog owner with two actual left feet. It's noticeable, and made a great gag for the film.) I was miffed that I hadn't been believed in the first place.

"Oh, I see," the orthotist said. "Well, we can make you another one. But meanwhile, you can wear this one; I'm sure no one will notice."

"No one will look," my mother chimed in. "It will be fine."

"*I'm not going to wear it,*" I said. "I'm not walking around with two left calves. People *will* look. Everyone will think it looks worse than my leg the way it is. It looks stupid!"

I was fourteen. I was starting high school, the beginning of my adulthood. I cared more than the vainest teenage girls about looking good. They re-made a prosthesis correctly, and this time they mailed it to me.

The first iteration, and also the revamp, zipped up the back, with a foam tab that was supposed to fit down into the heel of my shoes but didn't—it just bunched above the shoe. The slit in the foam was pretty obvious back there, too; it didn't close completely.

The orthotist and also my mother said encouragingly, "You know, that's where the seam in your stockings goes anyway."

Which decade are you living in? I thought. Seams up the back were quickly giving way to modern, stretchy nylons.

I asked them to make the next one with the seam up the inside of my leg, where you couldn't see it so well. This idea had to come from a teenager who'd never seen one of these before. (Not too many women in the orthotics field, even now.)

The next one I received had a zipper on the inside of my little leg that disconnected at the bottom. The zipper tab rested right at the ankle, a factor which led to a red scar and permanently broken blood vessels there from its rub. But at least you couldn't see the zipper gap as easily.

It was necessary to wear a pair of heavy, opaque "flesh-colored" (pale, beige-peach white girl) hose—much heavier than normal support hose—to try to mask the fact that I was wearing this apparatus. I had to wear the hose on both legs so I would not have one leg opaque and one with normal skin showing. Over these I wore regular nylons, which made the whole arrangement look just slightly more normal, at least at night and assuming no one was inspecting. I mean, you could tell something was odd there, and that I was wearing some pretty thick stockings, but the two-inch limp was mostly what made you look.

Colored tights didn't come into style in northern California until my first year of college, and I bought a plethora of them then. What was in style, much to my chagrin, was short skirts and then mini-skirts. The high school would not allow us to wear minis; if a teacher thought your skirt was too short, you had to kneel on the floor, a ruler was brought out, and if your hem was more than four inches above the floor, you had to go home and change. If you didn't have a way home, your mom was called.

I wore my skirts as short as I could without the tops of my nylons showing, and even shorter in college. I was determined to be "in," despite how the short skirts emphasized my leg differences.

The prosthesis was hot, especially during our sizzling summers. When I took it off at night, my leg was sweaty and I sometimes got heat rashes. I'd usually sprinkle baby or talcum powder all over my calf and ankle, plus a cotton "stockinette," which was essentially a lightweight piece like the top of a sock, prior to donning the prosthesis, the heavy hose, and nylons. All this was held up by a garter belt or girdle; panty hose didn't exist yet—and even when they did come out, the thick hose underneath still needed a garter belt to hold them up.

I wore one of these prostheses almost every day for four years of high school and a couple of years afterward. After that I chucked the thing and wore pants, granny dresses, muu-muus, maxi dresses, or jumpsuits all the time until ballet-length dresses came back in style (and even those I've worn only rarely). You have to know me pretty well to see my vastly different calves and thighs.

The other girl I knew in high school who had an obvious leg difference from polio did not go the prosthetic route, and no one seemed to care.

ᗑ

I have always loved dancing. My mom said that when I was a toddler, I used to stand in front of the TV, plant my feet shoulder-width apart, and bounce my body up and down in time to the music. She'd say, "Pick up your feet!" and I'd lean over and grab my feet and try to pick them up. Clearly, music was thrilling to me at an early age.

In grammar school summer days, I recall making up elaborate dances with the other girls. Daralyn took ballet and tap, and I was envious, partly of the costumes she wore in recitals, but mostly of all those steps and doing them to music. I liked making up my own ballet-looking movements, throwing my arms into the air, spinning around on my strong leg, and throwing that Other Leg out in some way resembling a kick, singing while I danced.

Mother was a remarkably graceful dancer. I only saw her dance a few times—once at an Arthur Murray exhibition dance (where she took lessons after my dad died), and several times at church dances. She sat out a lot of dances because she was a widow, however. I realize now that if men had asked her to dance, Church People Would Have Talked and Made Assumptions. There also were few single men at the church.

Mother thought I should learn to do the hula. As a child, I thought she must be right, that the hula would be a dance I could do, whereas other types of dancing would be hard for me. Obviously, ballet was out of the question, and tap as well. What she did not know is that the hula requires a great deal of thigh strength, because much of the dancing is done with bent knees. And a paralyzed foot would have made some of the moves pretty difficult, especially the one where you have to set your foot down flat repeatedly. The feet do move a lot in hula; you just can't always see them through the long muu-muus or grass skirts. So hula was out.

At church, they taught us ballroom dancing: waltz, foxtrot, jitterbug/swing, and cha-cha, all the simplest forms of ballroom. In high school, also, there was some ballroom dance taught on rainy days. None of it was easy for me, especially the part where I had to go backward. (As my husband will tell you, since our one-time foray into learning the foxtrot for our wedding dance, I am about 200 percent more stable walking forward than I am walking backward.)

Then along came the 60s, with the Twist (both traditional and Philly style, which you'll have to find on YouTube American Bandstand clips; it defies description but is much sexier), the Mashed Potatoes (plural on the record of the same name, later described by historians as a single potato), the Slotsun, the Watusi, the Monkey, the Swim . . . it was do-it-yourself on the dance floor. Thank you, Dick Clark and American Bandstand. Slow dances required coordinating your steps with someone else's, but doing all this other new stuff, I could be a little off-balance from time to time and even incorporate it into movements so that it looked like I was doing it on purpose. And the Jerk! You barely had to move your feet!

I really felt a kinship with these dances originating in the black communities of the US. There was a lot of hip action and cool stuff. I could feel those things in my body. Though I could not move my feet in entirely the same way, I did *feel* like I was doing the same movements as the kids on American Bandstand and the black entertainers, even though when I saw myself in a mirror it didn't look quite as cool. But it at least looked *kind* of cool, and it felt really good. Hip at last, hip at last, great God almighty, I was hip at last.

I had gone to only one middle school dance—my eighth-grade graduation dance—and there I'd had ONE sweaty-handed dance with a very self-conscious, sweet boy named Brad. I don't know if he was prodded to ask me, or was simply brave. After that, though, I was at every high school dance in our town and in Marysville, across the river, from 1962 through the summer of 1966, unless I had strep throat or was grounded (for talking back or coming home too late). And the weekend dances at the local National Guard armories, with live rock and roll bands, were the center of my social life. Missing one felt like social suicide; if you wanted a boyfriend, there was about a 95 percent chance that a teen dance was where you'd meet him.

Me & Mom, ready for 8th grade graduation dance and hopeful at age fourteen.

into boys and rock 'n' roll

T began having crushes on boys when I was four or five years old. I used to think that this early interest was because my dad died when I was seven, but the truth is, my interest in boys predated that. I am sure, though, that being fatherless contributed greatly to my thinking for much of my early life that it was very important to have male attention.

Probably part of this preoccupation with boys was because my mother and father were so smitten with each other. They were really affectionate, and the best times for me were when we were all together. There was never any arguing—although I now think perhaps there should have been. Because my father died so early in my life, I held for decades the view that people who loved each other never quarreled. For that reason, I had a hard time developing skill in discussing things in a quiet, equal way with men I was involved with. I was easily upset by their anger or criticism and just didn't know what to do with it; I often took it to mean I was at fault, would subsequently try to make sure I behaved in a way that would never make them angry, and then, when I reached a breaking point, would end up sobbing in grief or blowing up—or just leaving (the house, the conversation, or the relationship entirely).

Given my frequent arguments with Mom over the course of our being housemates alone for over a dozen years, I never felt unequal to women and was not afraid to simply state what I thought in any non-sexual relationship—which may have intimidated other people. Women were supposed to be shy, evidently, or at least not say what they thought.

So, it was clear to me in early childhood that the best thing that could ever happen to you was to fall in love and get married, and the next best thing was to have children, because . . . well, I don't really know why that was. Perhaps because it was what women did, and because churches and women kept saying it was the most fulfilling part of a woman's life.

My mother, to her credit, after having one divorce and being widowed by the time she was in her mid-forties, did emphasize to me that it was important that I be able to support myself. This was due not to early feminism but rather to the fact that she had lost two husbands and had not met the third and fourth yet, and also to her concern that I might not get "chosen" as a wife.

⚓

I was a teenager with a crush most of the time, but usually it was on someone who either was not asking me out or someone I probably should not have been attracted to as a realistic match. I liked the slightly bad boys a little bit, partly because they would flirt back and partly because they had an air of mystery. What were they doing while they were not playing sports? Probably just sitting around smoking and watching TV, which didn't interest me, but the mystery was there. The baddish boys, somewhat like me, didn't totally fit in—and they may not have wanted to, given that the draft for the Vietnam War was looming. And some of the boys I was attracted to were not so much bad as they were looking to the Rolling Stones rather than the school counselors or their parents for guidance.

Being in a rock band was attractive, but boys advanced enough to do that might be having sex, too, and I was going nowhere near that one, believing in those years that intercourse before marriage was immoral. (Not to mention dangerous; birth control pills, rarely even heard of, could not be obtained until one was twenty-one or had a note from an adult.) And that longer hair—Beatle or Beach Boy. The school was measuring the length of boys' hair (not below the collar!) just like they were measuring our skirts.

I dated a couple of boys throughout high school, but none of the relationships progressed very far. My freshman year, I had had a big crush on a nice, bright, homely but popular older boy I danced with a lot at dances, who was killed in an accident. People were surprised by how much I cried at his funeral; I thought everyone had known how much I cared for him.

Then I dated a boy who was a year younger, very sweet, blond, and not for me. I encouraged him to turn his head toward a girl who liked him more than I. Not long after that, I had a weird "meet at the dances and kiss in the parking lot" thing with another younger blond boy named Milo—very sexy, and possibly from the wrong crowd in another town.

For the first three years of high school, no one else asked me out, and it wasn't until my senior year that I at last met a boy I was truly interested in. I was at one of the weekly teen dances and our eyes locked—his green, to go with his freckled face and red hair. I thought he bore a *slight* resemblance to Mick Jagger, something he found immensely attractive in me when I told him later on.

The next time I saw him, he showed up at our school's homecoming football game and dance. He came with me to the dance—a big deal, since he more or less hated the moneyed, scholastic bent of our side of the river. But we both loved to dance, and he was pretty uninhibited on the dance floor, with moves not unlike Jagger's. And that was it, we were a couple.

Possibly the primary thing of value about my relationship with "Mick" was finding I could attract a male I was also interested in, and stay in a relationship with him for an extended period of time. In terms of emotional content, he was all over the place, probably manic-depressive. The relationship was a roller coaster.

We'd go out to a movie, usually at the drive-in so we could make out. If he was in a bad mood, the evening would go something like this:

"What's the matter?"

"Oh, Granny's giving me grief." (He lived with his grandparents.)

"Why, what happened?"

"She's just crazy."

"But what did she say?"

Silence.

"Come on, cheer up; this is a good movie [or a good song, or a nice evening]."

"Just sit there next to me. I like it when you put your hand on my leg. Just don't talk to me."

I'd cry when we had an evening that ended badly, especially if he was unhappy with something I'd done or not done. A lot of nights and weekends of tears and trouble and silent riding around in his truck ensued. I did not know, when I was nineteen, that I was settling; I thought that was the best I could do in a boyfriend.

Mick and I dated and tried to keep our love alive for nearly two years, but eventually the mostly unfulfilled heavy petting we were doing drove him into the arms of a younger, wanton woman who was not saving herself till marriage. When I graduated and moved away, he stayed at home—and, I heard, later got into a lot of trouble. To his credit, I will say that during our heavy petting he unwittingly taught me a lot about my body and how it responds sexually. He'd probably read up on things a little, whereas I didn't have access to any porn other than the *Playboy*s at the corner mom and pop. (We were *not* supposed to read those, but you could put one inside another magazine.) I did not know about induced orgasms until I met him, and before then could not for the life of me imagine why people would want to have sex—other than to have children, once I finally understood that sex was necessary for that purpose.

～

I had been listening to rock and roll on the radio every night since I was seven or eight. Daralyn's brothers were in a dance band ("Earth Angel," "Why Do Fools Fall in Love?") and we knew all the current pop songs. Daralyn could also read music and played the piano. I'd walk to her house and we'd sing, even while the boys practiced, if we were allowed in the room. Later, there was a radio program called Shan's Band Stand, named after a hamburger drive-in in the middle of town. If you bought something to eat or drink, you got a request slip to fill out: "Play 'Purple People Eater' from Francine to Stanley." (Once or twice in several years, a song was dedicated to me.) This ensured that a lot of kids were listening to the program at night.

In the mid-60s—late high school days for me—rock and roll became politically interesting, from the standpoint of both left-wing awareness and openness to sexuality. You did not have to be married to have sex, and this was no longer a secret, thanks mostly to popular music. And it might even be acceptable to not be in love with the person with whom you partnered, though I found this thought appalling at the time. In this way, we moved from "Be My Baby" and songs that portrayed the longing we girls had for the one, the only boyfriend, to "Will You Still Love Me Tomorrow?"—a song indicating that boyfriends were not necessarily the answer—and, later, "Love the One You're With," while also singing "Blowin' in the Wind" and "Eve of Destruction."

I went to a lot of concerts in the sixties: I saw the Rolling Stones twice with five-dollar, second-row seats, the Beach Boys, Paul Revere and the Raiders, Jefferson Airplane, Big Brother and the Holding Company with Janis Joplin, Cream (Eric Clapton, Jack Bruce, and Ginger Baker) at the Fillmore, Ravi Shankar, The Chambers Brothers, The Youngbloods . . . on and on. It was a fabulous time—"groovy," we called it then— with a lot of unparalleled music and dancing. I wore low-cut paisley jumpsuits I had made, thanks to sewing classes I'd taken when I was fourteen, and I loved the music nearly as much as I thought I loved the boys I met at concerts and in my college classes. Now I wish I'd spent more time singing and playing guitar than paying attention to boys.

life as a co-ed

*T*had a National Merit Scholarship I had earned on the basis of my high school grades, SAT and ACT tests, which gave me free tuition to any college in California—and I chose to use it to go to San Jose State when I could have gone to Stanford. Today, my husband relates this to people and shakes his head. But I was young and I had done all right in art classes in high school, and though I had made excellent grades in accelerated English, history, French, and geometry, and good grades in most of my other courses (enough to get that scholarship), I was most interested in fiddling around in art and thought I was good enough to Be An Artist. I didn't take the meatier subjects as seriously.

San Jose then had the best commercial art department in the state; Stanford's was mediocre in comparison. Plus, I'd still been attached to the boy with red hair and green eyes when I was applying to colleges, and had wanted to be within bus-driving distance of Yuba City. Mom thought it would be great if I became an artist as well, because from the time I was little I'd liked to draw, and it was a profession I could do sitting down. So San Jose State it was.

College opened me up to a much more diverse group of people than I'd encountered in provincial little Yuba City. We had Bobby Seale and Angela Davis speaking on campus. The Vietnam War was in full swing and I felt it was immoral, especially compared to WWII. A squadron of police with tear gas bashed heads (a teacher who was dating a friend of mine ended up in the hospital) when we demonstrated against Dow Chemical Company, which made napalm. (I permanently stopped buying Saran Wrap.) On the day Martin Luther King died, we heard the news on the radio and my better-informed roommate cried.

I was attracted to hippies, artists, musicians, and liberal politicos. I had one friend who did nude modeling, another who was a cartoonist who later introduced me to some of the more famous cartoonists of the 1960s (though I was too unsophisticated to know whom I was meeting), a roommate who made a film for her art project (A film! Imagine! In her twenties!), and another friend whose Unitarian minister boyfriend wrote me the note that allowed Planned Parenthood to give me birth control pills, which saved me from flirting with disaster in more ways than one. At home in the summer, I was listening to the Beatles' *Sgt. Pepper* album with my friends and smoking pot (which, at the time, did improve my art through greater concentration to detail, and a deeper emotional involvement; I'd smoke pot and paint all night sometimes).

Despite all this socially liberal activity, I still considered myself a Christian. I wanted to visit a Mormon temple, so I set up an interview with the San Jose church patriarch, who turned out to be a kindly old fellow.

"I'm interested in visiting a temple," I told him as I sat across from him in his library-like study.

"Well, you have to be in a pure state for at least six months before you enter the temple," he said. "You cannot smoke cigarettes, drink coffee or tea, eat too much meat"—*Check, check, check,* I was thinking—"or have sex for at least six months, since you are not married, and you cannot enter the temple if you have committed adultery."

Oops on unmarried sex. I'd have to think about it. I said in my most convincing, optimistic tone, "Thank you. I will have to think about when I would be able to go."

We shook hands, and I left.

I was new to sex, and so far, it was not all that great, but it seemed like it had potential. Plus, it involved boys, and I was just getting to be attractive to them. In this new college environment, there were more of them that didn't care if I was handicapped, at least in the short run. It didn't dawn on me right away that their interest might be because I was acting physically interested.

I thought about abstinence for about a week and decided I didn't really need to go to the temple. I figured I could go later, at some time when I was either married or sure I didn't want to have sex for six months. That's a clue regarding how committed I was to the church.

⸎

My freshman year, I took my first psychology class from Dr. Thomas Tutko, a teacher I loved. I had caught his attention when I had spoken up in class. We were discussing the effect the Bible had on society. He'd asked what some of the topics illustrating this point might be: what the Bible said that might be controversial, what about sex outside of marriage, etc.

"It says that men can 'do it' and women can't," I piped up.

The fraternity guys all turned around, looked at me in my seat near the rear of the room, and whooped and hollered. Then the bell rang.

After class that day, Dr. Tutko asked if he could speak with me for a moment. He told me he thought I was particularly honest and asked if I would participate in IQ and personality tests voluntarily.

I agreed—and subsequently scored high in IQ, but had

some things on the personality side that piqued the researchers' curiosity. So they asked me and some others to come back and answer some questions that the associates or grad students were almost salivating to ask.

On a hot spring afternoon, I sat down at a student desk in an empty classroom in the psychology building and answered their few questions.

"We see that you checked, as one of the things you *don't* want to be, 'normal,'" one of the grad students said. "Could you explain why you answered this way?"

I looked at them for a moment. They were dressed so conservatively—the young man in khaki slacks and a button-down shirt, with a short haircut; the young woman in a dress and nylons (warm day, pre-pantyhose)—for this non-professional, casual meeting, that I was tempted to say, "Like you; I don't want to be like you." At this point, I was an art student wearing jeans, turtlenecks, loafers, and flower child beads most of the time. I looked like I was suspended between the beat generation and hippiedom.

"What seems to be considered 'normal' in society is not appealing to me," I told them. "The emphasis on fitting in, on being the same as everyone else, on buying things so that corporations can make a lot of money, on making sure your personality is not too different, seems superficial to me. Especially the willingness of people—parents in particular—to follow along with the government's military intervention in Southeast Asia as a normal thing for a non-communist government to do . . . if all of that is normal, it isn't what I want to be."

The two young people just nodded their heads and made notes.

Now, this is contradictory if you look at my life up till this point. I had done everything I could think of for at least fifteen years to be seen and accepted as "normal." I had worn mini-skirts with colored tights that covered up my foam prosthesis, had hairdos like everybody else, and accepted social mores like everybody else (white girls don't date black boys, there are things you don't talk about, don't be too weird or nerdy, and so on). But college had freed me. I suppose this was my time to look over my shoulder and say, "Since I'm not normal physically, 'normal' in general will be something that's not important to me."

A girlfriend pointed out to me recently that we all want to be seen as normal, and everyone is concerned about that. I still do not want to stand out. I experience my life, when I'm not in physical difficulty or pain, as normal. I still forget that I limp, and I sometimes flush when people stare at me, at the way I walk. But when they are embarrassed, I now feel worse for them than I do for myself, for that moment. I want to tell them, "It's okay. I would probably stare too."

❧

I'd been paying attention to all the black power and racial marches and beginning to realize how pervasive racism was. There were perhaps two or three black families in my hometown, and although nearly all their sons were sports stars going to college, we white girls were not supposed to date them. As a child, I had simplistically thought, *We have Negroes, Hispanics, and Asians in addition to Anglos. People just don't date across races because races don't intermarry.* But aside from that blockbuster of a young prejudice, I was not really aware of racism.

In the spring of 1967, I had a visit from the Mormon monthly visiting teachers. Here at college, I was visited not by an old lady who thought I was too meticulous about my appearance but a couple of young married men in their twenties. I liked these guys; they seemed casual and trustworthy. We'd meet in the lobby of my dormitory on campus for about an hour and talk about church philosophy and how I was doing personally.

I knew that the Mormon Church did not allow black men to be in the priesthood, though they could be members of the church. This seemed strange to me—that black people would even want to be Mormons, given this exclusion. The reason the church gave was that Cain slew Abel, and according to the Book of Mormon, all black people were descendants of Cain.

How could anyone know this? What about evolution, which seemed clearly true? What about all the Asian people that the church was making such an effort to convert? What the heck was going on here, and who was setting these rules? (Note: The Mormon Church did lift the ban on blacks holding the priest-hood in 1978. Somebody had a vision, I guess. This is called out with clever humor in the recent Broadway musical *The Book of Mormon.*)

One Wednesday evening, these two nice (and white) young men came by and we chatted a bit, as we always did. And then I had a query for them—one that I'd been waiting for weeks to bring up.

"I'm not comfortable with blacks not being allowed to hold the priesthood," I said, "and I'm also not in agreement with the 'Cain slew Abel' reasoning. What do you think about that?"

They gave each other a long look, which seemed to say, "Any question but this one." Then one of them turned to me wearily and said, "We're not comfortable with it either. We don't have a good answer for that."

At that moment I ceased being a Mormon. I didn't tell the guys this, as I didn't want them to feel responsible for a young woman leaving the church. I could see they truly believed in their religion and were grappling with the parts of it that did not feel right to them, as any sincere believer may do, as he or she delves more deeply into questions of faith, dogma, ethics, and morality. It's challenging to know when to follow, when to leave, and when to go along with some things while secretly not believing in parts of what's taught, so that one can remain in the religious community, the family, the relationships based on this set of tenets.

But I, Carol Francine the Christian, had been falling away from the church for some time. I hated it when Sister N., the mother of the catty girl in sixth grade, said to me in the foyer of the church in Yuba City after my absence of a couple of months, "Oh, Carol, you've come back to the fold!" as if I were a lamb who had wandered away from Jesus. I had nothing against Jesus. I just was beginning to think he didn't have much to do with the way different churches had structured their religious teachings. I hated it when people in the church talked behind others' backs about their behavior and then were sickeningly sweet to those same people in person. It didn't seem Christian to me. Not that I haven't talked about people—I've done it a lot—but the gossip amongst these women who were so outwardly pious seemed hypocritical. My sister hated that about the church too.

And why was Jesus so Anglo-looking in that chapel picture? He was Jewish! If the Jews were the chosen people, as both the Jews and the Mormons often said, why did the image they used for Christ make him look like a white hippie with light brown hair and blue eyes?

When I was around eleven I asked Mother who had painted that picture of Christ that hung in our church and how it had been preserved for all those centuries. She told me it was "an artist's conception"—to which I did an inner, *Tch! What the heck! I've been duped.*

As a young adult, the church tenets suddenly seemed very unsupportable to me, on top of being racist, despite the loving relationships and friendships I did have within the church. Today, I still have Mormon friends for whom I hold great affection; it's just hard for me not to think, given my change in philosophy, that they've been taken advantage of, because they are such nice people.

So, I was done at nineteen. No looking back, and no regrets.

⤙⤚

There was a big variety of maleness at college, from the varsity jocks through the hippie guys, and I gravitated to the latter. Frequently. Frankly, I had too many boyfriends in my very early twenties (and later again in my late twenties); I was sort of a serial monogamist. I made this possibly poor choice for several reasons, one of which was a desire to prove to myself that I was attractive to men, and prove to myself and them that I was a viable life partner. Evidence had been to the contrary in high school; I hadn't, after all, gotten very many dates. Besides my leg being unattractive, that may have been because I had developed a sharp wit and a sometimes-sharp tongue, which teenage boys in the 60s did not necessarily equate with attractiveness. I also had not been "easy" in high school; I'd been saving myself for somebody special.

I was naïve in my college days and the couple of decades after that, and it did not dawn on me till many years later that if you were willing to sleep with men early in the "relationship" (if there ever was a relationship), of course you were going to attract a lot of "partners." I thought I was holding tryouts for a marriage partner, while most of the guys, I now realize, were just out to have a good time with any nice gal who was willing. Birth control, particularly The Pill, had liberated us girls in one respect, but being on a more equal footing with the guys also meant it was harder to come up with a good reason not to have sex. This was, fortunately, long before AIDS was a specter.

I did learn that there are different kinds of lovers and had both successes and failures in relationships in my twenties, which taught me other lessons: how to compromise, when not to push too hard, when to give in, and when to insist. (I'm still learning about all that; bet you are too.)

I cried a lot in my twenties—and on into my thirties—over men. My forties, too, at least a little bit. I blamed myself for failure with several boyfriends I thought would have made good life partners, although in retrospect, they may not have. I deeply grieved the loss whenever I fell in love and it didn't work out, even if I thought I was not to blame. *Where is MY mate?? Why am I attracting the wrong people?* My grief echoed my mother's perspective that the most important thing in life was a husband, and if he died or left, your life was nearly worthless.

It took me decades to learn that developing a sense of self and what was important to my own heart and mind—for instance, finding fulfilling work, creative pastimes, and friendships, which I was doing concurrently—was more important than relationships with men. I did also begin to learn to work things out without feeling it was the end of the world if someone was upset or disapproving. And a lot of the time, I was enjoying the ride; I just hated permanent good-byes. Each time a relationship ended, though I wasn't conscious of this at the time, I viscerally re-experienced the painful finality of losing my dad.

I didn't really think much about disability rights in my twenties. I was able to walk better then, for one thing, and I already knew that I was in a small subset of people—and of women in particular. I knew that I wasn't everyone's dream girl, but I thought that physical and social discrimination was something I'd leave in my small home town with my childhood, and my new college

and adult world would be full of mature, intelligent, unbiased people. I was trying so hard to be like everyone else that my self-image did not involve identifying with the group called "disabled." It would be a long time before I'd sit in a workshop and listen to one person after another share their impressions of my handicap and what it meant to them.

I was living in the "I'm Not Really Disabled" bubble in those days, and exhausting myself with long-distance walks and stairs at San Jose State. I worked hard to keep up with everyone else and keep my mouth shut about it, as I'd been taught. However, at the end of my freshman year class scheduling at San Jose, when we had to physically go to each department to get our next semester's classes (I actually spent the night on the sidewalk in front of the art department to get my first-year art classes, popular with graduating seniors who needed units), a wise teacher approached me and quietly said, "You can pre-register; didn't anyone tell you that? You don't have to do all this walking."

Nope. Didn't know that.

She didn't say, "because you are handicapped or disabled," and I appreciated her not drawing public attention to me more than my limp already did. There had been nothing in my application that asked if I had a handicap, and nothing had been mentioned at freshman orientation.

⚬

After three years of art school—two at San Jose State and one at California College of Arts and Crafts in Oakland—I quit. I loved making art, and I liked hanging out with artists and musicians, but by the time I transferred to CCAC, it was becoming clear to me that although my renderings and photos were good, I was not particularly inspired. I did skillful, sensitive line work in my life drawings, but about the only thing I could imagine I'd be able to do with that was greeting cards or book illustrations. DaVinci or Ansel Adams I was not.

I was not an outstanding talent; artists had to live in a city to make a living; and I was running out of money—I didn't have enough for the next year of college. So I dropped out. Mom was profoundly shocked and accused me of wasting the money "your dad died for," the $10,000 in VA insurance that I had mostly used for art school. Although I had a "full scholarship" for any college in California, it did not cover living expenses, books, and supplies (which is why my husband says I should have gone to Stanford and gotten my money's worth). I was surprised by the strength of her reaction, but in hindsight I think it was because she was artistic herself and had never had a true career of any kind. I suspect she had a romantic attachment to the idea of me becoming an artist and wanted to live through me vicariously.

I moved north to Sonoma County, where I met people I really liked—back-to-the-land folks, musicians, students of yoga and mysticism—and landed in a temporary business partnership with another woman, creating handmade clothing in a little consignment shop.

drugs lite

*T*ook a few psychedelic drugs from age twenty-one through thirty-nine, most of it in my twenties. I do not regret this, though I would not generally recommend it. I have a strong will, mind, and sense of self, and even on my very few bad trips was able to steer myself either on my own or with help to normalcy and what we know as reality. But I knew people in the 70s and 80s who were damaged irrevocably by psychedelic drugs— some because they were mentally unstable to begin with, most because they took too many.

The good trips were worth the risk, for me. I took LSD, psilocybin mushrooms, and mescaline, with a sense of adventure and seeking an expanded sense of what the world was. I was looking for deeper meaning in the late sixties, with friends going off to the Vietnam war and a few of them getting killed over there. I was protesting and signing petitions. I was hoping to find a greater spirituality than one that dictated, "There is a male god in heaven who controls much of our lives and leaves us to make our own mistakes and then later punishes or rewards us."

Also, the drugs were fun. I learned that not everything was as it might seem in life, that there was an "I" in me that was an observer beyond the limited mind and personality I had defined as Myself previously, and that the apparent barriers between objects might not actually exist—that maybe all things *were* one.

These are the kinds of deeper threads to which psychedelics led me in those days.

⸺

When I was twenty-one and in my junior year at art college, I had taken some THC and was sitting in my room, looking at my feet. I was living in Oakland with a fellow artist, Rich Wilbur, at the time, and I called him to my room from the kitchen.

"Look at this foot," I told him. I was staring at my little foot and could see its unusual circulation with its blue and red and purple coloring, and its small, paralyzed toes, which were a babyish mirror of their sister toes on the other foot. I studied this nearly inanimate, discolored, and helpless limb, perceiving its strangeness, especially compared to the other one.

Rich sat there with me, I on the bed and he in my little 1930s thrift shop easy chair. After a few moments, he said, "That weird foot. It's probably the best thing that ever happened to you."

I never asked him what he meant, exactly—but what I understood him to mean was that every seeming major difficulty has some payoff or lesson. I knew he was into yin and yang, opposites, understanding duality. At that time, I chose to believe that he was right. Maybe it was the best thing, not the worst thing, that ever happened to me.

Okay, I thought, *if this hadn't happened, what would have been different? What different path might I have gone down that wouldn't have been as good for me?*

For starters, aside from the good things I missed out on, I might have chosen a more superficial life, a life that did not include the richness of experience I now sought out as a result of being physically odd. The things I loved—art, music, mysticism, liberal politics—might not have pulled on me. I might not have ended up hanging out with the people I had recently chosen as my friends, who accepted a broader spectrum of options and social choices, who also were not part of the mainstream, who found new ways of relating and doing things that might not have been acceptable to me when I was a middle American kid. This was the beginning for me of not just clomping around on my leg without asking what it meant to be handicapped and what choices it was causing me to make.

༄

Two or three years later, I had taken LSD and was dancing in the afternoon to some music, Joni Mitchell and then Leon Russell, in my small living room in Forestville, and I suddenly began paying more concentrated attention to how my feet were operating. I realized that I was treating my polio foot like it was a stump at the end of my leg, just slapping it down. When I walked, since I didn't wear any kind of support device, my drop foot just hung at the end of my leg; no flexion was possible with my ankle paralysis. I have never been able to do the heel-first, roll-to-toes movement that comprises a normal walk. The ball of my foot slaps down first if I am barefooted, and at that time it did so even with a shoe since I did not yet wear an ankle brace.

My ankle hadn't rolled in since the surgery Dr. Mearns had performed on me years earlier, but on this day I thought, *Perhaps there's something else I can do so this little foot will behave a bit better.* My toes at that time were beginning to curl up and under, so that one of them was actually staying stuck, like a hammer toe. It did not hurt, but it felt strange, and I could see that left unattended, it could become a painful problem. This was a revealing moment for me: I saw that I was neglecting the needs of this foot and that this could be detrimental to how it functioned later on in my life.

⤳

Recently I heard an interview on NPR with a drug researcher from the Buckley Foundation at Oxford. They have found that administering controlled doses of LSD to patients with mental illness has resulted in their being better able to unify different parts of their brains. Patients on LSD or the drug nicknamed Ecstasy have exhibited a feeling of unity with the world—its flora, fauna, and, perhaps more importantly, its people. These sensations tended to have a lasting value even after the drugs wore off. That's exactly the experience I had.

It's possible that a lot of handicapped people are drawn to substances and sometimes substance abuse for several reasons. It is a relief to leave reality behind a bit when reality includes being physically deformed or being in pain. With marijuana, since what is going on in your mind and/or emotional being begins to take precedence over what you look like, pot can be an equalizer, and issues like having a paralyzed leg or being in a wheelchair become just additional aspects of oneself more quickly than they do amongst folks who might be concentrating on other standards. Not to say you can't get to a less judgmental place in sobriety, or that pot smokers have no judgmental tendencies. Maturity is the best equalizer of all. But there's something about psychedelic drugs that breaks down social mores, particularly the superficial ones.

What I was seeing on psychedelics gave me the sense that just about everything was alive in one way or another. I felt more connected to the world and more respectful, and, yes, loving toward it. I saw human beings as remarkably vulnerable, dealing with limited knowledge about a vast universe, trying to come up with explanations for everything when there was always going to be more that we did not know. A tenderness emerged because of this.

It seemed as if I had previously missed that there were many more layers to life, to people and their emotions, and to what humanity might potentially be. Could we have more inner knowledge than we realized? Could there be many more dimensions to life and existence than what we had classified, categorized, tied down, figured out, defined, equated, and written down? What was spirit? Was it material as well as etheric? Was there any real separation, given we exchange molecules just sitting in a room together? In the late 60s, I had sensed for the first time an "I" that existed apart from my body or mind. I had opened up to the possibility that I might in fact be one with the universe. Did human beings have a consciousness other than intellect? Was that the same as spirit? Could we know our spirit? What was the difference between spirit and soul?

Over a period of about twenty years, I took psychedelic drugs perhaps thirty times in an attempt to answer these questions for myself.

What did the Buddhist say to the hot dog vendor? "Make me one with everything."

love the leg you're with

*A*fter my psychedelic revelations about my foot, I felt more kinship with it. I saw that I had been treating it like it didn't matter and was just an appendage. I realized I needed to love my little leg—that it had worked really hard for a couple of decades, despite its severe limitations, and I needed to treat it with respect and kindness and try to stop blaming it for my situation. Many people had referred to it as "your bad leg," and still do, particularly physicians. To this I started saying, "It's not a bad leg. It's a weak leg." Mother was right in a sense when she called it my "lazy" leg, but even that had a stigma.

This leg is anything but lazy. I would characterize it as the leg that never gave up.

I began to wonder if there was a possibility that I might be able to strengthen my right ankle and correct the drop foot. The idealist in me didn't trust the initial prognosis, which dictated that polio patients only gained improvement in the first year.

I located a physical therapist in nearby Sebastopol. I told her I was a polio patient and wanted to look into learning to strengthen my foot. She said I'd need to get a prescription from a doctor, so I made an appointment with Dr. Anderson, an orthopedic MD in Santa Rosa, several miles from my home.

~

During the initial examination in Dr. Anderson's office, I said, "I'd like to see a physical therapist regarding improving my drop foot. I realize I've been ignoring how I walk on it, and am hoping I might be able to strengthen the ankle." "Mm-hmm," Dr. Anderson said. To his credit, he did not try to dissuade me. He was very interested in looking at my gait and the general condition of my leg. "Walk across the room for me," he said, and watched me ambulate back and forth a few times. He then inspected my lower limbs in the concentrated way I rarely see in today's sports-oriented orthopedic doctors.

I realize now that I was a study case to him. He did not see that many polio patients, particularly those who were not yet having severe new problems.

After examining my leg, Dr. Anderson made a comment that surprised me. He looked closely at the scar from my triple arthrodesis, and the resulting stability of my ankle, and asked, "Who did this work?"

"Robert Mearns, in Sacramento," I answered.

"I thought so," he said. "Great doctor."

I was astonished that he could recognize the work, just as you'd recognize the painting of a renowned artist.

Dr. Anderson did give me a prescription for physical therapy, and then we talked about how to correct the problem with my toes.

I told him I thought that if I had a little pad in my shoe under the curled toe, it would hold my toe out straight and keep it from hammering. He agreed, and in turn suggested that I sleep with a lightweight cast shoe on my foot. At the time, these were just a flat piece of plywood with an upper mantle of plastic stapled on, with a Velcro closure. He cut the one he gave me down in length so the covers would not pull on my flaccid ankle while I slept, then took some piano felt and cut it down to fit under my toes, crafting it until it put them into a normal position. He thought this would probably train the errant toe to stay straight, keep the others from following suit, and give me some relief from the tight feeling in the curled toe.

I had a pair of sandals made at the local (hippie) sandal maker with the pad I'd thought of, which relieved the hammering tendency when I walked around during the day, and began wearing my cast shoe to bed. From the start of using this device, I began to see a difference in my toe. It did not feel so stiff, and after a year or two mostly stayed in a normal position.

I continued to wear the sleeping shoe for a couple of decades, until trials of not wearing it seemed to make no difference, and I declared the toes corrected and healed.

～

I saw the physical therapist regularly for a few months. She had had arthritis from the time she was twelve (she was probably in her sixties when I met her), and she taught me that it was important to keep moving, regardless of how we feel. Without that movement, she said, my structural components would become stiff or even rigid.

We were working with the possibility that I might be able to regain ankle motion. She had me concentrate on moving my foot while she made little stroking motions with a finger along the top of my foot and ankle—an approach that was part of Sister Kenny's original program, intended to engage the mind and muscles by touching the area and concentrating on the concept of motion.

After doing this for some time, I began to have hints of movement in the top of my ankle! At first, I could only sense the motion inside my foot; later on, if we watched carefully, we could see a twitch of movement. However, this was after months of meeting once or twice a week and doing a half hour daily of concentrated isometric exercise.

We finally had a "come to Jesus" meeting where she told me that if I increased the time I spent on my ankle, doing the exercises for three or four hours a day, and kept at it for years, I might eventually be able to move the foot a bit, but it was never going to be a normal foot.

I felt a bit deflated, but I had known this project was a long shot. I accepted that the initial prognosis had been correct. (This is still the standard in polio rehab: the first year is when nearly all of any possible improvement happens, particularly with permanent paralysis.)

I made a decision to give up the exercises. The amount of time it was going to take, with little and uncertain success, was time I felt I would rather spend on music (plus, I had to earn a living). I was singing and writing country blues songs and wanted to improve my ability in that talent more than I wanted to spend three or four hours each day hoping for negligible movement. I saw that in some respects, at some times in our lives, devoting oneself to what feeds the soul, the mind, and creative instincts can be more rewarding than time spent improving the body. It was not a choice to neglect or ignore my body but rather to keep my life in perspective.

❧

I bought a cane at a flea market three or four years later. I thought it would look cool with my limp, and discovered it actually did help me walk in a slightly more level fashion when I used it on my strong side and leaned on it a little. It took the stress off both legs, as if I had a third leg. Generally, canes are not supposed to be leaned on—they are to be used to stabilize and keep balance—but I've always leaned on mine. (Sometimes I pay a price for that, with wrist and elbow tendinitis.)

I went back to Dr. Anderson's medical office to have the cane cut down to my height. (Now, my husband cuts my canes down with a saw; simple to do, but I didn't know this in my twenties.)

Dr. Anderson looked at the cane, which was an English-style stick, made of a thin hardwood branch and an antler handle, and said, "This is such an interesting cane; it'd be such a shame to cut it down."

I'm short—five feet tall in bare feet. And this is a good thing: if I'd grown more, there would be an even greater length difference between my legs. I need my cane, like everyone who uses one, to be at the approximate height of my mid-hip. A cane should allow your arm to be slightly bent with your hand resting comfortably on the handle. I see so many people whose canes are too long, and I always want to tell them they need to get them cut down.

In light of that, I thought Dr. Anderson's comment was rather thoughtless; what good was the cane to me, its owner, the woman who would be using it daily, if it were too tall? Did he think I should give it up, hang it on the wall, sell it as an antique to a taller person? He seemed to be suggesting that I wasn't deserving of a truly interesting cane—that I should save this one, and get myself a drug store cane. I know he didn't mean to offend, but, still. Just one of those remarks we crips can do without.

I hesitated a moment while I had these thoughts, then said, "Well, I'm the one who's going to use it."

He cut a couple of inches off the bottom with no further discussion, but he also went down a couple of notches in my esteem that day.

ᔐ

Despite the cane incident, I remained a patient of Dr. Anderson's, and when I was twenty-eight I went back to see him after tearing my Achilles tendon. (I was wearing boots with two-inch-high heels on an unstable pathway. Stupidly vain, and a seriously painful outcome!) I wore a limiting plaster cast for a month before Dr. Anderson put me in a walking cast. When I wore the second cast, I felt like I could finally walk normally, because the height of the heel made up for the two-inch difference in my leg lengths. I actually enjoyed wearing that walking cast quite a lot. I saw a movie two years later, *Just the Way You Are*, about a woman who had some deformity that caused her to limp—maybe it was even polio— and she actually got an unnecessary cast put on her leg when she went to a business conference so she could flirt with men and they would not think she was handicapped, but just had a ski injury. I could *so* relate.

All these experiences made me realize that I'd had a prejudice against my own body part and was expecting it to try harder and make up for its disability, just as some people had expected me to do over the course of my life. I started treating my leg with additional kindness, massaging it more in the winter and resting sooner when my extreme fatigue set in. I even told it sometimes, "You're a good little leg; thanks for trying so hard!" But old habits die hard, and we polio survivors, according to research, tend to have a lot of goals that we hate to give up. So, forty-plus years later, I'm still not resting enough.

in and out of marriage and back to school

$\mathcal{W}$ ithin a few months of moving to Sonoma, I met, quite by accident, the man who would become my first husband, Bob Haley. Actually, he moved in with me and we later declared ourselves married, thinking California recognized common law marriage.

Bob, who was nearly eighteen years older than me, lived upstairs from my two-room apartment in Rio Nido on the Russian River in northern California. When his "old lady," Mickey, author Richard Brautigan's ex, who was all of about twenty-six, left him, he moved into my place without my express permission, which I took as a compliment at the time. He promptly came down with mononucleosis and I devoted myself to nursing him back to relative health, thus abruptly ending my early twenties dating and free-love experiences.

He was very intelligent and, for the most part, kind, and had a variety of interesting friends (professional musicians from Ohio who worked for Bill Graham in sound engineering, independently wealthy people who were into astrology and mysticism, ex-bikers who were writers, ace sports car mechanics). A couple of these people are still among my closest friends, more than forty-five years later. The problems were that he was both an alcoholic and manic-depressive, and this expressed itself in bouts of bombastic diatribes, arguing, and public embarrassment alternated with many weekends and evenings of, "I don't feel like going anywhere. I've done that before. I'm a little down tonight. I just want to sit here and read. Would you make me a cup of coffee?"

I thought that if I could just be a better wife, anticipate his needs, never make a mistake, he'd stop drinking.

We bought a little cabin with the limited but appreciated down payment assistance Mom offered. ("Are you living with him . . . as man and wife?" "Yes, Mom, we consider ourselves married. I go by Francine Haley.") Our arrangement was not easy for her to accept, as a religious woman born in 1908, but then, she also thought she might go to hell for smoking and drinking coffee. And there was a part of her that was glad I was with someone at all. She had, after all, approved of my first serious high school boyfriend, who would have been even more of a disaster as a husband.

∾

More than once, while we sat in the living room, or at our round oak table, or lay in bed, this discussion ensued:

"Wouldn't you like to have a baby? Would that make you happy?"

"Someday, Bob, yes, I want that. But I'm not ready right now."

"Well, we could get married. Wouldn't you like that?"

"I feel like we're already married. Getting a government stamp for it won't make it any more spiritual, or real."

I soon realized that these proposals were a trap; Bob knew that legal marriage and having a baby would make me feel unable to leave.

At this time, I didn't fathom the huge physical drain it would have been for me to have a baby, a child. I now see the potential great difficulty, particularly having waited until I was in my late forties for a stable marriage. I'm not even sure that carrying a baby to full term without going to bed for months and essentially living in a wheelchair would have been possible for me, since it is very difficult for me to walk, and always has been, while carrying more than about five or ten pounds. Having twenty or more pounds out in front of me would certainly have been hard on my already stressed back, not to mention its effect on my precarious sense of balance. Plus, my badly deformed hip and pelvis would have been stressed and compromised by labor, if I could even manage a natural birth.

Lots of polio patients have had children and made it through. Some women—with, I should note, lesser paralysis and pelvic deformity than me—have told me it "wasn't that hard." I asked one of the women in a polio group how she handled it, and she said she had a Caesarian, for one thing, which compromises already weak pelvic muscles. I told her I thought it would have been hard for me to pick up a child and walk with her, if she weighed more than ten pounds, and my acquaintance told me that it *was* unusually hard: she could not lift and carry her child due to her back and leg issues, which had resulted in the child bonding more with the father. She'd had a lot of help from family and her husband.

I did not have family nearby who could have assisted me, and neither Bob nor my current husband would have been the baby-tending type. If I'd had a child with Bob, when I left him I would have been a handicapped single mother working full-time and barely able to support two people, let alone take care of a child. So fate did me a favor, though I have sometimes regretted having no children. I wonder if anyone will come see us when we're older.

❧

Bob and I knew a young man named Leslie Scardigli, who was a quadriplegic, and people hung out at his house in Rio Nido. He had a caregiver, Alan Hardman, and both of them were intelligent and hospitable.

Once, in the early days of our relationship, when we were relaxing with after-dinner coffee in the spacious living room of Lani and Al Krauss, our closest friends, Bob said, "I don't understand why women are so attracted to Leslie. What is it, Alan is the body and Leslie is the mind? I mean, Leslie's body is useless. How could he have sex?"

Then Bob looked at us with a half-smile, like it was a perverted type of attraction women had for Leslie, and as if he expected one of us to answer.

I reflected a moment, then said, "I think Leslie is an attractive man. He is still fun to talk to, even though he's in a wheelchair. And who knows what he can or cannot do."

Lani chuckled and said, "Yes, who knows, Bob?"

I was a little uncomfortable with the conversation and we dropped it and went on to different topics, like astrology, gardening, and whatever else was on our minds that evening.

But this diatribe of Bob's—and he went on it more than once—bothered me for two reasons. One, Leslie was very handsome, engaging, and charming, so it was easy to see why anyone would find him attractive. He gave you his full attention when you spoke, with big brown eyes that often twinkled as if there were some joke he was on the verge of divulging. I believe he thought his condition was a huge, absurd, damnable joke. You could see that before his accident he could have dated just about anyone he wanted to.

The second reason Bob's comments bothered me was that I, Bob's partner, was handicapped. I was not paraplegic, but didn't my boyfriend see some similarities between me and Leslie? I sure did. I had full paralysis below the knee, and partial from knee to hip. I was very clear what having paralysis in other parts of my body might mean. Didn't Bob see that to give a critique of Leslie's probable sexual inadequacy and almost make fun of it to others was bringing into the line of fire my possible inadequacy as well? My limitations in that realm? I might be able to do most of what others could do, but some things needing two strong legs were out of the question. To people who were more physically active than Bob, my inability to hike or do whatever else people might like to do on a date might make sex with me seem out of the question, especially given the unattractiveness of my little leg. Who'd want it? I took personal offense at his comments about our friend.

Bob's dissing Leslie's body actually made Leslie more attractive to me and Bob less attractive. If I'd been more mature I would probably have thought, "Hmmm . . . Maybe Bob's not the guy for me, actually." But at that time, I looked up to Bob as a more knowledgeable person than myself, and I was also invested in having our relationship last no matter what. Plus, I loved him and was willing to overlook a lot of faults.

❧

I "married" Bob in 1970. After a year or two, he got tired of supporting me, so I went job searching. First I got a job soldering printed circuit boards ($1.80/hour, minimum wage); soon after that I found another job pounding pegs in wooden puzzles at a cottage industry where some of the employees camped out behind the factory—not a career, but at least these were sit-down jobs.

One day my boss walked through the games factory, on his usual rounds to see how things were going. I was seated on a high stool, pounding pegs into holes with a wooden mallet at a huge work table, and when I saw him I called him over.

"Dick, you know, because the drill press is set a little too small, you are losing about 10 percent of these blocks when I put the pegs in, because the pegs split the holes. Then when the blocks go to sanding, the pegs stick out and tear up the sanding belts, so you're spending more on belts, and you lose some puzzles because they go flying off the belt. Maybe another 10 to 15 percent of them."

He looked at me as if he had not seen me before, though we'd said hello many times. "Really . . ." he said, not as a question but an observation.

The next day, he came to me and said, "I think we have you in the wrong position." He brought me up to the front office, such as it was (we all wore jeans and smoked expensive brown paper Sherman's cigarettes on Friday afternoons; I just puffed, never inhaled), promoted me to cost estimator, and had me start doing time and motion studies.

Unfortunately, part of why my boss wanted all this accomplished was because the company was bleeding money. He was hoping I would tell him where the greatest wounds were. Once I'd accomplished this, I was laid off, and once again, I was afloat career-wise, unsure of my next move.

⌁

Meanwhile, Bob and I were about four years into our relationship. We were now making love only once a month (not my idea, in my twenties, of a typical relationship), we were arguing more often, and his drinking was escalating (he had apparently been in a temporary "alcoholic lite" phase when I met him). I came home more than once to find he'd puked in the bed.

What the heck am I doing here? I wondered. I had my whole life in front of me.

I lost most of the twenty pounds I'd acquired as a wife/cook. I had two or three brief affairs in short succession, partly to reassure myself I was still attractive and partly because I was frustrated and wanted a sexual relationship, not just a housemate.

Bob loved me dearly and was a sweet man and a good friend to many, but he did not love himself nearly enough, though he blustered and feigned a huge ego. After too many binges on his part and too many weekends of my running away, leaving him alone while I saw friends, in an attempt to try and get him to go to AA, or counseling, or anything that might help our relationship to become what I was beginning to realize it would never be, I left. Five years of effort ended in 1975. It was a difficult decision, but I had a lot of support. Bob tried to get me to come back, but I stood my ground. I still saw for myself a hearts-and-flowers future, with hubby and one or two kids, and I was only twenty-seven.

I spent a summer going to parties and bars, exercising my freedom, though I felt lonely and upset. I wrote a lot of country western songs—some of them not bad: "Insomnia, we're here together again; sometimes I feel . . . you're getting to be my best friend"; "You planted the seed . . . of bitterness in me. It grows like the devil's grass, so uncontrollably"; "Oh, why does a woman's mind wander, when things are so good at home?" (Perhaps one day I'll look for celebrities to sing them.)

⌒

That summer, I also took some aptitude tests (and, concurrently, a typing class). They showed I had unusual ability in spatial relationships and that I should be a mathematician, an engineer, or maybe an architect, and definitely not a nurse (too much aversion to hospitals!). Going back to college in those fields would require moving far away, however, and I had a lot of established friendships, a big Airedale-Malamute dog named Mollie, and no money to relocate.

I was getting discouraged and did not have a steady way to support myself. I inquired at the Employment Development Department in Sonoma County whether I could get a job doing lettering or some other beginning art vocation, and they told me there were seven hundred unemployed artists in the county.

So I went to the local college, Sonoma State (nicknamed Granola State, and later re-classified Sonoma State University). I researched what majors I could take which would be math-related, point me toward a career that would provide steady, sit-down employment, and would be an equal opportunity job in terms of gender. I had most of my general education from my first three years. If I obtained grants and loans and worked part-time, I could get my BA in two years.

Accounting came up as the only thing that seemed to fit my criteria. Oy. This was so very far afield from my original desire to be a commercial artist, and so removed from my own nature and interests. But the tides were against me. I decided to go for it.

Over the next two years, I tried to balance having a social life, meeting friends and boyfriends in the local bar (even though I, of all people, after five years with an alcoholic, should have known a bar was a bad place to meet a boyfriend), studying harder than I'd ever studied, and working anywhere from twenty to forty hours a week while carrying a full unit load. I was sleeping a scant six hours most nights.

After being an art major, the stress of learning accounting and simultaneously taking on bookkeeping jobs to support myself was significant. It was like learning Swedish and learning to fix a Saab with a Swedish manual, all at the same time—and I felt I had little, if anything, in common with my classmates. I took Expressive Arts as an elective in order to get through the two years, writing poetry and songs and sometimes performing to feed my soul. There I met people who were more like those I was used to hanging out with.

NOT A POSTER CHILD   185

I got two loans and two grants. I sold ounces of pot to close friends so that I had a tiny amount of spending money outside of what I was making through my bookkeeping work. It was grueling, but I made it through, with above average if not exemplary grades.

At Sonoma State University, I discovered the Disability Resource Center, which was like a Disabled Students' Union. Its founder and director, Anthony Tusler, educated me about handicapped parking license plates (now DP, for "Disabled Person")—who could use them, how to go through the process of getting them, where to expect the parking to be, and so on. I remember thinking that it was interesting that disabled people had a center, and feeling impressed that some people at the school (primarily Anthony, I learned) had determined that disabled or handicapped people might have special needs.

At that time, there was not much in the way of handicapped parking in most places, other than in front of hospitals, doctors' offices, and schools. The Resource Center's existence was a wake-up call for me that special needs were being addressed. It was interesting to me that anyone other than a family member would care that some people had physical difficulties. I was still in my "I'm not disabled" attitudinal bubble much of the time, however—I barely thought of myself as a person with special needs—and I did not want to identify with a group that called itself "disabled" or "handicapped." I'd rather have spent my spare time in the Expressive Arts department, which is exactly what I did.

21

—

wake up, little sufi

*I*n the middle of all this, I more or less got religion. That first summer after Bob and I split up, in 1975, I went up to Ukiah, in Mendocino County, to stay with our good friends, Lani and Al Krauss. Lani was twelve years my senior and was both a mentor and a very entertaining and close, loving friend to me. She and Al had a piece of property on the McNab Ranch, a lovely, big old house that Bob had helped repair and remodel, and acreage with a barn.

One day during my visit, Lani and I took either LSD or psilocybin together, and I took a short hike by myself, hoping to clear my head of my divorce.

I found a shady place in the foothills to sit for a while. I thought I would try doing some chanting—"Om"—which I had learned was best done as three sounds: "ahhhh—uuuu—mmmm." The "ah" was supposed to open the heart chakra, the center of love and openness; the "u" the throat, the center of communication; and the "m" was said to reside in the third eye to stimulate intuition or intelligence. I found that I had good breath control and could hold these syllables for an extended amount of time. I was also pleased to discover that on the "uuu" sound, there were two or more harmonious notes, like a chord, emitting from my throat.

After practicing my new experience for perhaps a half-hour,

I thought, *I don't know what effect this might be having, and holding my breath for so long, even though on the exhale, might be dangerous* . . . I felt like there was the possibility of breaking a blood vessel in my head, or worse. I didn't think of passing out, though that was probably a more real danger.

I hiked with my maple sapling walking stick back down the hill to the house. Lani studied esoteric things like astrology and bioenergetics, so I suspected she'd know something about chanting, too.

She greeted me with a fond, "Hi! Did you have a nice walk?"

"Yes, 'high' is right," I said, chuckling. "But I was up there chanting 'Om,' and I heard these overtones in the notes, like on a guitar—like harmony with myself. I can kind of control it and make the sound go up and down the scale. But I was holding my breath a long time and I began to be afraid I was going to break a blood vessel in my head or something. Do you know anyone who knows about this kind of stuff?"

She laughed. "I don't think you would break a blood vessel . . . but, oh, yes, I do know people who know 'about this stuff'!"

She put on an album she thought I'd like, by The Sufi Choir, called "Stone in the Sky." There were songs like, "It's Coming Back to Me," about remembering one's spiritual self. One of the singers, a man named Vasheest Davenport, had a perfect tenor voice. I sat in the Krauss's music room and read the liner notes while listening to the whole album, enthralled and even brought to tears at times.

"I want to sing with this guy!" I told Lani at the end of the record.

She smiled. "Well, these people are in the San Francisco Bay Area; you might be able to hear them sing, at least."

That night near Ukiah, we attended my first of thousands of Sufi meetings. We sang, danced (the Dances of Universal Peace as initiated by Murshid ["teacher"] Samuel Lewis in 1960s San

Francisco, commonly known as Sufi Dancing), meditated, and listened to a paper on practices of Sufism. This philosophy is described variously as the mystical branch of Islam, the Way of the Heart, and a philosophy in which you learn to become one with God and learn to see from the point of view of others. I wanted to dive into this stream of wisdom.

I started going to Sufi Dance classes in Sonoma County. These were based on fairly simple folk dancing steps, circle dances, set to various music using the words of many world religions. We sang "Sri Ram, Jai Ram," from Hinduism; "La Illaha, il Allah Hu," from Islam; "Kwan Zeon Bosai," from Korean Buddhism; "My House Will Be a House of Prayer," from Christianity; and many more. (In western Sufism, we studied all major religions—at Universal Worship services, there were always at least seven religions represented—and I loved this inclusiveness. I have felt a special affinity for the Buddhist enlightened being or bodhisattva Quan Yin, since I read that she was an independent woman who had a lame leg and walked with a limp as she traveled around teaching and assisting humanity. She is said to be a goddess of mercy and compassion who hears the distress of worldly beings. A small statuette of her resides on my dresser.)

It was not easy for me to do all the steps in some of the dances, such as the grapevine, but at that time I was able to stand up longer than I can now, and I tried to do all I could to keep up in the dances, since I didn't want to slow down the circle or jeopardize others' steps. When I became too tired, I sat one out.

I suspect that few of my Sufi friends ever realized the degree of difficulty the dances presented for me. Years later, when I began to sing in the center, I was still often encouraged to "stand up to sing"—which, if I'd had the strength in my little hardworking leg, I would have done. Thankfully, we always sat down at the midpoint of the meeting for a lesson or reading.

⌣

I called Lani (who had a new Sufi name, Farida, "The Unique" in Arabic) in the spring of 1976.

"Hi, can we talk for a few minutes?"

"Sure," she said. "What's up?"

"I am really depressed and lonely," I said. "I go out on the weekends and the guys I meet are not the right ones. I know it's stupid to hope to meet someone in a bar, but that's where everyone goes. Plus, I hate accounting and I realize it was probably not the best subject for me to study, but now I can't afford to change majors. I am completely overwhelmed; I wake up anxious every day."

"Oh, I'm sorry you're feeling like this," she said, her voice full of tenderness.

"And . . . I was used to having my own home, and now here I am renting in a house with people I barely know, with one small bedroom to myself. It's a place to live, but not a long-term home. I know it was right to leave Bob, but I miss my old life. I don't know what to do."

"Listen, try doing this meditation: just breathe in and out and concentrate on your heart, gently, imagining the breath healing your heart. Do it daily for at least five minutes, and then you can work up to twenty minutes."

"Okay, I'll try that," I said, thankful. "But you know, I would really like to meet someone who could help me make my life okay. Like, someone who could give me a mantra or something to make my life better."

She chuckled. "Oh, well, you should come to Sufi camp in Mendocino this summer! There will be a lot of nice people and music and dancing and meditating . . . I think you'd enjoy it. Kalyan and I are both going; you could share a cabin with us."

And I did just that, hoping, at idealistic twenty-eight that some teacher at this camp in the woods near the coast might give me a mantra that would make my life blissful and perfect.

I shared a cabin with Farida, another friend, Kalyan, and a gentle young man named Neil Klotz, who was a journalist from Colorado.

A couple of days into the camp, I was alone in the cabin with Farida during a break and I told her, with tears in my eyes, "I'm just not good enough for these people!"

"Why do you think that?" she asked with concern.

"I'm not like them," I said. "I still like to drink a little alcohol. I'm not going to give up having sex, or become a vegetarian. I just am not *holy.*"

"Listen," Farida said, "these people do all that. There is no set of rules that you have to eat something in particular, or that you can't drink. All things in moderation."

That was a relief, since I was generally moderate in most habits anyway. I saw that my Mormon upbringing was coloring what I thought "good" people did and did not do. This community seemed to be much more based in the "God is Love" than the "God is Judge" mentality. This was a group of mostly formerly hippie folk who had channeled their energy into doing spiritual work with a musical and artistic bent. Perhaps I fit in better than I thought.

↝

On June 11, 1976, I had a couple of experiences that were unusual for me. We'd moved the ancient metal cots out on the porch, and were sleeping on the floor on our skimpy old mattresses, which was more comfortable, and just after we turned in I heard a *tap, tap, tapping* on the floor near the head of my bed. I shone my flashlight in the direction of the sound and a scorpion raised its head and waved at me. I grabbed my cowboy boot, smashed it in two, and pushed it over to the old stone hearth, my heart racing, then told the others what had happened. I now wondered at the wisdom of sleeping on the floor, but we left things as they were.

During the night, I had two dreams. The first was of Christ on the cross—impressive, since I'd never had a dream such as this before, not during all my devout years as a Mormon and not even during times of taking psychedelics or doing yoga, mantra, or breathing practices. I had never had any symbolic dream of any kind that I could remember.

Next, I dreamed that I swallowed the scorpion!

Holy mackerel. I awoke thinking, *Something in me is changing.* I was not sure what all this might mean, or if my subconscious was trying to tell me something . . . all I knew was that being at this camp was greatly affecting my psyche. If there was some meaning beyond that, it was not specific enough for me to decipher. After considering my dreams, what I did decide was that I was being led to make a huge spiritual transformation—to basically crucify my old lifestyle—and that I needed to express my desire to do that despite my fears (the scorpion in the throat).

The next day, I took initiation into Sufism from Pir Valayat Khan, leader of the Sufi Order.

❧

In one session, days after my initiation, Pir Valayat looked long into my eyes—a practice called "darshan" in which a teacher gives a transmission of love or conveys the sense of his or other great teachers' spirit. (This could be darshan of Christ, Mohammed, Buddha, or other advanced beings.) The teacher also often looks for a need in the student and tries to understand him or her, and possibly make suggestions based on intuition.

After his intent gaze, he gave me one practice: to concentrate on the fragrance of the rose.

Over time, this meditation on the fragrance of a rose served me well: it was a comforting and peaceful practice; it helped me to remember the beauty and essence of life despite my difficulties; and it incidentally improved my already keen sense of smell. (I have prevented at least three electrical fires in office buildings before the wires actually began to smolder and, less relevantly, have detected an open jar of peanut butter twenty feet away.)

One of the philosophical ideas I heard Pir Valayat address in a talk that week was in response to a set of questions about depression, being happy in one's work, finding a relationship, and not being lonely. Essentially, how to maintain happiness.

"If you are not an executioner or a butcher [and I take exception to the latter, given I am a cautious meat eater], any profession is honorable," he told us. "Just choose something and if it doesn't work out, change professions. As far as relationships go, appreciate where you are now. When single, you have much more time to do as you'd like, though you do not have the joys of relationship. As to being happy, you must remember that there is always someone who is not as happy as you are. You could be eaten by a tiger. Many people in India, where my father was born, have died in this manner. So if you are not being eaten by a tiger, maybe things are really not so bad."

I still sometimes think when things are tough: *I am not being eaten by a tiger.*

Sufism eventually gave me a body of practices to take my mind and heart off my difficulties, whether physical or emotional, and help me be at peace—and it gifted me with a spiritual community of friends, most of whom have not seen me as a person who was deficient in some way.

〜

The following week, Valayat was gone, and the remaining time at camp was devoted to the teachings of Murshid Sam, so there was a lot of singing and dancing—in fact, there was "Sufi" dancing every night. This was very tiring for me, but it brought me so much joy that it was irresistible.

One day I got an interview with a local teacher, Moineddin Carl Jablonski, who was a student of Samuel Lewis. I walked up a hill to his sunny cabin.

"Hello," he said with a gentle, welcoming smile. "What is it you'd like to see me about?"

"Well, I took initiation with Pir Valayat last week, and he asked me if I was working with you. Then I came to understand that he's rarely in California. I wanted an interview with you since I'll be going to your meetings in Marin County."

"Oh, I'm glad you'll be joining us," Moineddin said. "I can give you some practices. Did Pir Valayat give you any?"

"Yes, he told me to concentrate on the fragrance of a rose."

"Very good. After you do that each morning, I'd like you to chant the word 'Hu,' the essence of spirit, on one note thirty-three times. You can get a *tasbih*"—prayer beads spaced with the right number for different practices—"or you can count on your fingers." After also explaining a *zikr* (a phrase meaning "God is the only reality"), which he wanted me to practice singing, Moineddin asked me, "Would you like to have a spiritual name?"

"Yes!" I answered, elated. I thought perhaps with all the practices and the new name, I might finally leave behind my disquiet.

He traced the outline of a winged heart, the symbol of Sufism, on my forehead with his index finger, and said, "I give you the name 'Sabzpari,' which in Sanskrit means 'Green Soul' or 'Water Fairy.'"

I loved the idea of being a fairy, especially a green one or one who was attuned to water. The story of Sabzpari, however, which comes from Hindu mythology, is also one of great pathos. Sabzpari was a devic (fairy-like or angelic) being in the temple of Indra, the Lord of Heaven, and she was a favored dancer in Indra's court. (Given how I loved to dance, this also was appealing to me, and possibly meant to be an inspiration—that I could dance in one way or another, despite my physical limitation. Moineddin saw that I had at least the *nature* of a dancer.)

Sabzpari was often called to court to dance for Indra, but on one of her trips to Earth, she fell in love with a human prince, Gulfam. (Oh, those human princes! How I knew the pitfalls of that path.) She told Gulfam that their love could not be, that earth was earth and heaven was heaven and they could not be mixed. But he was seductive. On his request, Sabzpari took him to heaven with her.

Gulfam was mistrustful and jealous, as only a human could be, and whenever Sabzpari was called to dance before Indra, Gulfam accused her of going off to see some other fairy, of having another lover. Finally, in desperation, she let him talk her into bringing him to court. She knew that no good could come of this, so she told him to stay out of sight, yet near her. She hid him behind her veils as she danced skillfully before Indra.

But one of Indra's devas saw Gulfam and cried out to the Lord of Heaven that there was a human present in his heavenly court. Indra grew red-eyed with rage! (Not only the Bible has an angry god in its legends.) He stood, pointed his fiery finger at the offenders, and decreed as only an incensed god could, "Throw the human out! Send him back where he belongs, to the Earth! And tear off Sabzpari's wings and throw her also to the Earth to live there, if the ways of Earth are what she desires!"

Thus Sabzpari, the earthy, water-loving fairy, was separated both from her lover and from the ecstasy of heaven, to more deeply learn that the two could not be mixed, and to spend her days in the green world she loved so well, with its joy, drama, and trials.

Awfully intense! Especially the symbolism of not being free to fly. Punishment in general was also something I'd had quite enough of in my life. But I was entranced by the tale, and enamored by the lovely name, the green soul/water fairy aspect, and the idea that I might have the soul of a dancer, so I was very happy to be Sabzpari. I thought perhaps I needed to pay more attention to the ways of heaven than of earth.

I now had a mantra, a concentration, and an inspiring name. I settled in to see what effect they would have upon me, hopeful and somewhat expectant that my life was now going to be joy-filled and fully repaired.

not exactly bliss

*A*fter my initiation, I began doing the "Hu" chant (*wazifa* in Arabic, pronounced "wa-ZEE-fuh"), and within a day or two began hearing those overtones I'd heard back at Farida's house on my hike up the hill. When I formed my mouth in a particular way and the air passed through in just the right fashion, two or more notes resonated at once, in harmony. It was quite other-worldly, more like a flute than anything I'd heard from a human voice before, and not unlike overtone harmonics on a gui-tar—beautiful, and joyful. (I now know that this is called "throat singing" and is popular in Tibet and Mongolia.)

I was glad to find that this was something I could do with-out the use of psychedelics, given my quest to find something higher up the emotional scale than the despair I sometimes felt and the frustration and loneliness I often experienced. I thought, *Okay, pretty good, I've gotten a mantra that brings me joy—step one.* The concentration of that practice and imagining the essence of a rose took my mind off my personal considerations.

Given that this Sufi group was human and not unlike other groups, it wasn't long before members of our well-meaning, big-hearted community began offering me advice about my leg, my personality, my work, my approach to life—anything that came into their heads, it seemed. The ones who had been initi-ated as teachers often felt a responsibility to do this, and perhaps because I was an advice giver myself, in some respects, I was attracting the same qualities in those around me. Maybe.

That first week at camp, someone approached me and told me that nerve cells were now being replaced and regenerated and I should look into this; perhaps I could get my polio-damaged nerves regenerated. I naively thought, *Gosh, I wish I'd heard of this before 1976, but I'll get right on it.*

After a dance class ended that day I approached Saul, a fellow at the camp who was head of the healing order segment of this Sufi branch or "order."

"Can I ask you a question?"

"Sure," he said, looking into my eyes inquisitively.

"Someone told me there's a nerve regeneration process of some sort . . . I had polio, and I wondered if you knew where I could find information on that kind of thing."

He kindly put his hand on my shoulder. "You know, people mean well. You, given your unique condition in life, are going to hear a lot of things from a lot of people. I know of no miraculous cure such as this, and if there is something like that, it's surely only in the research stages. But healing occurs on all levels. It's not all physical. You want to take care of your own health and healing in whatever way you can. Just take people's advice with a grain of salt."

I was disillusioned by Saul's response. I was so eager to believe that there was some faith healer or some Western MD who had come up with a cure for nerve damage, muscle regeneration, bone growth, anything. (Today, of course, nearly forty years later, we're on the verge of something like this, with stem cell research, but even now any regenerative cure for humans is many years away.) At least my disappointment was brief, and I learned early on that lots of spiritual people, in their naturally sensitive way, were liable to want to "help" me with my disability. I did hear what Saul said about healing taking place on many levels, not just physical, as well. In any case, I had become used to people telling me to try things that they thought would benefit me even though they knew nothing about polio.

⟿

When a split between the more meditative Sufi Order and the more outgoing, dancing *Ruhaniat* order required us to make a choice in 1977, it seemed obvious that I belonged with the singers and dancers in the San Francisco Bay Area. I moved into a Sufi property in Petaluma, Sonoma County, California, where nine to fifteen of us—including Moineddin and his wife—lived together for several years.

The house was a huge Victorian mansion with ten bedrooms, lovely grounds, and a pool. It was a great place to hold Sufi seminars, and I was soon organizing these. I then was offered the barely paid position of bookkeeper for the organization, in addition to my bookkeeping job with a CPA firm.

What a leap into the fire. I lived in the same house as my Sufi teacher, who had years before been diagnosed with kidney disease and thought he was probably going to die soon. We had classes in Petaluma six nights a week, and I attended all of them. My housemates and I prayed together every morning, and we ate together twice a day. Cooking, cleaning, shopping, and house maintenance responsibilities were all shared by house members, most of whom were working full time, as was I. About a year into living in the house I was asked to be volunteer CFO of the Ruhaniat, and began meeting one full Sunday each month with the board of directors, who were all teachers in the organization. I was responsible for organizing the accounting for all the branches of the organization, which was taking more and more time. And I wondered why I didn't have a boyfriend.

It was interesting how my relationships with people shifted as I took on more responsibility for the organization, especially those related to finances.

It started when I was only the dues secretary. I was told by one person that when she saw me, she felt guilty, because she knew that I knew she had not paid her dues. I could rarely remember who owed what, but people thought I did, so they'd avoid me sometimes.

This was the beginning, for me, of realizing how many issues people have going on about money. I tried to learn to be relaxed with people (especially if I did happen to recall that they were not paying dues at all) and tried deliberately to forget their balances, a challenge for my detailed memory. I worked at using the knowledge I had of names in the group as a way to recognize people. But my position did create a distance I regretted.

We in the Sufi community concentrated more on spiritual growth, music, dance, and compassion than we did on income, or at least that was true for more than a few of us. So it was particularly ironic that people thought that I was financially successful and sometimes measured their own success by mine, when I never made more than a lower-middle-class income in my forty-year career.

These were spiritual lessons I had not expected. I had signed on for bliss and learning to live with adversity; instead I was finding trial after trial. But these experiences did help me to further develop depth and compassion. Jumping into roles others didn't want—and sometimes didn't respect—taught me a great deal about how to relate with people, and also how to take a little less seriously what they thought of me. I was now in my early thirties, and at last beginning to grow up. Everyone in this age group had life lessons to learn, and these were some of mine.

In everyday life and conversation, I found that within the Sufi community, language about cause and effect and what was God's position on this or that was similar to how people had spoken in my Mormon Christian congregation. There was a lot of "If it's God's will" and "There must be a purpose in it, or it wouldn't have happened." As a polio patient, I could not imagine that God really willed things like terrible disease or was okay with a myriad of human troubles, such as war. The concept that we were paying for previous wrongs, whether Adam's transgression or the Eastern philosophy of karma (which made more sense to me than western Christian tenets), seemed ludicrous to me. *If this is God's way of teaching lessons,* I thought, *well, God must not be particularly nice.*

It was hard for me to accept disinterested punishment and enforced tough education as the nature of God, but I did surrender to this thinking for several years in my early Sufi studies as I had when a Mormon. I came to see this as dualistic, black-and-white, and non-inclusive conceptualizing.

It will always be true that we do not know what result may come of any experience, but I don't believe that God either causes or allows things to happen. I believe we instigate much ourselves, and that there are also many random occurrences. I am willing to consider the possibility that we might come into this life to learn particular lessons, and these lessons do show up.

I took several solo Sufi retreats from 1977 through 1988—usually three or four days of doing breathing practices, chanting, and meditations for about nine hours a day, which was very intense. Sometimes there were tearful searches through my faults and seemingly limited perceptions, and sometimes a deep sense of peace. I found that afterward I nearly always felt like my spirit and mind had a clean slate and I was inspired to be more creative and understanding, and to meet more of my potential as a human being, than I had before the retreat. I was always exhausted and sometimes got very sick during these retreats, and always left with a desire to just do what was in front of me rather than think about the meaning of my life so much. I was ridding myself of emotional baggage and negative states.

About three or four years into my discipleship, around the beginning of 1980, I noticed that when we said our daily prayers, which acknowledged God in "all the names and forms, known and unknown to man," I could barely relate to the idea of God as form.

I had grown up with Jesus and God, who were holy and aspirational models—one apparently an all-knowing, disembodied, male personage, and the other his human son who had been sent to save humanity and now lived on in the spirit world with his father. After I left the Mormon church, I hadn't stopped praying. Before discovering Sufism, I'd had a quick affair with existentialism and atheism. Now I had come to a place where I felt like my relationship with God was not all that definite. I wanted to explore this more deeply and from my own experience, not from accepting the wisdom or platitudes of others.

I began to wonder if I was an existentialist by nature. I could more deeply relate to the idea of "God in all things"—a spirit flowing through all life—than I could to God being a male overseer I had to surrender to, ask forgiveness from, thank for everything; I didn't feel sincere when I prayed. And the Mother God I was beginning to hear about in Sufi classes, as presented by the few women teachers and some of the men, seemed like she might be either a bit intrusive or maybe too passive, one or the other, the apparent Ideal Mother. Always forgiving, always compassionate, always waiting, always knowing what was best for you, just ask Mother, all those stereotypes. I had such a contradictory relationship with my mom. I loved her so much and thought of her as the person who loved me more than anyone (after my dad died). But I also endured her spanking the bejesus out of me, stonewalling me when I made her mad, and conveying the feeling that I would never be good enough and was generally a disappointment to her. I felt like she never knew me (right up through her funeral), and given her secretiveness, I'm sure there must be things I never knew about her as well. Mother God seemed more untrustworthy a personage than even Father God or Son God.

Prior to my involvement with Sufism, a couple of friends had told me they thought that the seeking of happiness was probably a lost cause and not the purpose of life, but my philosophy is that as long as you are a person who looks at life in depth, there is nothing wrong with seeking love, harmony, and beauty. Those aspects cannot help but bring a certain amount of happiness. Sadness and trouble never seem to have a problem finding us eventually, so why not concentrate on the best of life when we can?

On one retreat in the 1980s, I spent some time reading one of Inayat Khan's books, *The Sufi Message*, which contained a section called "The Alchemy of Happiness." In it, Khan discusses how knowledge of God must be approached from both a personal side and a universal side. The personal side is where you relate to God: your prayers go to God, you thank God, and you seek guidance from God. The universal aspect of God was the one I could easily embrace. I could imagine the Spirit of Guidance, God, or Divinity flowing through people, cats, trees, even rocks. The idea that all of creation had a certain divine presence felt true to me.

Khan goes on to say that you need to cultivate the aspect

you lack, because only then can God be fully experienced. His advice on cultivating a relationship with God in the personal sense is to assign to God the trait or personality with which one feels most natural—God as Judge, as Kind Father, as Loving Mother, as Benefactor, as Teacher, etc. Reading this, I knew without a moment's thought that there was one personality and role I needed to assign to God in order to experiment with this concept: God the Friend. I had to have someone I could fully trust, someone I could tell things to honestly and even complain to sometimes. God had to be someone I was not afraid of— someone with whom I could even be angry, if circumstances warranted. And I had certainly had a lot to be irritated about over the years.

I'm not saying I had blamed God for the unhappiness in my life; on the contrary, I blamed myself. But this was like blaming God indirectly, especially if you believed that everything came from God. (This, to me, is the discrepancy in the viewpoint of those who consider themselves too shy to accomplish things and then say it must not be God's will. That's like saying God wants mediocrity or a lack of enthusiasm.)

I began to talk to God a lot, now that I was assuming he existed and was my very best friend. (Or She? For some reason, gender for my deity always seemed to be male, or at least a very strong, definite essence—maybe due to the loss of my dear father, or my inability to fully trust my mother, or my associating particular traits with masculinity.) "Wow," I'd say, "thanks for the parking space"; or, "Listen, I have *no* idea what to do about this; you really have to help me out here." That was how I prayed now. Not addressing God in a way that was placating or begging, as I had in the past, or asking, as I had, way too many times, "Why is this happening to me? Why am I so alone? Why can't I see what is wrong with me?" I now see my pre-God-as-Friend self as a sniveling wimp.

204 の FRANCINE FALK-ALLEN

With this, things started to change for me. I found that more small coincidences occurred. I'd be wishing I had some company and within a half-hour someone would call just to chat or ask me if I wanted to go out to coffee or a movie. Or I'd be sad and a favorite song I loved to sing would come on the radio and I'd just have to sing it, and then feel great. I'd had coincidental experiences previously, of course, but now it was becoming so common—when I asked for help, my prayers were answered in some way within a day—that it was difficult to deny a cause-and-effect relationship between prayer and help from God, or whoever was hearing my prayers, even if it was merely my best or higher self. This was a divinity I had not been in touch with in this way before. (For the record, I am not always able to maintain this state. And I find that the more time I spend alone, the fewer the challenges.)

I was still lonely some of the time, but overall, I was becoming pretty happy. This was a real improvement!

singing as prayer

*W*hat first drew me to Western Sufism was its uplifting choral music and Dances of Universal Peace, which are like folk dances done to chants of various world religions. When I was living in the Sufi house in northern California, one of the dances we learned was the dervish turn, which entails spinning in one spot with one hand lifted to heaven and one palm down, "anchoring" one's physical being to earth.

The turn is quite an ecstatic experience when done so that the spin does not make you dizzy. It takes you out of the mundane world, into appreciation for the divinity of life. I never knew if I was doing it right until my spiritual teacher said, after I'd spun for only a few brief moments, "Very fine." He was not given to compliments, so I took it that I had assimilated the teaching—a welcome confirmation.

Later on, Jelaluddin Loras, who is the head of the Mevlevi Order from Turkey, the original whirling dervishes in the lineage of Mevlana Jelaluddin Rumi, told me after seeing me spin that he could teach me the advanced dervish turn, though I probably would only be able to do it for one ten-minute set.

The turn is a sacred spinning (nicknamed "whirl" by others) that is said to have begun when Rumi reached ecstasy and started turning, his robe inscribing a perfect circle in the dust at his feet. His disciples reasoned that if he turned when he reached ecstasy, they might reach ecstasy themselves if they imitated the turn. Now the ritual is taught with great discipline and performed publicly on December 17 of each year (the day Rumi died and was married to God). There is a long evening of poetry, talks, and Turkish music, and then the turn is performed by practitioners of a year or more. There are three or four turning sets of ten or fifteen minutes each, accompanied by mystical music, though the sound of the white robes whooshing through the air is almost music enough.

Having been told that I could possibly learn to do this, I was greatly encouraged that I might have a small amount of grace, even with my two-inch limp. I declined to learn the turn, however; at this time in my thirties, I was on the cusp of realizing that my physical energy and strength was slightly diminished compared to recent years, unexpectedly early. And I was already spending most of my free time singing.

Less than three years after I took initiation, and a few months after I moved into the Sufi house, Bill Allaudin Mathieu, director of the Sufi Choir and former musician and composer with Duke Ellington, had announced that he was going to start up another Sufi Choir (the original one had not performed for a few years).

I couldn't wait to audition. I sang something for him, and he looked at me kindly and said, "Very nice." Then he addressed me more seriously: "I think you have a deep well of music in you. And I believe you are like me: you have to work very hard at it. If you want to do the work, I'd love to have you."

I was elated—and then spent a couple of days mulling it over. I'd had so many short stints of musical training, but certainly had never pursued it on a professional level. I grew to understand that Allaudin truly was being kind by comparing my learning style to his. He might have to work hard, but if I was like a kid with a folk guitar and twelve chords, he was more like a student of Mozart. Hard work, yes, but on a very different level.

There would be rehearsals, plus the extensive practice I'd need to do at home, not only to learn the music itself but also to work on my voice, particularly my range and strength. But I decided to go for it.

For the next three or four years, aside from earning a living and keeping up my responsibilities in the Petaluma Sufi house, the choir and my voice were my foremost concentrations. On Sundays, one other household member and I would drive to Sebastopol (seventeen miles each way on narrow backcountry roads). Rehearsals started promptly at ten in the morning and went till four in the afternoon. This was every Sunday, except for two or three months in the summer. I don't know that I ever missed a rehearsal other than for illness. Which, of course, meant there was even less time for the elusive and longed-for boyfriend. In my early thirties, I thought I heard my biological clock ticking.

At rehearsals, in addition to singing "Ah" on one note for long periods of time to improve our pitch (and hopefully open our hearts), we also practiced blending our voices so no voice was louder than any other. This blending of volume and tone can result in a section sounding like one voice, even though each voice has a slightly different quality. Chills went up my spine, goose bumps traveled down my arms and I felt not just happiness but ecstasy when we achieved this perfect harmony, filled with a sense of emotional and spiritual unity with the other choir members.

It became clear to me during this time that music (along with friendship) was my spiritual path. I had always loved it, and had been singing in groups since I was nine. Now I did it daily in solitude, not just to improve my voice or memorize parts but for the effect I hoped it was having upon my being, my spirit, my emotional and mental state. It brought me peace and joy, and was something I could do that did not always involve standing. It felt like something I could offer the world that might bring beauty and harmony. It was also prayer.

The prayer we used at every Sufi meeting was this: "Toward the One, the perfection of love, harmony and beauty; the only being; united with all the illuminated souls who form the embodiment of the Master, the Spirit of Guidance."

No words ever spoke to me more strongly than "the perfection of love, harmony and beauty." To me, music and compassion were the means to this end.

෴

I had not had a steady boyfriend in my first six or seven years as a Sufi initiate. I'd had a couple of short affairs, but mostly I had been celibate and longing for a life mate. I was starting to get older; Planned Parenthood had told me I could have children "at least up through my late thirties," which had sneaked up on me too quickly.

As the years passed, I came to feel that I carried the story of the name Moineddin had given me, Sabzpari—the woman who lost her lover and her wings. After so long with barely a date, I was beginning to see that it was a long shot that any future mate was going to come from the Sufi community. So I wrote to Moineddin, who had separated from his wife and moved to Hawaii, and asked him to change my name.

He responded in a considered note, "I've been thinking that for a couple of years, but I did not feel well enough to change it." (As a dialysis patient, he had undergone two kidney transplants by this time.) "I will ask someone else to come up with a name for you, unless you have one in mind yourself."

Jeez, I thought, *you might have mentioned this a while back*— but going through kidney failure and a divorce was overwhelming, even for a spiritual teacher. I also had been pretty self-absorbed with my loneliness, feeling that being single had been the result of a spiritual deficiency, and my expectations were unrealistically high with regard to his guidance responsibilities. I kept my complaint to myself.

With involvement of several other teachers, I was given a new name in 1982. One teacher got the name in a dream and sent it to Moineddin in a letter. When Moineddin was in San Francisco, he handed the letter to me and asked me to give it to his ex-wife, Fatima, also a teacher. She talked it over with her current husband, and after they decided it was a good name she called Vasheest Davenport, the great singer who had originally inspired me on the Sufi Choir record Lani/Farida had played for me years earlier.

On April 15, after singing a zikr with our local group, Vasheest jumped up from his chair, suddenly remembering he had an important task to do, and gave the name to me in ceremony.

Tracing a heart and wings on my forehead, he said, "I give you the spiritual name 'Qahira.'" Pronounced ka-HEE-rah, this name comes from an Arabic root having to do with divine power coming through one's being and taking responsibility but not credit for it. It means "The One Who Has Overcome." This is what my Sufi friends still call me.

࿇

I had begun attending zikr classes led by Vasheest in Marin County in the early eighties. Partly because he had given me voice lessons and knew my voice, and partly because I could not stand up for the forty-five minutes most zikrs lasted, Vasheest began using me to sing solo Arabic phrases over the beautiful choral chanting. My soloist role allowed me to sit in the center of the group rather than outside the circle of chanters and singers. Vasheest also suggested that I be a part of it all by using my voice in musical leadership rather than just sitting there and singing quietly. He began teaching me and a few others to lead the zikr.

I continued to find great joy and fulfillment in my musical pursuits, but even so, I wished for a partner—something that, despite my name change, still continued to elude me. In search of answers, I requested a spiritual interview with Vasheest on the matter in the mid-80s. He was not my primary teacher, but I was going to Sufi classes with him at least once a week, and he had seen my solitary life as a theme for a few years; he'd even suggested particular men from the community to me at various times.

In the interview I told him, with an ache in my throat, "I am so lonely! I just do not seem to meet the right guy—or, if I do meet someone, he may not be interested in being my life partner. It seems like it's never going to happen." It was, essentially, a similar plight to the one I'd described to Farida some years before.

What Vasheest said to me was forehead-smackingly illuminating.

"It's one thing to be attracted to someone as a lover. You are an attractive woman"—always a welcome surprise to me to hear that—"and I can see that there would be no problem in finding men to have fun with or even sleep with. But it's another thing to look for someone who is a life partner. He might want someone to play tennis with . . . or to go backpacking. He might be concerned that you would have trouble carrying a baby around on your hip. These things are much different than being someone's lover, or even than being in love."

We both knew that although there were rogues in our midst (Vasheest sometimes operating as one of them), many of the men I knew in spiritual work would not enter into a relationship lightly. Many of them really wanted a wife, unlike some thirty-to-fortyish men at that time. That they were not approaching me was a compliment, in a way. They might have been afraid of hurting me if it didn't work out or if it looked like I might not be able to handle the full role of wife and mother.

I'd like to believe that this was why I was not finding a mate; it's far better than thinking that I had some deep personality flaw. Yes, I was strong, but I was also sensitive. I had what I thought was a fair portion of redeeming qualities, not the least of which was an irreverent sense of humor, something I was sure a lot of men could appreciate. I was working on being less outspoken, though my friends tolerated, accommodated, or appreciated my transparency and honest blurting. Usually. Everyone likes those traits with a little more sugar and less salt, something it's taken me some decades to learn.

This was major stuff. I had not previously seen myself as possibly lacking the ability to be a "whole" wife, in terms of the physical role traditionally expected of a wife and mother, as hard as that may be to believe. I had been looking from the inside— from how I felt, from the kind of person I was, my intelligence, my humor, my music, my devotion, my emotional makeup, and my personality limitations, which I thought were no worse than most people's. I had seen that my emotional strength might be detrimental, but I knew strong married women. I was working hard on understanding men and their challenges, and attempting to keep my opinions to myself more often, without folding to a male-dominated society. I cooked every night, I did shopping, I did housework regularly, and I worked full-time. But what would it mean if I added child rearing to that mix? I still felt that I could do it, but did others think I could?

My friend the Sufi teacher gently added this: "You need to consider the type of man. Perhaps someone who either doesn't want to have kids, or would take on more than most fathers would in order to be with you. Or a man who doesn't care that much about things like walking and sports, or at least is not looking for a woman who could share those things."

Tears had come to my eyes, but I knew that this was very helpful advice, if very late in coming. I had always held it that the main problem was how my leg *looked* and how unattractive my walk was, and that someone, someday, would overlook this. Bob had, and my first boyfriend, and a couple of other guys. Until this moment I had always seen myself as bringing more to a relationship than I took from it, and though this might be true, whatever I had to offer might not make up for what I could not do. I now saw that a man who chose to be with me might be giving up something.

↝

Some disabled people, especially when young, believe that they will never be able to have a mate because of the limitations of their bodies. My mother seems to have thought this about me, though I was not aware of it till I was mature. I had long thought my inability to get into a life partner relationship was because of other reasons, including the possibility that I might have some awful traits I was not aware of (the cause of a lot of torment and tears) or that it was just serendipity, it simply hadn't happened (also the cause of a lot of tears). In my thirties, for a couple of years, I did affirmations: "I am now attracting my perfect life partner." I also did meditations, visualizing myself in a loving relationship; I chanted, using phrases with meanings such as beauty, peace, manifestation and so on; I prayed; and I went to psychics, one of whom said, "I see you beating, beating on the doors of heaven."

Yeah, well, I was. It was easy to fall into negative thinking sometimes.

I read recently that a young fellow with cerebral palsy saw that he was partly the source of his lack of relationship because he had believed for a long time that he would never have one. He feels he bought into a belief of the dismissive part of society: "no one will ever want you." The young man with CP didn't want to face rejection, but he saw that everyone in any body fears that, and now he hopes to have a mate and family one day. His physical limitations are much greater than mine, but he has a loving attitude and is a successful professional comic, so I believe his chances are good.

We can all say that true love conquers all, and for a long time I believed that, but not many people get so caught up in love that all daily life considerations are put aside—and those who decide to throw all reason and caution to the wind may face a life of difficulty.

So it was sobering advice I received from Vasheest that day, and though it was enlightening, it did not solve my problem of being alone.

on the ropes

$\mathcal{I}$ volunteered in the 1980s, when I was in my thirties, as an assistant for the Six-Day, a seminar the old est network (est was short for Erhard Seminars Training and was always written in lower-case letters because it drew attention to the Latin meaning, "is" or "to be") held in Southern California. It was six days of intellectual and emotional "processing" meant to assist people to confront their fears and celebrate their courage, and included a ropes course where participants swung over canyons, learning to trust. I had heard it was an exhilarating experience, and given I was never going to be able to actually participate in a ropes course, I wanted to assist so I could watch people go through this life-changing program.

We had weeks of preparation about learning to be the background for others' experience, to be invisible as a team so the paying participants would have a seamless experience and be able to concentrate on their own needs and insights. We'd be there ten days to serve their seven-day workshop. We were going to do whatever it took to keep a small resort running while the presenters talked, the ropes course instructors led, and we all cheered the participants on. We had to buy particular clothing (including shorts, which had not been in my wardrobe since my teen years, since they exposed the vast difference between my legs; I wore Bermuda socks with them to help hide my skinny calf, though of course it was hot and no one else was wearing Bermuda socks).

The day before the seminar began, we rode eight hours in a large, limo-style bus from San Francisco to the San Bernardino Mountains. That evening, prior to the arrival of the participants, we had an orientation. During the meeting, we were asked to say what we expected to get out of assisting in the course and what we were looking forward to. When my turn came, I piped up, in front of the hundred or so people in the room, "I am really looking forward to being at the ropes course and watching people confront their fears and get past them. This will be the highlight for me."

The leader looked at me. "You're not going on the ropes course," he said.

I stood silent, sure I had either misheard him or he had been misinformed. Then I began to protest: "But that's the main reason I came."

"I'm sorry," he said, "but you won't be going on the ropes course."

I began to tear up.

"Someone take her in the back room and process this," he said.

I left the room with a young man who took the task. I was beside myself with disappointment; I felt I'd been deceived. All the participants and leaders in my training group knew I was looking forward to the ropes course. Had they not discussed this? This bunch discussed things *ad nauseum*. How could this misunderstanding have occurred?

The young fellow who was "processing" me was basically talking to a wall; all I was able to do at that point was calm myself.

"You will be working in the kitchen, and will also be on a towel folding team," he said. "But when others in your group go out on the course once during the week, you won't be going."

I returned to the room with my face hot (similar to the middle school bathroom scene twenty years before), feeling humiliated that this had been a foregone conclusion of the directors—that the handicapped woman would not see the key experience we'd all come to see—and no one had thought to tell me.

◁

The next morning, we went on about our functions, folding towels, doing food prep, with me in numb disappointment, thinking I would not have come, or have done the weeks of preparatory meetings, or bought the shorts, had I known.

At lunch time I was outside chatting with several people, and the course doctor, who was an athletic, sweet man, approached me.

"Can I talk to you about what happened in the room last night?"

I cautiously answered, "Yes . . ." and we stepped away from the group.

"Are you still upset?" he asked.

My eyes filled with tears. I could see that he understood my deep disappointment.

"Francine, you can't go on the ropes course because handicaps dominate," he said. "Your handicap would dominate the mountain. Do you understand what I mean?"

"No, I have no idea what you mean," I said, trying to regain my composure.

He quietly explained. "If you go, everyone there will be concerned for you, your safety, and whether you are okay, because you are handicapped. They'll be worried you might fall or get hurt. The course will be about you instead of the participants."

It was as if a curtain had opened on the drama of my own

life. I had never, ever seen myself that way. I was so independent, and I handled my own problems—indeed, always *expected* to handle them, and rarely asked for help, even when I needed it.

In fact, I felt so powerless about the condition of my leg that the concept of handicaps dominating any situation at first seemed absurd to me. But in hearing the doctor's gentle explanation, I saw that it was true. I was at this program to be invisible and facilitate others, not to be the center of attention.

"I'm so sorry that no one told you that you were not going to go on the ropes course," he said.

How healing is apology, even when the one saying "I'm sorry" is not at fault. My conversation with this compassionate doctor enabled me to remain there on the course with enthusiasm instead of with resentment, anger, and regret.

I find that there's an assumption that, as a disabled person, I should not expect some things like activities and access, and that it should also be obvious to me that I should not want these things. It's rather like the way the wealthy sometimes consider that the poor should lower their expectations and desires. But being limited does not change desire—in fact, I believe that restriction stimulates desire, like dieting might. Resignation does set in, and acceptance calms the spirit. But wanting to do what others can has never completely left me. Everyone's life has limitations. Most people don't have as many physical ones, though, or at least don't expect to have them until they are in their late elder years.

⟶

At the seminar, we were required to attend a short session daily where we paired up in dyads and disclosed to the other assistants any distracting thoughts we had about them. This could range from being attracted to someone to needing to tell someone they'd done something you disapproved of, or anything else that kept us from focusing on the present. In my case, one time I had to tell a young man that his shorts were too short and I had been uneasy with seeing his genitals. (He was embarrassed and wore longer shorts in the future.) The purpose was to keep relationships in the assistants' team "clean" so that we would function as one being and not let issues build up, whether those issues were romantic leanings or annoyances that took people's minds off what they were doing.

For the most part, these dyads were an enjoyable part of the day. You might have thought someone was a jerk on day one, but by day three you'd have seen his other qualities and could laugh about or forget the annoying aspect and really begin to appreciate the dedication of the team.

In the first dyad, I paired with a woman I didn't know but felt I had had a nice connection with in passing. She wasn't on either of my teams. We sat facing each other, with our knees a few inches apart.

"I've enjoyed seeing you around," I said on my turn, "and I'm interested in getting to know you."

On her turn, she said, "I have the thought that you want people to feel sorry for you. That you are sad and that your life must be really difficult and unhappy because of your leg, and you want people's pity."

Once again, shades of the sixth grade. I was really taken aback. We were supposed to just listen and not counter the things people said.

One person after another told me the things they thought about me with regard to my being handicapped or disabled, not about who I was as a personality or whether I was attractive, or wondering what I did in my life. What they had to get out of the way was my paralyzed leg and the way I walked and who they thought that must make me, and essentially that they wouldn't want to be me. I was amazed at how much stuff people had going on about handicapped people, and I learned that not only children had a huge amount of bias about disability. It was a prejudice, just like racism or ageism or any other *ism*.

Several people told me that they anticipated that I would want them to feel sorry for me. I believe they saw this was very far from my nature after they got to know me, but this was an assumption they had about handicapped people. They had lots of ideas about how I must see the world—that I must be sad, that I must be angry, that I must be this or that. This was projection, I assumed, based on what they thought they would feel if they had a paralyzed leg, and also upon my disappointment the first evening when learning my activities would be limited. And though of course I had experienced these things over and over in my life, they were life assessments that came and went for me, like watching movies: you cry when there is something sad, but then the next scene comes and there's something to be inspired by or laugh about. I've never been one to hide my emotions well, and over time, I've learned that many people not only don't express many emotions, they are not even aware of what they feel. But here I learned that people thought I must feel depressed, needy, wanting more from people emotionally and physically than others wanted—most of the time!

Wow. What a life view. This was what people who were willing to trust me with these musings thought about my mental and emotional makeup. This was probably what many or most people thought but would never have the courage to tell me.

The truth was, the most emotionally upsetting aspects of my young life had actually been that my dad had died when I was so young, and that I had thus far not been able to get into and maintain a love relationship that nurtured me. I had been far more sad in my life about not having a husband or life partner than I'd ever been over having a paralyzed leg. My deepest hurt was not my paralysis, it was not sharing my love—a problem any able-bodied person might have.

I learned so much from these people who needed to unload their concepts about disability in a safe environment. I had to be a little brave to hear it all, especially at first. This, after all, was my ropes course.

❧

Not long after I came home from the est seminar, a spiritual teacher I was working with responded to a letter I had sent him, and it caught me off-guard. I had told him that I was finally feeling secure in being single and had come to a place of peace about relationships. I felt relaxed about the prospect of eventually meeting someone I'd spend my life with, and if that didn't happen, I had so much in my life that gave me satisfaction and inspiration. His reply was something like, "Have you thought about what having one side of your body damaged has done to your personality, and how it may have hurt the male and female aspects of your being?"

I'd expected that he'd be glad to hear my news. After I picked my jaw up off the floor, I thought, *Oh, no. Never gave it a thought. Only every day for the last twenty or thirty years.*

So on the one hand, I had people who thought I must feel sorry for myself, and on the other, someone who knew me well (or so I'd thought), and possibly others, who thought I didn't realize how being handicapped had affected me. How naïve; that's like asking a cancer patient if they've thought about why they got it. For a sensitive or deeply thinking person, these are the first questions that come up: *Is there a reason this has happened to me? Have I lived inappropriately? How is it going to change me?*

To his credit, a decade later, the teacher wrote me another

letter, more or less out of the blue, after seeing a letter I'd written to someone else, and said he realized he had not really "seen" me, and that he "probably said some really stupid things" to me over the years. Could I forgive him?

I wrote back and said I'd done that long before. I knew he couldn't help what he'd thought, but also, forgiveness feels better than holding a grudge.

the hazards of walking

*I*magine if every step you took were difficult. If you have a birth defect, a back problem, cerebral palsy, spina bifida, or multiple sclerosis, or have had a serious injury, or are seriously overweight, or have arthritis in your feet, knees or hips, or are older and now have plantar fasciitis, flat feet, or anything similar, you may know what that's like. But generally speaking, other than experiencing pain from bad shoes or from being on those doggies too long, most people probably don't consider walking a serious daily problem.

I've always experienced a lot of fatigue. (These days, pain does play a bigger role, though there are some days when I have little or no pain). When I walk barefoot, my polio foot just hangs there and I am required to hike up my hip a bit so my big toe clears the floor. This weak foot just slaps down on the floor, toe first, if I am not wearing my orthotic, putting me at risk of catching my toe—even in shoes—on sidewalk cracks, sculpted or shag carpets, door sills, tree roots (even tiny ones), and so on.

As I've already mentioned, I learned early in life that when I lose my balance, I usually cannot retrieve it. I see others slip and catch themselves; I find this fascinating and almost impossible for me to do. I try to plan ahead: I scope out stairs (which I avoid if possible), stay away from slippery surfaces, and avoid walkways that have a lot of trip hazards—because once I trip, most of the time I either go down or must catch myself with or *on* something, such as a banister or handle or bookshelf, which has been the source of a lot of bruising and wrenching of joints.

When I slip, my weak leg usually buckles under me, and I'm on the ground before I can react, let alone think. So I've landed on my polio foot a number of times and it has been very forgiving, though it has often been injured.

It is common for me to trip when I'm in a hurry. I try to allow myself sufficient time, but when I fail, I fall. I have sprained both ankles and both knees repeatedly and both wrists a few times, broken both my knees and one foot, torn my Achilles tendon on my polio foot, badly dislocated a toe and broken it in several places (it was sticking out at a forty-five-degree angle from my foot), bruised my coccyx, bruised the bone in my elbow, broken a finger, and cracked a wrist bone. All this in the course of normal activities like shopping, walking into my closet, going to an ecological display, stuff like that—not in extreme sports (other than one skiing mishap where I broke my strong knee).

When my first husband, Bob, and I were looking for a home to buy, I slipped (wearing cowboy boots, stupid indulgence) on the way down the steep, painted concrete hillside walkway—basically a slide—to the backyard, and I badly sprained my big toe on my little foot.

"I guess that this must be the place," I said, "because I won't be able to look at any more properties."

We did buy it, and I wore hiking boots with Vibram soles thereafter to go down that walk.

Over the years I've been told by some well-meaning friends, orthopedists, and my sister that I should wear tennis shoes because they are more stabilizing. Most polio people find that they are really dangerous, however, because they grab surfaces and we end up twisting our ankles or knees. They may sometimes prevent a fall, but so far, they've been more detrimental than helpful to me.

ᔥ

By the time I was about forty, I had finally accepted that I would continue to fall throughout my life. I know, you'd think I would have gotten clear about it long before that, but I was optimistic and believed in my younger days that life was a continuum of constantly improving circumstances. Ah, the folly of youth.

Right around that time of acceptance, I badly sprained my knee while trying to walk down a carpeted ramp wearing—you guessed it—tennis shoes, and had to be taken to a hospital emergency room. I had not done myself this much damage since I'd torn my Achilles tendon twelve years before.

By this point I had moved out of the Sonoma Sufi house and was living in a rental in San Rafael. The challenge this time, once I got home from the emergency room with crutches and began looking for a good doctor in my new area, was finding anyone who knew even an iota about polio. I knew that my recovery was going to be different than that of a normal person with a sports injury. The orthopedist at the hospital had been in his sixties, but when he'd looked at the x-rays and then at my legs, his perplexed comment had been that it looked like I had arthritis in my leg. He hadn't even noticed that the leg was atrophied and partially paralyzed—something an orthopedic doctor should have been able to see at a glance.

I made ten or fifteen calls trying to find an orthopedist who knew anything about polio in my county. I ended up calling physical therapy offices for referrals, and finally located one doctor who knew polio. She lived an hour away and only came to Marin one day a week. I made the appointment.

I always drove with my left foot crossed under the steering

column over to the accelerator—something I couldn't do with the brace they'd given me at the hospital, which held my right leg straight out, no room for it under there with no bend at the knee—so I had to take a cab to my appointment. (I learned at this time that there were no subsidized, or free, transportation services in my county for handicapped people unless you were over sixty or permanently unable to drive. Many people seem to believe that there are a lot of services for injured or handicapped people, but in fact they are limited for younger patients who are not on public assistance.)

This all happened right in the middle of an intense work phase for me. Every hour that I was not working on a non-profit tax return put it closer to being in jeopardy of filing past the due date in three days, or my having to stay up all night to prepare it. When I arrived at the rehab clinic, I was asked to wait in the reception area, since they were fitting me in as an emergency. I waited an hour or two, in pain and having a hard time finding a position I could sit in comfortably with my leg up on a chair. My back was starting to hurt. There was nowhere to lie down and elevate my injured leg.

Finally, someone came out and said, "Dr. Clark doesn't have time to see you today. She has to go back to the East Bay. She will be back next week and you can make an appointment to see her then."

"*What?*" I replied with subdued anger. "I have been waiting here for two hours in pain, after taking a cab to get here, because I can't drive. I have called all over Marin County trying to find a doctor knowledgeable about polio. I'm supposed to be working. I want to talk to her for at least a couple of minutes."

Soon Dr. Clark—a dark-haired woman in a full-skirted, white-with-red-polka-dots dress—came into the reception area and asked coolly, "What seems to be the problem?"

I told her I'd been waiting for two hours in pain and had a

very badly sprained knee on my polio leg. "I appreciate that you fit me in, but I have called all over Marin and could not find a doctor who knows anything about polio and the more complicated healing involved," I told her. "My time is valuable too. I'm injured, I'm a tax accountant, I have already lost time from work, and am supposed to be preparing a non-profit tax return which is due this week."

I was fuming from her sense of self-importance, and had a feeling she'd figured that since I was a polio patient and disabled, I had nothing better to do but sit in that office for hours and then go home and come back at her convenience. Maybe not, but that's how it seemed.

Dr. Clark briefly examined my knee. "You should see Dr. Ed DeMayo here in Marin," she suggested. "He is an orthopedic surgeon, and knows something about polio. Then you could come here for rehab later on."

I thanked her, she left, and I asked the receptionist if I could use their phone to call another cab.

ᴄ⌒ᴗ

Dr. DeMayo proved to be a great orthopedist and was very helpful in explaining my options and eventually prescribing physical therapy. He understood that my leg would heal more slowly than a normal leg due to its circulation and atrophy problems, and that I could not stand on it alone for more than a second, even when it was in excellent health. He also took the time to ask me a lot of questions about how I was doing in general and how I took care of myself, and checked to see I was using my cane on my strong side. (He knew the right way to use a cane, unlike some orthopedists—impressive.)

In that first interview, while I sat on the exam room table, Dr. DeMayo said something surprising: "My polio patients are among the most intelligent and innovative people I encounter in my practice. Polio survivors have a knack for adaptation and figuring out how to do what you need or want to do."

(There are stats on this: we tend to be highly educated, with a much higher percentage of college graduates than the national average in the US and a higher number who go into professional work, and are often described as "type A," overachieving personalities.)

"I have always wondered if polio selected for intelligence," Dr. DeMayo continued, "which would seem like a cruel twist of fate; or if polio people just had to become more intelligent as an adaptation in life."

"I don't know," I said, "but for me, it's true that I've come up with things like shoe modifications that helped me walk better."

I would think that if Dr. DeMayo's theory is true, it is because we've had to think things out for ourselves in order to overcome a lot of obstacles, and thinking creatively does increase intelligence. It was a flattering statement and I appreciated his observation and opinion. It was one of the few positive observations on a handicap that I've heard.

❧

The physical therapist I worked with after seeing Dr. DeMayo suggested that I needed an ankle/foot orthotic, called an AFO. This is a lightweight plastic brace that keeps a drop foot in a closer-to-level position. It has a partial cuff around the calf where a Velcro strap is attached. I wear a nylon knee-high under it and another over it to keep it firmly against my foot. When I wear pants, few people notice it. It's quite noticeable with ballerina length or shorter dresses, however, even with panty hose over the knee-highs.

Wearing an AFO helps prevent catching my toe on so many

minute obstacles, and also allows me to not hike up my hip so much so that my toe can clear the floor. My gait has improved slightly since I started wearing it, and my hip does not get as tired. Except for the times when I am going in our pool or taking a break from wearing shoes, I wear one of these AFOs all the time.

I hadn't worn what is essentially a brace in thirty-three years. I was at first disappointed to be told to wear a brace again, and also had to throw out all my old shoes and gradually buy new ones in a larger size to accommodate the AFO. But the featherweight device soon proved its worth with the reduction of fatigue and greater safety it provided. It's the first thing I'd save in a fire (after the cats).

I saw Dr. DeMayo for every serious injury I had for many years to come.

making way for mr. right,
and a new challenge

*I*n 1991, at age forty-three, after the breakdown of yet another inappropriate relationship—the first long-term one (two
years) I'd had since my marriage ended in 1975—I started going
to Adult Children of Alcoholics meetings. I saw that I had some
codependency issues that were causing me to choose the wrong
men (ya think?!). I'd learned as a young adolescent, probably
seven years after Daddy died, that he had been an alcoholic,
though he never drank at home and was a sterling fellow by
everyone's account. My mother described the behavior of her
previous husband as that of an alcoholic, and my first stepdad
was a severe alcoholic, taking money from Mom's purse and
hiding vodka bottles throughout the house. Mom had married
three alcoholics in a row; I'd married one, and had had alcoholic
boyfriends as well.

I had read a little about codependency and saw that Mom
had passed on the worst of these habits to me—things like expecting others to know what I thought, and stonewalling them
when they misbehaved. I had acted like this in my twenties,
without successful results.

In one particular ACA meeting, I was listening to a woman
share about her fear of visiting her father over the holidays (he
had beaten her and her siblings when they were children) and
thinking, *I am so lucky my childhood was never that bad; I had a*

happy childhood. Then a picture flashed before me of my mother slamming my backside repeatedly with a wooden paddle when I was tiny, maybe five, less than three feet tall. I was crying, "Mommy, Mommy, stop! I won't do it anymore!"

I flushed inside and thought, *My gosh, what else am I in denial about?*

I soon began attending Co-Dependents Anonymous (CoDA) meetings as well, and I found that working the twelve steps (for my "addiction" to my expectation that having a committed man in my life would solve my emotional problems) was the most whole and effective spiritual practice I had followed.

There are many people who just go to the meetings—and they are very beneficial, don't get me wrong. They help you see your habits and traits, and that repeating the same behaviors and expecting a change is, well, crazy. There's a story told in these groups about going down the same street and falling into the same hole over and over, and that eventually you go down a different street. Going to the meetings is a support, but not a full practice. The steps themselves are what teach acceptance of life as it is, especially the knowledge that one has no control over other people.

The inventory step is the most psychologically and emotionally enlightening work I have ever done. I made a written list of the personality traits I had that came from habit or as a reaction to the negative influences in my life, and included what I got from them and how they held me back. Then I shared this written work with a sponsor, another person farther along in my program. I meditated and worked to remember to not let these things control me. They still came up, of course, but now I was more aware of where they came from and better prepared to not let them rule my life.

After a couple of years of this program, I felt revamped and renewed, like I had an ongoing white canvas for my life. More than anything I had done previously, the steps had assisted me to live from my authentic self.

࿏

For New Year's Eve 1992, I asked a friend I didn't know well if she knew of a party where I could wear a really great dress I'd bought. It was a dark green velveteen column with spaghetti straps and a slit on the side—the side of my pretty leg, not my gimpy one.

It happened that she and some friends were having just such a party at a rented venue, sixty miles south of my home, on that dark and very stormy December 31.

I rode down with a handsome guy about two years younger than I was with whom I had quite a bit in common—singing, music, math, other stuff. As soon as we arrived, he acted like he'd never met me. It was a party of mostly dates, and he and I were both looking for romance from the options there. It was clear I was not an option for him.

I noticed another younger man early in the evening. He had a tall, lanky frame, collar-length, perfectly curly dark hair, and a moustache, and wore a double-breasted, well-fitted suit. He was all over the place talking to people, so I assumed that he was one of the organizers. Really cute, but he didn't show an interest, so I paid little attention beyond my first impression. One guy asked me to dance one time in the whole evening, and I couldn't wait to go home after a couple of hours.

With no one for me to kiss, I was glad when midnight came and went. Once the chaos of the countdown died away, I went to the restroom. As I walked back to the stool where I had left my coat, the bandleader announced, "This is going to be our last number, and while we break down, we'll play some CDs for you."

When I approached my seat, I saw that the cute guy with the curly hair was sitting on it, and on my coat as well.

I really wanted to get one more dance in and said to him, "It's the last song! Do you want to dance until your date comes back?"

"I don't have a date," he said, shaking his head once.

"Oh!" I said, surprised, and we moved to the dance floor.

We danced and talked about our love of rhythm and blues. Then he asked someone else to dance, and then someone else, who was voluptuous and a bit tipsy.

I asked the hostess, Leslie, "Who is that guy?"

"I don't know," she said. "He came with Sharon." She gestured toward the voluptuous woman he'd danced with. "Do you want me to find out?"

"No, never mind," I said, thinking, *Too young and too cute; probably a salesman, and dangerous.*

A few days later, Leslie called me. "That guy you liked? His name is Richard and he would like to go out with you." She'd seen him at a party and they'd talked. She hadn't given him my number, but she'd gotten his. So I called him, and during the course of the relaxed and enjoyable conversation that ensued, he let slip that he was a computer programmer and thought of himself as a nerd. I was relieved to hear it.

On our first date, we met halfway between our respective homes (he lived in the South Bay) for dinner and dancing at Harry Denton's nightclub in San Francisco. They had a great rhythm and blues band, and we danced off and on for two hours, taking frequent breaks. He didn't seem to mind my needing to take breaks when I told him I was a polio survivor and needed to rest every twenty minutes or so; it gave us a chance to talk more easily. (I'd learn months later that he was picked on for being geeky and scrawny as a kid, which has made him much less judgmental of people's differences.)

Our lively conversation that evening was almost non-stop. At one point he said, "What are the chances of meeting someone you really hit it off with? One in ten thousand." (I thought he was actually quoting a statistic, but on another date, he told me he'd just made that up.) That night of dinner and dancing was the easiest and most fun first date I'd ever had. But when it came time to say good night, he just gave me a quick kiss.

I guess he's not that interested, I thought.

❧

I soon found this was not the case when Richard called from Boston, where he was on business, to invite me on our second date.

I was flattered that he thought to call when he was away for work.

"I'm putting together a ski trip at Tahoe," he said, "a bunch of us are going up. Do you ski?"

I thought he was inviting me to sleep with him for a weekend and was a little taken aback. "Ummm . . . no," I said, "I've never tried to ski. My right leg is pretty weak and I don't think I could do it." I realized he didn't fully understand the extent of my limitation.

"Well, do you want to try?"

"Mmm . . . well, I've heard of handicapped adaptations so I could look into that . . . where exactly are you going?"

"We're going to Alpine Meadows. Would you be okay up there if you couldn't ski and everybody else was off on the slopes? Would you still feel like you were having a good time?"

I appreciated his concern for my happiness and desire to

include me. I was also glad that my potential inability was not an issue for him. "Oh, yes," I said. "I always take a book everywhere I go, and can be happy sitting in front of a fire reading. But . . . what are the sleeping arrangements going to be?"

"The women will have one bedroom and the men will be in another," he said.

My initially perceived pressure was off, so I said, "Okay, sure, I'll come."

"Great!" he said, and we chatted a few minutes more before hanging up.

I researched whether there were any facilities for disabled skiers. Happily, Alpine Meadows had a school, Tahoe Adaptive Ski School (TASS). I called them; they said to rent boots before I came up, and the special skis we'd deal with at Tahoe. Then, of course, I had to go out and get some semblance of ski clothing, which amounted to some snow pants to go over my leggings.

I spent significant time that first morning in the mountains just getting fitted for the skis, because they said my legs had to be level and they had different heights of wooden lifts to put on the skis. We were going to try cross-country first, because it's safer and less challenging.

"Are we ready to slip and slide!?" my female instructor said when I finally had all my gear in order.

Wrong phrase to use with me.

"No, I'm not," I said. "Slipping is definitely not something I like to do, having done a lot of it. Plus, I'm forty-five."

She laughed. "Oh, this will be different," she said. "You don't look even forty—but either way, lots of people learn to ski when they're in their forties."

(Really? I still doubt this.)

So the moment comes, and we get up there on a little mound—and I mean really little, like, two feet high—and I've got the poles, I'm wearing the skis, and my very kind, optimistic, and patient instructor is telling me what to do, and . . . whoosh! My little right leg flies out to the side and I'm down.

I hate falling. I've done a lot of it, as I've already explained, and I've hurt myself repeatedly that way, so my habit is to really watch where my feet are and what might be on the ground, because, as my mom used to say, I can trip over my own shadow.

I'm down on the snow, and in my first five minutes of skiing, I've already slightly sprained my right knee.

"You know," I told the nice instructor, "I don't think this is going to work. I just don't have enough control over my right leg. I sometimes don't know where it's going to go even when I'm on solid ground. I have no control over the ball of my foot and little over my thigh, so I can't keep my foot pointed ahead of me." I was ready to take off the equipment, go have an Irish coffee, and read.

But she was undaunted. "Okay then, we'll put you on one ski with outriggers and try downhill."

I thought she must be remarkably naïve—but then again, she was working with all kinds of handicapped people, all the time. I was interested, but barely, more focused on nursing my newly sprained knee.

"We have lots of guys with only one leg who do this," she said. She had already interviewed me about what I *was* able to do, and she knew I swam and had upper body strength—a little, at least. She had also asked me how my balance was (not bad) and if I could stand on the one strong leg (I could).

Okay, she said, good to go. I was still not convinced, but she made it sound like skiing on one leg was a cinch. I agreed to try, hoping these outrigger things were going to be like big pontoons, with me as the canoe.

Ha! If only.

Before we tried the outriggers, we tried me on a walker with skis on it, and over the next day and a half, we found that

I could almost get the knack of skiing that way. She had me lean lightly on it, telling me to consider the walker to be "just in case" and coaching me to try to keep my weight on the ball of my strong foot and center my body over it with a bent knee, using primarily my thigh muscle for support. It was a lot to put together, both mentally and physically, but I made some progress.

Finally, we actually went on a ski lift. My instructor had the operator nearly stop the lift so I could learn to lean forward to get off, and then we went down a bunny slope, me with the ski walker. There was one point for a couple of minutes when I actually felt what the attraction of skiing was—that sliding, smooth, gliding, almost speeding feeling (she was behind me, with reins on the walker)—and I laughed. I was enjoying it. Slipping and sliding, indeed!

Then, of course, my determined teacher would not allow me to continue to use the walker (geriatric thrills), even though I was eventually able to get off the lift without slowing it to a virtual halt. Oh, no, we had to conquer the outriggers, too.

Outriggers in skiing terms are ski poles with level handles, rather like canes, but with the handles pointing forward, and little, sawed-off skis at the ends. The skis matriculate somewhat, up and down. You're not supposed to depend on them; you're meant to use them only to corner and for emergency balance. But you can use them to "pizza," as they tell the kiddie students to do with their actual skis on their actual feet—make a V in front of yourself to slow down and stop. You can do this all the way down a hill, in fact, and I was teasingly chastised for doing just that.

By the end of that first ski season I looked somewhat like a normal downhill skier, just with one foot held up next to the other, almost resting on the boot of my strong foot.

But far more important is the fact that Richard and I were a couple from 1993 on, excepting a couple of short breaks. (Oh, and we did sleep together—on a makeshift bed in the basement—on the last night of that first ski trip. Couldn't wait.)

what people think

*R*ichard was not particularly concerned about me being handicapped while we were dating, until we started getting serious. Then we had conversations about what I could and could not do, and what life for me might be like going forward.

Some members of his family said I had "three strikes" against me: I was older than him (by eleven years). I was of a different and, in their eyes, "opposing Judaism," religion (they saw Sufism as being more Muslim than I did; Western Sufism has a very universal attitude, respecting all religions, but they did not know that). Lastly, I was handicapped. I would be a burden on him. For these three reasons, and at the request of another family member, Richard's parents told him they would no longer see us as a couple.

⸎

People can't help their thoughts. They can't even much help what they do or say, all that being a product of accrued knowledge or stimulus or training. Hopefully with maturity we do develop a chat regulator, learning more by listening than opining. I can't say I'm there yet.

Often people say things they don't mean to be unkind, rude, or inconsiderate. As with some racist remarks, comments about handicaps and disabilities can be blurted out either with naïve good intention or without forethought, often stated as "obvious" fact that we crips surely must know or accept.

I've had people say, for example, "Oh, *you* aren't crippled!" To this I always want to say, "What the heck do you think crippled *is*?" I don't usually voice this thought unless I'm speaking to someone I know really well and we have an understanding about my candor. I realize the speaker is trying to be considerate. I guess to some people "crippled" means all gnarled up and basically unable to get out of a wheelchair. I have a paralyzed, deformed foot, a deformed hip, and an atrophied leg that's two inches shorter than its mate. One doctor has called my limp "horrendous." That's crippled.

Crippled means, according to the dictionary, deformed or having the inability to be used normally, to lack considerable strength. The dictionary also says it is a synonym for lame, which it circularly defines as crippled; having at least one limb that cannot be used normally; having a limp. So, I fit the dictionary definitions of crippled or lame, handicapped or disabled.

Now, "lame" unfortunately gets thrown around a lot, as in, "a lame idea." I've probably even said that, and it's not been unusual for people in my presence to say similar things. I once had an employer—a great gal—who would say things like, "You can't just be limping along with this work or you'll be here all night," or, "I am tired of this place's policy of hiring the handicapped" (in reference to their hiring anybody who wanted to work there more than people who were trained). When I drew her attention to how freely she threw those metaphors and similes around, she was appalled at herself and apologized. I told her it was okay—that I knew she didn't mean it to be about me, I was just uncomfortable with those kinds of terms being used to negatively describe something I did. This came out in a three-way meeting with her manager. In the end we all laughed over the *faux pas*; they were so obvious in their extremity that I could only be amused. The alternative was to be offended. And who wants to live there? Considering all that, no, I don't want you to refer to me to my face as crippled or lame. But within the disabled community, I have no problem referring to myself as a "crip"—I'll use that term with normies sometimes, not to shock them but to make it casual. Within most cultures, it seems to be okay to use slang and nicknames that, thrown around by an outsider, would be a slur. Once, at a relationship seminar in the mid-1980s, the moderator had the cheek to ask me, "How does your boyfriend feel about you being a crip?" I think now that he just wanted to put the disability issue out on the table and get me to think about it, because it was probably an elephant in the room to him. I was shocked at the time and told the guy, a bit defensively, that my boyfriend didn't care. But I didn't actually know that; I only hoped it.

If you see yourself in a negative light while reading my experiences and observations, please know I'm letting you off the hook and did so long ago. We're all human. Or perhaps you'll be able to say, "I do that, I'm helpful that way." I came to realize while writing this book that most people who are careless about disabilities are unlikely to read it.

For every person who has let the door slam in my face as I approached on crutches, there've been at least half as many who have held the door or apologized for cutting in front of me, standing in my way, or even just being too close to my cane or crutch—an apology that sometimes carries a "Please excuse me, I'm sorry you're disabled" aura. Occasionally I can feel an attitude of, "I have not got time to hold the door for this crip; I'm late." I find it particularly funny when I stand with my crutches holding the door for someone carrying packages. But I have this hope that it makes an impression of sorts. Someone asked me if this action made me "feel whole." It simply makes me feel like I'm doing the right thing. Righteous, maybe. I have never felt "un-whole."

A few people have told me that I am heroic. I have tended to pass this off with an "Uh, yeah, no choice, there," but I do appreciate having what I navigate daily be seen. Disabled people are treated with far more respect in this century than we were in the twentieth or especially before that, and better in the US than some other countries. We've a way to go, especially given what I see with kids, cyber-bullying, and celebrity personalities like President Trump. Still, I find that young people—especially young women—are most frequently the ones who hold the door or apologize for cutting in front of my crutchy path.

❧

All of my life, I have had moments like this one: I'm walking along a sidewalk downtown somewhere, see my reflection, and am stunned to see that I am limping badly. Another handicapped friend says this happens to him too—that he's surprised to see the difficulty of his walk in mirrors and windows. I want to just ignore it, but I know that many normies cannot. If I am alarmed to see it, after having lived with it all of my life, what must go through their heads? What went through the head of the middle-aged man in an expensive sports car (and haircut) who stared at my polio foot without looking at my face while I walked into the library? While I was waiting for eye contact? I felt like an anomaly, an object, not a human, barely a woman, when he did that.

I've also lost count of how many times I've turned to see a child behind me trying to mimic my walk. It was always disconcerting in childhood, and of late, simply a reminder, as when you realize toilet paper is stuck to your shoe and trailing along behind you. As I matured, I could finally smile at the panto-mime, think, *Do I REALLY walk like that?* and assess the imitation for accuracy instead of its potentially pointed accusation: "You walk weird." And those occasions have given me many opportu-nities to tell children the reason I walk like this, even when their parents were grabbing their arms and telling them, "Stop it! That girl (or woman) is crippled! Don't make fun of her!" (Often they were not making fun; they were just imitating.)

How the adults respond to their kids is usually worse for me than what the kid is doing. Sometimes the mom apologizes with embarrassment (always a tinge of "sorry you are disabled") and sometimes she just scurries away with her kid, too embarrassed to look at me. It's actually more painful to hear someone say, "That woman is crippled," than it is to see a child imitate me. I'm not sure why; more fodder for therapy. I prefer the eye-contact moms, because then I can say, "It's okay, don't worry. Happens all the time with children; they don't know what is wrong with me."

I used to tell little kids I had a disease "when I was about your age that caused my leg not to grow, so one of my legs is small and short." I especially did this if they asked (which, again, mothers will often try to stifle, but I think it's healthy for a child to show curiosity about differences). A couple of decades ago, I realized that my explanation scared small children, because it made them think that they could get a disease that would de-form them as it had me. So I simplified my story to, "One of my legs is shorter than the other." If the *whys* ensue and we come to my having polio, I always throw in, "But *you* won't get polio, because you have had your vaccinations. They didn't have vacci-nations when I was a little girl."

If they *haven't* had their vaccinations, they can talk to their moms about that. Let the anti-vaxxer mothers deal.

After I put aside the shock and hurt I felt when part of Richard's family rejected me, I viewed their objection to my handicap as ironic, given that I was far more physically active than he was! At that time, we went dancing frequently and sometimes went for walks (if I could get him away from a computer or TV). I was swimming a lot, and I regularly cooked, shopped, and cleaned house, while his exercise program consisted of skiing two or three times a year and walking from his house to his car and from his car to his office and hiking once a year with friends. Twenty-five years later I am still more physically active than he is, although it is now difficult for me to dance for more than a few minutes at a time. This is due to the increased weakness and back problems my in-laws foresaw, and that I thought would not accost me before my seventies or eighties.

Still, I know people in their fifties who are not handicapped and do far less than I do, or have more back problems. As one of my best friends said to me during Richard's and my challenged courtship, "We're *all* going to be handicapped eventually." Another friend generously contributed, "Francine, at least people can see what's wrong with you up front. I have an obnoxious personality, and they don't see that until they get to know me."

My father- and mother-in-law accepted me completely once they saw that Richard and I truly were committed to each other, and these days most of the family feels that I am an asset and treats me with great affection, despite my not being able to stand up for as long as the rest of them.

Richard Falk and I, November 22, 1997
(would have been my mother's 89th birthday if she had lived)

Me skiing on one ski (for the last time), about 1998.

personal best

.

*F*or the first several years after I started dating Richard, I went up to the Tahoe Adaptive Ski School and took ski lessons the first day or morning I was there. Then I practiced on my own on the runs, either in the afternoon or the next day. Richard would periodically ski over to see how I was doing and was proud of my perseverance. His kiss hello and good-bye were definitely encouraging. I made *one* run down an intermediate slope, and it was terrifying. The rest of the time, I went down that same bunny slope, over . . . and over . . . and over. Sometimes I was really exhilarated by it, and many times I fell. Learning to fall is one of the skills of skiing.

I particularly liked the image of being a handicapped skier. Fully capable black diamond skiers told me they thought skiing on one ski was very challenging. I think that they were being more kind than truthful, because I saw a lot of ski instructors skiing on one ski with no poles. Still, it was nice to hear. I was proud to go down those slopes, even when I had to stop myself with the outriggers. I liked that I was a special member of the skiing community, not just up there to hang out with people who might be there to show off their great bodies, blond hair, or expensive ski outfits. I met an extreme challenge and overcame a big fear.

Then, when Richard and I had been married for a year or

so, around my sixth season of skiing, I rented a different type of boot—one that came up higher on my calf. My strong leg was rigid in the boot and that prevented me from moving my knee appropriately.

I had a new instructor that day, as was true almost every time I went. There were only two with whom I'd had repeat lessons, both of whom were really patient and helpful. The fellow I was assigned for this time was doing little besides repeat the others' advice: "Keep your knee bent and your toe pointed forward. Keep your weight over the ball of your foot. Don't use the outriggers unless you have to; use them just for balance in a turn when you traverse the hill."

He wasn't keeping a close eye on me—I think he thought I was not a novice anymore because I'd been up for several seasons—but after a couple of runs, I was still having trouble getting down the mountain in smooth long glides. I fell repeatedly in a short period of time, which was unlike other years, and frustrating.

"I think this boot is too tight on my shin and comes up too high," I told him. "I feel like I can't control my leg as well as I usually can."

"Oh, don't blame the equipment!" he chided me.

But the falls kept happening, and I kept complaining about the boot. Then I fell a few seconds after coming off the lift, and I felt my knee twist in an unusual way—like it had popped out of place or cracked, something bad. The pain was sharp, and I was disappointed that I might not make it down the run. Worse, it was my strong knee. The knee in the leg I depended upon in order to stand and support my limited walking.

"Now, get up and we'll get down this mountain," my instructor said, trivializing my pain.

"I think I may have broken my knee," I said. "I heard it pop."

He gave a frustrated sigh. "You can do this, even if it hurts a little. Come on, get up."

I gave it another try, but it is not easy to get up on a slope on skis in the snow when you have a very weak leg, and harder if the strong leg is injured.

"*Owwww!*" I cried out. "No, it hurts too much. How am I going to get down the hill?" I was almost in tears.

Another ski instructor came by, and mine told him, "She keeps blaming the equipment for her falls!"

The other fellow leaned down to my spot in the snow and said, "Are you hurt?"

"Yes, it's pretty bad," I said. "It's my strong leg; the other one is paralyzed, so I haven't been able to get up."

He called the ski patrol to come and rescue me. They lifted me onto a toboggan sled, jarring my hurt knee.

"I'll go down to the TASS office and tell them what happened, then I'll meet you over at the medical office," my instructor said. "I'm sure it's not broken, though."

The rescue team pulled me down the hill to the medical facility—a very unpleasant ride because it was hard to keep the leg still, and every time it moved, pain shot through my knee.

The young male medic at the emergency facility did a fairly quick and gentle exam of my leg after we gingerly removed my ski pants and tights.

He looked at me and kindly but matter-of-factly said, "Your knee is probably broken at the top of your shin bone, the tibia."

Great. I had had enough injuries to know that this probably meant at least a month on crutches, and, during tax season.

I called Richard on his cell phone and he eventually got reception and came down from his much bigger mountain. The instructor never showed up at the med center. I know he was embarrassed that my injury had happened on his watch, and that I had told him repeatedly that I didn't think my boot fit correctly, but still—it would have been nice of him to show up and see if I was okay.

We stopped at the Truckee hospital on the way home and got an X-ray, and the doctor there said, oh, no, it wasn't broken, it was just a sprain. Later, at home, when the injury did not seem that minor to me, a very good orthopedist had me get an MRI, and we found that the first young medic had been exactly right: my knee was fractured at the top of my shin bone.

I had to wear a mobile brace with gears at the knee for a month or two. I was living an hour's drive from my office, and was working long tax season hours. Fortunately, I could still drive with this gizmo on (by this point I had a left-foot accelerator pedal so I no longer had to drive with my left leg crossed over to the right). A different or more serious injury could have had me in an immobilizing cast and possibly put me out of business.

So ended my brief and tumultuous stint as a skier.

I still enjoy going up to Tahoe. I still like how I look in ski-ish clothes; I like hot chocolate with a little cognac in it near the fire; and I like to take my computer and write, or settle in with a good book. But I'm glad I got off easy. My broken knee healed fully, and today is a reminder that I was very lucky my high-risk sport didn't result in something more serious.

❧

Maybe having polio has caused me to be somewhat more compassionate. In some ways, though, it's made me less forgiving about what people say they cannot do. I have a harder time believing that statement—"I can't do it, I could never do it"—since I've found that I can do far more than I ever thought I could, because I had to. There is so much I've had to arrange just to function, so much I would have preferred not to have had to do. But it was that, or miss out on life.

I have traveled the world, hiked in the woods alone, climbed onto boats and (somehow) down their treacherous ladders, ridden on the back of motorcycles, danced for two hours in my youth, walked alone in Guadalajara and London, and skied on my one strong leg—all that with a deformed hip, a partially paralyzed, atrophied leg, and probably more fear than most women. I've never been fearless. I was scared to death the first time I went down a slight incline on skis, and when I climbed onto my first boat, scared that I'd lose my balance and fall into the brink, conking my head and becoming more disabled on the way down. So I'm really not the right person to whom to say, "I can't."

With maturity, I have also realized that people can be psychologically or emotionally handicapped as well as physically handicapped; there can be something within that creates a barrier to accomplishment. For me, that type of limitation has always seemed surmountable (barring schizophrenia or panic disorder, though I've known people who worked through panic disorder), whereas permanent paralysis is a different circumstance . . . it just dictates some literal impossibilities.

I know there are people with two paralyzed legs who have gone up mountains with the help of others. Paralympics. A president who contracted polio and stayed in office. I'm not talking about that heroic stuff we all hear about; I'm talking about it being impossible for those same guys to actually hike, with their legs, up those peaks, or stroll into anyplace at all, whether a hall at the White House or a shopping mall, without a wheelchair, an exoskeleton, a walker, a cane, or crutches. For me, strolling anywhere is nearly impossible without a cane or crutches, although I did just that in my youth, and sometimes to my detriment.

So that's how I define "I can't": to me, it's physically literal.

I took up yoga in the late 1960s; today, I do ten to twenty minutes of stretches and core strengthening on the floor each morning, plus pool stretches. This is partly so that I can continue to get down on the floor and back up again—not a very easy proposition. I have recommended this exercise regimen to other polio friends and even my husband, since getting up off the floor is important if one should fall, whether as an elder or a middle-aged adult. Although my body is not as strong as I'd like it to be and not nearly as strong as that of most others my age, I am fairly limber, and certainly stronger than I would be if I didn't do yoga and physical therapy. Besides, it feels good to stretch, and my routine ensures that I'll be able to do things like dress myself and bend over and pick things up for at least a decade or two more. When all that gets too difficult, I intend to do chair yoga. Our bodies evolved to move. Even one that is limited wants its parts moving and stretching.

Some might think, *But you could have been an athlete. All those guys with no legs, some of them getting into the Olympics . . . I mean, come on, stop your whining.* This is, after all, in keeping with my own intolerance of people saying, "I can't." And to an extent, I agree. However, many, if not most, of those athletic guys (and gals) have remarkable body strength in their upper bodies and/or thighs. Even a below-the-knee amputation does not reduce thigh strength to almost nothing; with exercise, the thigh and hip are still capable of propelling a leg. Polio, in contrast, is a neurological disease. It kills the nerves and atrophies the muscles, and trying to build up the muscles you have left only wears them out faster, unless you do it V E R Y   S L O W L Y. So slowly that it takes years to build strength by, say, 20 percent. For the most part, with damaged neurons, the best you can hope for is to maintain the strength you already have.

I started doing my pool therapy program about twice a week for forty-five minutes each session in 1999. It took me ten or twelve dedicated years to arrive at doing an hour a day. My leg was slightly stronger after this, but now my thigh muscles are declining a bit. The rest of my body is wearing out, just like everybody else's, but sooner and faster, by maybe a decade. I can walk perhaps a tenth as far as most people my age, even those in poor condition. I am doing these exercises just to be able to remain standing and moving.

Those who got polio as adults and worked really hard to rebuild their muscles have primarily been the first ones to get post-polio effects: new weakness and pain in the affected limbs, and also in the seemingly unaffected limbs. This usually occurs thirty to fifty years after the initial onset of polio. There is also a greater contrast if one regained a lot of use and then suddenly lost it. If there was always paralysis, the new loss of use is not as dramatic. But vigorous attempts at rebuilding did take their toll on many polio survivors, and that's part of why we are not supposed to "go for the burn."

With paralysis or extreme weakness, one uses other muscles to substitute for the movements the limb cannot do or support it cannot provide. I've used my strong leg, my back, my neck, and my arms to make up for my weak leg, and my tendons are showing the wear first. My bones are also very slowly deteriorating, like others with genetically-linked osteopenia or arthritis. I could have done more as a youth, and possibly—if it had been more acceptable for women crips to be athletes in the 1950s and 60s—I could have withstood the taunts of "Hopalong Cassidy" and swum competitively in the Paralympics (and, possibly, reduced the ridicule). But I didn't, and it's just as well, since competition probably would have caused my neurons to deteriorate faster in this later life.

I don't think I would have liked to compete in handicapped

sports anyway; I don't really like competition, though I do like teamwork. I do wish, though, that I could have run and hiked for miles—as a normie, not as the brave crippled girl.

I did climb the Cascades Trail up on Mount Tamalpais here in Marin once, in my mid-thirties. At that time in my life, I could walk perhaps a mile or a mile and a half—but only with difficulty. This hike was two miles, and it was simply too much for me; had I known the length beforehand I would not have attempted it. My very tall, strong, generous friend Mansur had to carry me down the mountain on his back. I was in bed for two days afterward recovering from the fatigue, and I had to use crutches the next day just to get from room to room. This more than three decades ago, was when I was stronger.

Walking is so fatiguing for me because hauling a partially paralyzed, atrophied leg and foot around is a lot of work, and also because polio people, like those who have MS, fibromyalgia, or chronic fatigue syndrome, tire much more easily from seemingly simple and mundane effort. People with these neurological challenges are better off spending their time doing something else. I don't think gardening, painting, writing, or getting a law degree are necessarily easier, but physically they are not as strenuous as going on a long hike—unfortunate, since in my view, there's nothing as inspiring, peaceful, and regenerating as a quiet walk in the woods.

I have always enjoyed feeling like my body was being stretched and accomplishing something. I like moving, and I often forget that I have one leg that is two inches shorter than the other, that it's very weak, and that my foot is paralyzed—except that I am exhausted by motion. Once in a while when I'm walking, especially with a vista ahead, I realize as I gaze down the sidewalk that the landscape moves up and down, from left to right, as if I'm on a tricycle with a flat tire. I remember in that moment that I limp, and that this is not the way others perceive the world.

For me and for anyone with a physical injury or impairment, particularly affecting a leg, personal best is whatever you are able to do. I always wish that I could do more, even as I am thankful for what I can do, where I can go, the ways I can move. It is hard for me to imagine why anyone with a normal body would not take advantage of this and climb every mountain, spend a lot of time dancing, go for walks with friends. Would I do this if I'd been able, or is it a desire born of forbidden fruit? I think I would, but who knows—maybe I would be a couch potato.

a crip by any other name

*W*hen I first decided to learn to ski, in 1993, Tahoe Adaptive Ski School was a subsidiary of Handicapped Sports USA, a non-profit that sought to bring sports to amputees and other handicapped people (including those with mental impairments such as Down syndrome) who were interested in winter skiing or summer water skiing. The challenge and the usual resultant success was often inspiring and regenerative, and Handicapped Sports' motto was, "If I can do this, I can do anything."

Then, one year, I noticed that the name had been changed to Disabled Sports USA. I called one of the directors in Sacramento, Doug Pringle, whom I understood to be a handicapped war veteran. (He's the one who first introduced me to the term "normies" for normally abled people.)

"Doug," I said, "I don't like that the name has been changed to 'Disabled Sports' from 'Handicapped.'"

"The board voted to change the name," he said. "I know, I am not that happy about it either."

"I'd rather be called handicapped than disabled. Handicapped sounds more positive and inclusive of all levels of disability. Disabled sounds more like we can't do anything."

"There were a lot of people who weren't happy about it and didn't want the change, both participants and donors," he said. "There was a lot of controversy, but in the long run, the board went with it because it is easier to get funding if the organization is serving those termed 'disabled.' So it was mostly a matter of getting access to funding, especially in the case of veterans and our being able to use skiing as rehabilitation."

I was disappointed but understood.

People have told me that they do not think of me as disabled, and I believe they meant that they think disabled means that you cannot function. My view is that "disabled" means you have an impairment severe enough to prevent you from performing tasks that most people can perform. I happen to qualify, but I still prefer "handicapped," especially for an organization's name. To me, handicapped means that you have some real physical or mental limitations and need to be allowed some time or perhaps emotional "space" to be able to function as normally as you are able. And I also fall (sometimes too literally) into that category.

People have asked me whether I think we as a group should be called handicapped, disabled, differently abled, physically challenged, or . . . ? And I'm sure there have been and will be other labels or euphemisms thought of for us "crippled" or paralyzed folks, as well as for mental processes that fall outside the norm. Those terms are really a mouthful. I like handicapped best, because it is true.

I no longer mind being referred to as disabled, because I am "ambulatorily" disabled, and always have been, just not completely. I can stand and I can walk, though on some days I cannot do much walking. But most people take that for granted, so in this sense, I accept that I am disabled. In the truest sense, my leg keeps me from doing some common daily activities as a normie would do them. Still, "handicapped" remains my preference. Disabled can imply that we have no abilities, though it actually means ability has become impaired. "Physically challenged" is true, but it sounds so cumbersome, serious, and correct. "Differently-abled" may sound great to some people, particularly those with learning disabilities, but for me as a physically handicapped person, "differently" just seems to be glossing over the fact that there's a lot I cannot do. *"Differently," no sh*t,* I thought when I first heard that term.

A polio survivor I know who also worked in social services has a lot of charge on this issue and says adamantly, "You are *not* handicapped. You are *not* disabled. You are a person *with* a handicap or a disability." I don't see the difference; it's a matter of semantics. One word is an adjective and the other a noun, but my body stays the same.

You may sometimes hear things like this said: "He's handicapped by his shyness"; "He's handicapped by his inability to find better solutions to problems." I get it, the expression is being used to describe someone whose traits limit him. But I don't think I've ever used "handicapped" in that way, to describe what is essentially a personality trait. When I say, "I just cannot walk another step," I don't mean, "Boy, I'm really tired, I'll be glad when I reach my destination or finish this errand"—I mean, "I may fall over if I don't stop walking, and then someone is going to have to carry me or go find a wheelchair."

I definitely do not like being called "a polio," as is true of numerous other polio survivors. But many elder polio survivors use that term, which was common in the 1940s. I heard a historian on Ken Burns's *The Roosevelts* TV series repeatedly call the patients at Warm Springs "the polios" and President Roosevelt "a polio." Jeez. I wouldn't call an HIV patient "an HIV" or a Parkinson's patient "a Parkinson's." Most of us like "polio survivor" best, according to a poll of three thousand of us.

With regard to labels, it's important to ask people what they prefer. When you, my reader, become even slightly handicapped, challenged, or disabled, which is probably going to happen if you stick around long enough, you'll find out how it is you perceive your own condition, and how you want others to label it.

polio, the gift that keeps on giving

*W*hen Richard asked me to go on that first ski trip with him in late 1992, he didn't really care if I skied or not. As long as I was happy, he just wanted me along. I don't hold the contrast between Richard and the guys who rejected me primarily for my handicap as morally or ethically superior. It's just lucky that Richard and I both happened to be more interested in watching movies than skiing. We figured out early on that there were few ways in which my not being able to walk long distances or my inability to do activities requiring two strong legs were going to affect what we wanted to do together.

In 1997, we decided to get married. Over the next eight months, I went through a number of stressful though mostly positive changes—including planning and having a big wedding, finding and buying a house, living with Richard for the first time, having to commute two hours a day, and having the scariest case of the flu I'd ever experienced. We were now living in San Mateo, closer to Richard's job in South San Francisco, but we agreed that it wouldn't be forever. "Five years max," we decided. "Then we move [for me, back] to Marin."

Between the stress of all these changes and living in a two-story house for the first time in about fifteen years, I noticed I was becoming much more fatigued than usual. I was also moving into menopause and was experiencing some severe symptoms, including insomnia. Suddenly, I was very interested in learning more about post-polio syndrome (PPS), something I'd heard of but knew very little about.

The first time I'd heard about PPS was in the 1980s at a tax seminar, of all places. A woman on a sit scooter approached me and asked, brashly, if I had had polio, having noticed my gait. A little stunned, I answered that I had. She said something like, "Well you'd better watch out, because people who have had it are getting it again!" She gave me a long hard look and rolled away.

I thought the woman sounded a little paranoiac, but I decided I'd better look this up—and found that there was reason behind her misconception, although no one was "getting it again." I learned that PPS struck people approximately thirty years after the onset of polio, and something like 25 percent of polio patients were experiencing it. *Good*, I thought, *I'm home free: I'm in my late thirties and it's been thirty-five years since my initial onset.*

In 1998, though, I wasn't so sure about that "home free" thing.

Post-polio syndrome is typified by new muscle fatigue, weakness and/or pain. It seems to be caused by prolonged wear on the motor neurons that have been compensating for weak or paralyzed muscles. My simple explanation of this neurological issue: When you contract polio, some of your motor neurons, which reside in the horn cells on the anterior or front of the spinal cord and are responsible for the control of muscles and all movement in the body, get burned out. The virus specifically attacks the horn cells. If there has been permanent or partial paralysis, some or all of the motor neurons are gone and it has long been assumed they will not regenerate. (A 1999 article from the American Society of Neurochemistry says that motor neurons *can* regenerate. The article was very technical, and while its claims may be true, neither my own motor neurons nor those of any polio survivors thus far have regenerated.)

An unlucky 1 percent of people who experience polio have permanent paralysis. About 75 percent of polio patients had non-paralytic polio, though about 15 to 25 percent of that group did experience temporary paralysis. There were also far more people who were asymptomatic carriers or had another type of polio, referred to as "abortive," which also did not cause symptoms. These four types account for all those stories about older relatives who "had polio, and they got over it; they had no remaining problems with it."

In recovery and beyond, we use other motor neurons to control the muscles polio left weak, or work other parts of our bodies—in my case, for example, my strong leg does nearly all the work when I walk, bend, or squat. Over time, generally in thirty to fifty years, the overworked compensating neurons also start to wear out. This is true for all aging humans—but we polio survivors have less neurons going into our senior years. And this includes those who did not have permanent paralysis.

Our sensory neurons, located all along the back or posterior of the spine, control feeling. Though polio patients may not be able to move a particular set of muscles, we can feel soothing, pleasant touch, and pain, to its fullest, just like everyone else. From my discussions with other polio patients, and from what I have read, it seems that we may have lower pain thresholds than most people. Possibly the sensory neurons were heightened, perhaps to compensate for the danger perceived by the neurological system in having damaged motor functioning. This is not something I've seen in any of my reading; it just seems logical to me.

It's been suggested to me that I get an electromyogram (EMG) to see where different pain signals in my body are coming from and find out if they are specifically related to polio. But this process is tortuous for a person with a very low pain threshold such as me, and the information gleaned would probably be mostly interesting to the doctor(s). My primary care doctor even told me that she once prescribed an EMG for a non-polio patient who did not expect the extreme pain, and that patient promptly fired her as her doctor.

The treatments generally prescribed for post-polio pain are exercises (mostly stretching and core strengthening), pain medication, dietary moderation, massage or other manipulative body work, rest, ice packs, cortico-steroid shots, and surgery, which does not promise relief.

I have managed to mostly control my back and tendon pain with a combination of non-invasive treatments. MRIs have shown problem areas in my tendons, wedged disks and vertebrae (from my two-inch limp), and narrowing of the spinal canal ("canal stenosis") that has resulted in a slightly pressed nerve, causing my back pain.

Other polio patients I know who had undiagnosed symptoms and got an EMG told me afterward that it was either "not that bad" or "pretty awful." Their doctors were able to tell them, based on the EMG results, whether their issues probably resulted from polio, but their treatment options did not change.

Thanks, but I'll skip the torture.

❧

Not too long after Richard and I moved to San Mateo, Richard's company went public, and we made a sizable donation to Easter Seals. I sent a note telling them that if it had not been for their organization funding my physical therapy in 1951, I might have lived my life in a wheelchair, and I was now happy to be able to give them a gift in return.

After receiving my letter, Easter Seals called me and asked if I wanted to visit their pool therapy facility, Timpany Center, in

San Jose, about an hour south of our home. It is a remarkable place for all disabled people who can benefit from water exercise: polio, MS, arthritis, fibromyalgia, intellectual disability, the works. On my visit, I was so impressed and inspired! There were several physical therapy rooms with attendant tables, weights, balance balls and other equipment, and men's and women's locker rooms. The pool was almost Z-shaped, nearly as big as an Olympic pool, and kept at about 90 degrees F so poor circulation would not cause chilling for seniors or people with atrophied limbs. There was a long, wide, gently sloped ramp in the shallow end for entering the pool, even facilitating being pushed in a wheelchair, followed by a shallow area for walking, stretching, and other exercises. The other leg of the Z was a deep-water area for swimming and doing kicks while floating with a noodle. Wow. As a swimmer, I was envious.

The head of physical therapy asked me if I wanted to come use the pool and they could teach me a routine, and I accepted.

ھ

When I had learned my water exercise set, I found a rehab doctor in San Francisco at St. Mary's Hospital who had been trained by Dr. Stanley Yarnell, a retired polio expert. I made an appointment with the young doctor and traveled to San Francisco to meet with him and his staff. They told me to bring my swimsuit.

Dr. Yamamoto was quiet but friendly. He tested my muscle strength and made some notes. He reviewed the water program as it had been written out by the Timpany folks, and said, "This looks good. I'd like you to meet with Margo Falk, our physical therapist, to see that it is appropriate for you. But before you do that, what kind of diet are you following?"

"I have recently reduced the number of simple carbohydrates in my diet and am trying to eat more protein and vegetables so I can get my weight down," I said. "I have gained twenty pounds in two years; I have been commuting two hours a day so am doing far more sitting than I used to."

He nodded. "Most polio patients do better on a high-protein diet. You need to be able to rebuild your muscle more than the average person since there is so much work for parts of your body that are compensating for weaker muscles, especially when there is paralysis. This is partly because protein is integral to regenerating muscle growth, but also, without walking much, you don't use up the carbohydrates and begin to gain weight, especially with aging."

(Of course, longevity has been proven to increase with a low-protein, high-vegetable-content diet. Toss a coin.)

He asked if I was having any new problems with regard to polio effects.

"Oh, yes," I said, "I am living in a two-story house now, and with my recent move and the added commute, I'm much more fatigued than I used to be. I read a magazine article this year in *Scientific American* about post-polio, and it seems that I do have new weakness and fatigue and occasional pain."

"I think you do have post-polio sequelae," he said, "especially since you say these symptoms have worsened recently and it has been about fifty years since your onset. But let's see if your exercise program will help you out by strengthening your muscles without fatiguing them. We also have an occupational therapist here and I'd like you to make an appointment with her, to review seating and work habits and other assistive devices that might make your life easier."

I donned my suit, was introduced to Margo, and went with her to a tiled room that contained a small warm exercise tank. I climbed down the stairs into the tank.

"Okay," Margo said, "let's see what you're doing."

I did every exercise on the list for just a couple of repetitions.

Margo nodded enthusiastically at the end of the twenty-minute mini-workout. "This is an excellent program," she said. "It's giving you a good all-over workout, and if you don't overdo it and increase your time and repetitions only after a particular exercise becomes easy, I think it will help you regain some strength. If you feel tired, or have any pain at all, stop and reduce the repetitions or the time."

I began reading more on post-polio, and the most helpful info I found was contained in a little book titled *Managing Post-Polio*, by Lauro Halstead, MD. One of the many useful suggestions in the book was that for any exercise program, a polio patient should determine, for each exercise, the maximum number of repetitions or time that the exercise can be done without fatigue or pain. Once that max was established, Dr. Halstead recommended doing 20 percent of the max for each exercise to begin with, then increasing that very gradually—by perhaps 5 percent at a time—when the 20 percent became easy.

I continued my pool work at the Mickelson Arthritis Center in San Mateo, a wonderful warm pool with a ramped entrance. (There are very few warm therapy-centered pools, even in the progressive San Francisco Bay Area.) Mickelson was full of very old people, and it was not easy to get my laps in with so many in the pool who were easily frightened by vigorous activity. But the facility was perfect for the rest of my exercises, and the pool was near our house. I started out in late 1999 doing about forty minutes of exercise twice a week, and by the end of 2002 was doing about two-plus hours a week.

Dr. Halstead's book also confirmed what I had suspected: our two-story house was a major culprit in my new weakness and fatigue. It takes ten times more energy to climb stairs than it takes to walk the same distance on a flat surface. This is why

NOT A POSTER CHILD   265

step aerobics are so effective in weight loss and strengthening leg muscles—unless you are a polio or MS patient. Dr. Halstead's recommendations were basically common sense: don't duplicate efforts in daily activities, store items you use near the place where you use them at home or work, and don't bother with things that don't matter that much, such as making the bed every day.

That was a hard one to let go of, having been taught that I could not leave the house as a child until my bed was made and my toys were put away. Neatness is a superb habit and I kept up with it fairly well throughout my life, always happy to come home to a tidy house, until we lived in that two-story house. Now I have admittedly become a little sloppy, and clutter is an issue in several areas of my home, especially since I do most of our non-grocery shopping from catalogs. But I like to save my energy, as Dr. Halstead recommends, for things that are either essential to me (working, cooking, gardening, shopping, exercising, managing our finances and house repairs, and taking care of the cats, Richard, and myself) or fun (writing, watching movies, reading, listening to or making music, traveling, and hanging out with friends). I can't wear myself out by also being ready for *House Beautiful* to show up with a camera—and that, I think, is not a bad philosophy for the last third of anyone's life.

Two or three years ago, I heard an Italian polio research doctor speak at a polio conference. His study has shown early results indicating that those who experience PPS often have a very low, non-contagious level of active polio virus still in their blood. He has found that giving his European patients a polio vaccination has stopped further advancement of the PPS symptoms. (My question about this protocol is whether these patients ever had inoculations as children or young adults *after* they'd had polio, as we all did in the US.) I tried to find a place in the San Francisco area that tests for presence of live polio virus; one said they did, but when I got the blood test results, they had only tested for polio antibodies, which indicates one has been vaccinated, and we already knew I had been. So I recently got a polio booster shot and am hoping for the best. It can't hurt and may slow the process of weakness, fatigue, and pain I am experiencing.

moving on

*R*ichard and I kept our agreement to move back to Marin County, where my work and many friends were located, within five years of marrying. Marin is full of beautiful hills, and most neighborhoods that were close enough for Richard's commute to south of San Francisco were hilly, foggy, or both. Our search for a one-story house on reasonably flat land that either had a pool or would accommodate one took two years. Then, because we each needed an office and wanted a guest room, and I wanted the kitchen oriented to the back of the house, and he wanted a media room for our stereo and TV, we added on 1,000 square feet, totally gutted the original house, and rebuilt it.

I had a surprising encounter with our architect during the remodel process. I may have put her on the defensive to begin with, because the contractor we'd hired had seen the plans and faxed them to me, and over the phone the architect said she was unhappy about this.

"I like to show the plans to the client myself, Francine," she told me.

"Oh," I said, surprised. "I asked John to fax them to me. Since I have architectural drawing background [minimal college-level], I wanted to look them over in advance and be prepared with questions."

She was a bit testy when we showed up at her office and sat down to go over the plans.

"I really like this plan number three you have come up with," I told her, leading with the good. "I think it will be very livable, especially since each part of the house has a circular traffic pattern."

Later, we were discussing the back of the house and a potential landscape and patio, which she was not actually going to design, and she said, "You'll want to have wooden decks with stairs going out from the back door."

"Oh, no," I said, "we currently have a wooden deck and stairs and it's been awful for me. Because my foot and ankle are paralyzed, I can't have an uneven surface as we'd have with a plank deck. When I'm barefoot, which I would be around our pool, they are a hazard for tripping and splinters. We've decided to have sloping cement sidewalks, ramping down from the house to the backyard, and no stairs."

I was envisioning something textured and non-slip and clay-colored, not just flat grey cement. But I think from my comments she may have pictured ramps with pipe handrails, like a hospital would have. We had already discussed widening all the doors in the house and creating a master bath shower that would eventually allow a wheelchair, if necessary.

Before I finished talking about the back sidewalks, she exclaimed, "Francine, you have to think about the value of your house and what the next buyer is going to want. You can't expect it to be handicapped heaven!"

I felt stung. I didn't breathe a word for the rest of the discussion. Richard, my hero, knew I was in a state of mild shock and took over for us. He asked a few questions while I summoned up all my emotional resources to keep from crying or giving her a tongue lashing. I did cry a few minutes later in the parking lot, alone with Richard.

He was quietly furious. I asked him what he thought we should do. We'd invested a few thousand dollars into these plans; I did not see how we could work with her now, but I also didn't know the protocol and whether we could use the plans if we did not retain her for the remodel.

⌒

The next day, Richard sent her a certified letter in which he told her we did, in fact, want our home to be "handicapped heaven." Our purpose in remodeling was largely to allow me to live in an easier way and accommodate my disability as I aged. He told her that she had to tone down her attitude or we would find a different architect, as expensive as it would be—in money and in time. But we were prepared to do that.

We didn't hear back from her for over a week. Finally, I called, and she was the picture of politeness.

"Sorry the meeting didn't go well," she said. "I really am not used to the client seeing the plans in advance." No mention of an apology for her deeply offensive diatribe. She wanted the job, however. The total fee, we already knew, was going to be nine times what we had paid for the initial floor plan.

Nearly a year later, when I was doing the walk-through of the rebuilt house with her, I told her that the one thing in which I was a bit disappointed was that she had made the living room smaller (though cozier) and the front hall larger, which I felt was going to be wasted space. This had not been pointed out to us and we had not noticed the change when reviewing the plans, until the walls were already moved and rebuilt.

"Well, I wanted to make sure you had room to turn your wheelchair around," she replied, and walked away.

⌒

That year before the move was another stressful one. We remained in the two-story house during the remodel, and I continued to commute two hours a day. I'd be on my hands-free cell phone with the foreman every morning while I drove to work, managing my life's biggest art project, and several times a week, I went to the new house to inspect, make choices, or answer questions.

In the end, we did get a lovely floor plan (though it was not precisely what we'd wanted), and we succeeded in moving back to Marin almost exactly on schedule—five years and two weeks after we had moved into the two-story San Mateo house.

32

—

taking care of business

A couple of years before our move to Marin, in 2000, Richard encouraged me to get out of accounting. The hours during half of the year are exhausting, and he was worried about the toll the stress was taking on me.

I'd had a complicated relationship with my work over the years. I was so clumsy with public general ledger accounting for the first six months I worked in a CPA firm that I was the employee left with no job when the firm split up, but I gradually sharpened my skills, freelancing for several CPAs, until people started asking me to do their taxes. Between doing that, having a few bookkeeping jobs, and managing the Sufi camps (big adult summer camps with a population of around three hundred), I gradually built up a practice of tax and bookkeeping clients—and I found that I liked working for myself so much that I couldn't just drop it and get a full-time job someplace, though I had nosed around for one from time to time. I took the CPA exam a couple of times and nearly passed it, but was sick to death of studying, especially accounting. So I took the federal Enrolled Agent exam and got that designation, which suited me, since I preferred dealing with tax and its infuriating changing laws. It was constant problem-solving, and I enjoyed doing tax planning to save money for my clients.

Still, it wasn't all good. I had to cut my hours sometimes or I would have been even more fatigued, putting me at greater risk for tripping and falling. I lose my balance more easily when I'm tired, partly because my strong leg and my back are tired and can't take up all the compensatory work they usually do. Also, if I'm fatigued, sometimes I am less careful about watching my steps. I hired help in order to keep clients, reducing my own pay to do so. Other accountants work too hard as well, but it is a little different when you have a serious physical limitation. It can limit what you can accumulate in terms of savings, too.

I also always thought I would eventually get out of tax work and become something like a CFO for a non-profit involved with art—maybe one that did programs for underprivileged kids, something like that. Something that would contribute to a better world, and to my soul. But once I had a hundred or more clients, it seemed daunting and irresponsible to switch career tracks.

ᦾ

It has irked me throughout my life when people have said, "Of course, handicapped people can't work, or don't work full-time." What an assumption. Along with this goes the assumption that someone with a handicap must be getting governmental aid. This is available to some, but unless family members subsidize those receiving it, their standards of living are distressing. I still hear this mindset, often from doctors, partly because I just turned seventy (though almost all people I know who are my age are still working). I know so many handicapped people— particularly polio survivors, who tend to be over-achievers, and veterans— who worked all their lives, just as hard as able-bodied people, and did it with greater fatigue issues than anyone knew they were absorbing.

The flip side of "of course you can't work," on the other

hand, is when our handicaps are discounted or ignored and we are expected to work just as hard as normies. There's a balance. The Americans with Disabilities Act has helped this, along with getting more accessibility in place, which is huge.

I know of polio survivors who have had careers as doctors or lawyers, and I am in awe that they were able to keep up the pace without experiencing serious health issues. A valiant non-polio paraplegic I know comes to mind: she went to UC Berkeley and met her nurse in her van during class breaks to be catheterized. She became a disabled people's advocate.

And there's the famous example of Stephen Hawking, of course. But not all of us are brilliant physicists.

⤳

Briefly, in the mid-80s, after I'd sung with the Sufi choir for four years, I thought I might become a professional singer. I auditioned with and took lessons from Judy Davis, a skilled vocal teacher in Oakland who was Barbra Streisand's West Coast vocal coach. My class included the musicians from Sammy Hagar's band, which was fun; we rode to classes together and they were nice guys, very funny. But I realized that in order to succeed in the genre I had the most talent for, rhythm and blues, I'd have to pay my dues singing in clubs at night for quite a while before I'd be ready to launch. I was past the bar scene and could not see myself spending a lot of time in those venues. I also ran out of money after my trip to India in 1982 and could no longer afford the voice classes.

Nearly two decades later, after singing in community choruses, choirs, a rock and roll chorus, and a jazz chorus, my polio leg nearly collapsed under me as I walked across the stage during intermission of a big show—pretty scary. I was in my early fifties then, and my voice was still good, but my polio leg was not made for show biz. Even light choreography was way beyond my ability, and it was getting harder and harder to stand up and sing; I needed to sit on a high stool most of the time, which didn't really work for the rest of the jazz group, who were also in their fifties and sixties but all had two strong legs. Plus, I was tired of 1940s jazz numbers.

So ended my erstwhile avocation as a singer.

One day I looked back and saw I'd been doing tax and accounting for decades, and that I may as well stick with it. By the time Richard asked me to consider retiring, it had been a long time since I'd truly taken stock of what had turned out to be my life's career.

I took a hard look—and saw that I loved my clients too much and was not quite ready to say goodbye. Quite a surprise for someone who spent so much of her life wondering if she'd made the right decision by going into accounting.

Eight years later, when we saved up almost enough for both of us to retire, I did sell my practice. I have been working as a tax temp for accountants and have one very small bookkeeping job—which, with all I do at home, plus writing and facilitating a writing group, feels like a full-time job. So, I've decided to give up the numbers work.

For a handicapped person, this has been a fair career. But I would not recommend tax work, given how fatiguing the hours are. You have to have a lot of physical resilience to do it, unless someone absorbs your tasks at home or supports you for at least a couple of months a year so you can take the breaks you need. However, being able to set my own (long) hours, being able to go out to the car and take a nap, and being able to say, "No, I can't meet with you that day," was helpful for my health. If a person has the entrepreneurial spirit, any self-employment that showcases a physically realistic skill is good for a handicapped person, especially if part-time work can be viable.

～

There are still so many places that handicapped people cannot go. And that doesn't begin to address the old factors that are gradually falling away, such as, "Crips don't look good, so avoid hiring them." My auditing teacher looked right at me in class when he said that the big eight accounting firms in the late 70s were very discriminatory and paid considerable attention to how you looked. You could not expect to be a person of color or to bring a brown bag lunch. Women at that time could not even wear pantsuits! This would have left me with my short, skinny leg and drop foot really exposed.

After I got my degree, I bought three-piece wool suits with skirts, interviewed, and did not get a job with a downtown San Francisco big eight firm. Probably just as well, but these were the kinds of employers where the ADA countered discrimination decades later.

I am glad to see that more developmentally disabled people are now being hired by a variety of businesses. But in general, career choices are somewhat limited for handicapped people, if they want to take care of themselves and be self-supporting, and particularly if they'd like to love what they do. This is true to some degree for everyone, but it's easier when one doesn't have to consider a disability. I wish for better outcomes for the people who've had no work or struggled repeatedly to find it. I'm just glad I've had work, and could support myself sitting down.

and now, for something different...

I had a slightly suspicious mammogram in 2002. We were just watching the films, doing a mammo every six months. My breast doctor felt, and I agreed, that too many women have unnecessary biopsies and mastectomies. But if you really do have breast cancer, it's important to find it early, to save your life and possibly your breast.

After one of my semi-annual mammos, my primary care doctor at the time called me and said, "Why don't you just get a biopsy? Are you going to get mammograms every six months for the rest of your life?" My breast doctor and I had thought that the latest film looked like the calcifications we were seeing were getting closer together. We surmised that maybe whatever was going on in there was shrinking. But the day before my primary had called me with her imploring message, I had read in *Harvard Women's Health Watch Newsletter* that the closer calcifications are together, the more probable it is that it's cancer.

I underwent a stereotactic needle biopsy in July 2004. This involves lying on your stomach on a table with boob holes, getting a basically useless shot of something like Novocain in your breast, getting an ultrasound, and having a needle the size of a pencil lead shot into your breast. It hurt like hell, even with "something to numb me." I cried, and most of the women I know who have had them told me they also cried. The radiologist told me that the chance of my actually having cancer was less than 8 percent; it was unlikely they'd find any cancer in the sample; and we'd talk about what would happen next only if there were cancer present.

I had several days of high tension waiting while the lab cultured the sample. My breast doctor called me from her cell phone on a Sunday. She wanted to save me from going through the rest of the weekend worrying.

"I have ___ news," she told me. "You ____ have cancer."

What I heard was, "I have good news; you don't have cancer"—so I answered, "Oh, good!"

Then she repeated what she'd really said, with more emphasis on the "BAD" news and you "DO" have cancer.

In my biopsy "material," otherwise known to me as a dearly beloved part of my breast, was a BB-sized tumor of stage one invasive cancer (smallest tumor ever detected in Marin County), and a lot of *ductal carcinoma in situ*, or DCIS, which is pre-cancer that stays in the eensy milk duct and is not life-threatening . . . until it turns into something more aggressive and invades the breast tissue. It's a slow grower, most of the time, but still—cancer.

Clunk. I let it sink in.

⤚⤙

Richard went with me to the initial strategy consultation with my accomplished surgeon. It's a good idea when faced with something like this to have another pair of reliable ears along, and to take notes. Additionally, there was the waiting, because we would not know if there was more and worse cancer lurking in there until a surgical lumpectomy was performed. In the weeks after the diagnosis, I was sometimes in tears, and a lot of the time I just tried to distract myself and not dwell on it.

At one point in an interview in her office, my breast doc said, "It's not fair, is it?"

I hesitated a moment, thinking, *Well, cancer is probably never fair,* but then asked, "What do you mean?"

"Well, having polio, and then having breast cancer, too."

"Oh," I said, and thought a moment. "No, I guess it's not." I had long before abandoned the concept of fairness in life experiences. Breast cancer was scary, but for me it was yet another thing to overcome. I hoped I would not have to have a mastectomy, and was definitely not happy that I was facing at least one surgery and would be anesthetized for it. But I'd been overcoming things I didn't want to deal with for fifty years.

⤸

A month later, I had a lumpectomy. In the initial interview with the hospital, I told them that I would not go into surgery until I had talked to the anesthesiologist, because polio people have very strong reactions to anesthesia. We sometimes need a little more to put us out, but we take forever to come out of it. And I had gotten quite sick in the past from anesthesia.

My surgeon had told me that Dr. Stephen Licata, the doctor doing my "cocktail" for the surgery, was very experienced and had formerly been a pharmacist, so he was an expert. The night before my surgery I got his call, which I'd been anxiously awaiting, and he listened carefully. He took great care of me on the actual day. I felt fine afterward and came out of the haze better than I'd ever done in the past. Later I asked him for the formula so I'd be able to pass it on to another anesthesiologist if I ever had to have surgery again.

Days of more waiting after the surgery, and then the sorry phone call that said good news, bad news: there was no more stage one cancer, it all came out in the original needle biopsy, but my surgeon had not gotten clear margins on the DCIS. This meant a second lumpectomy. ("Take it, take another little piece of my breast, now, dar-lin'.") Dr. Licata changed his schedule to be there for me. In this second operation, my nimble surgeon got acceptable margins.

Every tumor in Marin County is discussed at a tumor board. Some of the doctors there thought that the second margins were too small and I should have a mastectomy. My surgeon argued with them that I was a polio patient, that I had concerns about disfigurement. "She can have reconstruction," they countered. My doctor told them that I could not give up a back muscle, especially on that side, to support reconstruction. (The common procedure is to pull a back muscle around to support the substitute breast. In my interview with a well-respected plastic surgeon, he said that it might also be possible to take abdominal muscle, but of course I need that for core strength since my degenerated hip is so weak.)

I so appreciated that my surgeon was my heroine in this debate. In the end, the tumor board agreed that I could move on to radiation.

❧

You have to get radiation after a lumpectomy in order to kill off any stray cancer cells that may remain. Although there is some danger of radiation causing cancer, any new cancer cells stimulated by it are generally killed off by leftover radiation, which stays in your system for a while. This combination of treatments makes your chance of a recurrence about the same as if you'd had a mastectomy, but you still have a breast, or most of one—in my case, about 75 percent of what I'd had before. The drawback is that radiation makes future reconstruction inadvisable or even impossible, if one has a recurrence.

I took my beat-up breast to the radiological oncologist's office every weekday for seven weeks, with only one or two days off. The technicians were caring and friendly; they knew it was scary for all of us cancer patients. When I let the doctor know that I was a singer, she also made sure that the radiation missed my lung. (If it hits the lung, it can leave you with hoarseness or shortness of breath.)

Radiation was greatly tiring over time, and it also caused nerves in my breast to fire off painful electrical "shooters"—it took a couple of years for that to completely stop. I had to take a nap every day for months and then sleep nine hours a night. Fatigue on top of my normal fatigue.

I completed my course of radiation on December 22, and was back at work doing taxes two weeks later. That was not an easy season. I told my clients that I could not work such long hours that year; thankfully, they were all considerate about that. (The year my mom died, some of my clients were angry that I had to file more extensions and some found a new accountant, so I was relieved that for cancer, everyone had some compassion.)

⟿

When my radiation course was done I tried to take Tamoxifen, a hormonal drug that reduces your chances of having a recurrence in the first five years. But I began having more and more hot flashes and night sweats, which in turn were causing severe insomnia, right when I was still tired from radiation and was trying to do tax season—always grueling to begin with, without breast cancer lite.

I'd joined a cancer support group facilitated by a wise, considerate breast cancer survivor, and had gone from the "in treatment" group to the "moving on" group. Each group met in separate rooms at a building near Marin General Hospital.

One evening at the "moving on" group, fifteen of us sat

around a table, all survivors now. I decided to take a little poll on Tamoxifen vs. aromatase inhibitors (AIs).

"I am looking at taking AIs because I can't tolerate Tamoxifen," I told the group, "but I already have joint and muscle pain, and the pharmacology for these drugs indicates that 25 percent of women who take AIs have muscle and joint pain. So, how many of you are taking AIs?"

Twelve of fifteen hands went up.

"And how many of you are experiencing muscle or joint pain?"

Same twelve hands.

I know, that's only anecdotal, not a double-blind study, but still, that's 100 percent. A year or two later, I learned from a BC survivor who does volunteer coaching of new BC patients that all the women she knew on AIs went off them for a few weeks a year—on vacations or for special occasions—because they were in pain all the rest of the time.

I went back to my oncologist, Dr. Jennifer Lucas, an affable whiz kid from Stanford.

"I'm going off the Tamoxifen, and I am not going to take either of the AIs," I told her. "I feel that I am a whole person, not just a cancer patient, and polio affects my life on a daily basis more than the threat of cancer. On the Tamoxifen, I feel like my quality of life is so poor that after five years I would be a nervous wreck, totally debilitated by lack of sleep, even more at risk for tripping and falling, and, incidentally, a complete bitch. On the AIs, I am facing an increase in my existing pain issues from polio effects."

"I'm fine with that!" she said. "You won't be on hormones, and all three of those drugs increase your risk of blood clots, stroke, and uterine cancer."

"I also read that women who take low-dose aspirin over a long period of time have a lower incidence of breast cancer," I said. "What do you think about that?"

"I'm a big believer in aspirin," she said. "It can't hurt at that low a dose; go ahead. I think you have a good plan here and I am not worried about you not taking Tamoxifen or AIs."

So, there you are. A voice of sanity amongst those shaking their heads and saying they were concerned about my cancer risk. Heart disease kills more women than breast cancer. My wise breast surgeon agreed.

I did continue to take a battery of pro-energy, anti-cancer supplements recommended by a skilled acupuncturist (Michael McCulloch of Pine Street Clinic in San Anselmo, CA) who specializes in cancer and is also a Western epidemiologist. These have been tested in double-blind research studies. I still take them, fourteen years after treatment. I sometimes feel like I'm clapping my hands to keep the elephants away—but then again, I've had no recurrence. My doctors tell me that the exercise I perform so religiously probably has the most to do with reducing my cancer risk, and of course it's great for overall health.

34
—

doctors, doctors

*O*f course, surviving cancer did not put an end to all my other medical woes. After suffering another fall in 2005, concerned that my smaller foot was broken, I made an appointment with an orthopedist I'd never seen before. I would have liked to see Dr. DeMayo, but by then he'd developed arthritis in his hands and become a consultant for Kaiser, leaving me with no orthopedic polio doctor in the San Francisco Bay Area. This new orthopedist knew nothing about polio-affected limbs but had at least been recommended to me by Dr. DeMayo's successors.

A technician made x-rays of the foot and then had me wait in the exam room in the flimsy gown, my skinny polio leg getting colder by the moment as I waited for the doctor.

He finally walked in, and without looking at me said, "Hello, I'm Dr. X_____," and sat his young self down at the computer with his back to me. His first comment while checking my input form, without even having examined my leg, was, "What makes you think you had polio? We don't think most people who think they had it actually did . . . and we don't believe in post-polio."

I would have gotten up and walked out, but I was undressed and needed my underarm crutches with my hurt foot; I couldn't just hop down and take off. I defended myself instead, saying, "I was diagnosed with poliomyelitis in 1951 and hospitalized in a polio rehab facility for six months. And if you *look*, you can see that this foot is paralyzed and the leg is atrophied, typical of polio."

Still looking at my X-ray on his computer screen, Dr. X_____ said, "It looks as if the foot has been cracked previously."

"Yes," I said. "That was a previous fall; one of many."

"It looks like there is no new break," he said, while looking at my actual foot for a moment. "Just a sprain. Use the crutches, stay off it until it feels better, keep it elevated, and ice it. Take ibuprofen if you need it."

"Yes, that's what I always do. I just thought I'd get it checked out."

"You can make an appointment for a follow-up in a few weeks," he said. He nodded goodbye with a perfunctory half-smile and left.

I dressed, and crutched out to the car.

It is common for doctors to dismiss questions about post-polio effects or post-polio "syndrome," but even knowing that, I always find it infuriating. It probably goes without saying that I didn't go see this doctor again, even for follow-up.

∽

A few years later, in 2009, I was suffering from tendon stress and pain and couldn't find a doctor locally who knew anything about those conditions in polio patients, specifically regarding my strong leg and foot. So I looked for a post-polio support group—and I found one in Sonoma, the next county up from me. Just one problem: they had stopped meeting because so many of them were elderly, tired, and debilitated. Most did not have the energy to manage, run, or even attend a group.

I went to Sonoma's swan song luncheon with about forty polio survivors, some there with their spouses. It was a little strange to be in a room in which nearly everyone limped or was in a wheelchair! (Stranger still, though welcome, when I later attended a polio patients' conference of a couple hundred.) It was inspiring to learn that many polio survivors live into their nineties and enjoy life, despite having to use a wheelchair or walker. They may have a harder time getting around than other elderly people, but they are still getting around. I had not known previously whether simply having polio was going to mean a shorter life span. This can be true for those who need to use ventilators to breathe well, but it's certainly not the standard for the rest of us.

At the luncheon, I gathered names of folks who lived near me and might be interested in being in a group again. I found a location and put the word out to an email list and some physical therapy and doctors' offices, and started Polio Survivors of Marin County.

We meet quarterly to discuss physical issues and remedies, and also psychological or family problems that can result from disability. Generally, we haven't socialized other than a bit of chat before or after the meeting, or occasional emails between individuals, but we think of each other and contact one another when a news article or other piece of information is relevant. In one case, a member was having difficulty with Social Security and her health insurance program, and we rallied and found resources for her, including free legal advice. Since some of the people in the group are overweight, a hazard of not having full mobility, it was particularly inspiring when one member went on an anti-inflammatory diet, lost nearly a quarter of her weight, and found that her fibromyalgia also disappeared. I find speakers to address the group on topics related to polio, disability, and aging, when possible.

Even in the 1970s, there were few doctors who knew anything about the repercussions of polio, especially outside of major metropolitan areas—and today, their numbers have dwindled even further.

These days, I have an intelligent and gentle primary care doctor, Meenal Lohtia, who was born and schooled in India and probably has a greater understanding of polio than most American-educated doctors, and an orthopedist who is a "foot star," the staff physician for San Francisco Ballet. But I believe I'm his only polio patient. My only true polio doctor is a rehabilitation physiatrist whose office is over one hundred miles away from me.

This distance issue is common for polio survivors. I've only been able to locate a couple of polio-educated doctors (other than my physiatrist) in northern California who actually take polio patients. There may be more in Southern California, since the epidemic was worse there, but where I am, it's a struggle to find doctors who know what they're doing when it comes to polio and its aftereffects.

deal with it

$\mathscr{I}$ had a period of a couple of years—after the cancer scare, plus the two years it took for me to heal as much as was expected—where my physical life was fairly stable, aside from a lot of fatigue from working during the demanding tax seasons. But in 2010, after I had sold my tax practice, I slipped and fell and badly injured my polio knee—just two or three days before Richard and I were to leave on a trip to Germany.

I managed to get in to see a new-to-me orthopedic surgeon referred by my former orthopedist. He thought I had torn my AC ligament, inside the knee, because I was in such acute pain. I could still go to Germany, he said, but I was probably going to need surgery, so I would not be able to put any weight on it for the entire trip.

Being on underarm crutches for a big trip clearly would not work. I pictured staying home and having surgery while Richard was working in Europe. Ick.

I miraculously was able to get an MRI the next morning to identify the damage—*Hallelujah*, my ACL was not torn. My pain was probably worse than most people have with a sprain.

The good thing that came out of this was a pair of Lofstrand Canadian arm cuff crutches the orthopedist recommended, which have a hinged forearm cuff and are basically balancing supports that reduce fatigue over distances. They also can be used to help take weight off a foot or leg, though they are more tiring than underarm crutches when used this way since all the stress is on the arms and hands, whereas with underarm crutches, the rib cage supports some of the weight. The Lofstrands took a little getting used to. I found that I was also a lot slower with them than I am with just a cane or underarm crutches. As with the little Kenny sticks, I put one foot and the opposing crutch forward, and then the other foot and crutch. Since my knee was very painful, that also slowed me down.

However, when I wanted to pick up a cup or hand my ticket or passport over, I didn't have to take them off my arms and lean my crutches on something while I stood on one leg. I also later found that in a store, I could take things out of my purse, use my credit card, and write checks at the market without removing them from my arms.

I got a flexible knee brace and went to Germany with the Lofstrands. Not an easy trip, but the young hotel concierge gave me another useful suggestion: gel-padded bicycle gloves. I wear them when I'm going to go more than a block or so with the Lofstrands, and they diminish soreness in my hands. (They also look cool and athletic, and protect my hands when I'm using my motorized trike.)

❧

Prior to this knee injury, I had spent about six years of my life on crutches: first at three, in and after the hospital, in order to be able to walk at all; then after my surgery at thirteen; and then periodically as a result of my myriad injuries. Now I use the Lofstrands for distances of more than a half-block if I don't have my scooter, so they are a fixture in my life. Crutches are really limiting, and I've had my back "go out" (pinched nerve, actually), after using underarm crutches for a few weeks. That hurt more and was more debilitating than the initial foot or knee injury.

I wish everyone would try using crutches for maybe an hour, so that more doors would be opened when a person on crutches tries to enter Starbucks or the doctor's office. Doors are difficult: I try to swing them open as far as I can and then quickly stick my crutch down in front of the door as a stop, so I can get myself through, but if I'm carrying files, groceries, or anything else, this is frustratingly challenging. I can't carry anything without a handle when using two crutches, and it's imperative for me to use a crossbody purse. I've learned to carry less as a result. You will rarely see me with a tote.

People who have to use crutches don't get a break. They have to use them for a week, a month, several months, or forever, and they are tiring and limiting. But they allow us to walk farther than we could without them—or, in some cases, to walk at all. Those rolling kneel scooters are great if you're able to use them, but they don't work for all of us.

⌘

Unfortunately, not long after the pre-Germany knee injury, I also started experiencing joint pain. I had been taking statins for high cholesterol, and they can be pain culprits. (I was really glad at this point that I'd skipped the AIs post-breast cancer.) My primary care physician and I tried several different statins, and some were worse than others. Finally, I stopped all of them, and most of my joints returned to a normal, pain-free state—but even sans statins, I was left with stabbing pain in my thumbs, especially my right one (I'm right-handed) and in the top of my strong foot.

I went after a solution to my thumb pain first, because I could barely use my right hand some of the time. Given my new role (after selling my business) as full-time home manager, I really needed to be able to lift a frying pan without dropping it and do the grocery shopping without crying out when I put something into the cart (I was occasionally alarming other shoppers).

I went to a hand therapy center, where they told me that I appeared to have arthritis in my thumbs. They made a custom splint that restricted the position of my right thumb, and also made me a great little rubber-covered wire support to wear over my gardening gloves. I got a hot wax machine to relieve the pain, and a prescription for Meloxicam (generic Mobic) which is like heavy-duty Advil, plus one for Voltaren gel, a non-steroidal anti-inflammatory drug (NSAID) rubbed directly onto the joints, which is very effective.

❧

I was still in a lot of thumb pain and having difficulty using my hand(s) for necessary activities, even after starting the NSAIDs, so one of my hand therapists referred me to an expert hand surgeon in San Francisco, Greg Buncke. He and his dad are at the cutting edge of serious hand surgery: they have made big toes into thumbs for people who lost a thumb and reattached severed limbs.

Dr. Buncke x-rayed my hands and found, yep, arthritis. (Arthritis is common in polio patients, in legs, back, and arms. It's often caused by normal wear and tear on the cartilage in joints, especially by overuse.) Both Dr. Buncke and my hand therapists have told me that arthritic hands do not necessarily look abnormal. There are people with badly misshapen hands who experience no pain, and people like me, whose hands look almost normal but are in a lot of pain.

We decided that the best solution for the hand problem was

cortico-steroid shots directly into the thumb joint. God-awful painful; exquisite, you might say. I cried every time I went, which was every five months for four years. I would take half a codeine and four Advil before I arrived at the office, and the injection still hurt like hell.

These shots are controversial; many doctors tell their patients that they can only get them for a while and then they must have surgery to remove the thumb joint and replace it with a curled-up tendon (like an anchovy) taken from the wrist. These doctors also say that the shots deteriorate the thumb joint. Some say the limit is ten or so shots in your lifetime. Dr. Buncke, however, has been giving these shots for nearly thirty years to more than one hundred patients, and he has never had anyone get a deteriorated joint from the shots, though he has operated on several people with deteriorated tissue whose doctors put the injection into the tendons or ligaments near the joint in error. He also feels that the cortico-steroid reduces inflammation, which is a cause of arthritis.

So the shots, when done correctly, may stave off further damage. He says no more than three a year, and I usually made it with just two—lucky for me, given the acute pain. But as of today, my pain level has become manageable, my thumbs seem stable, and it's been more than four years since I had my last shot!

Having more or less dealt with regaining the use of my right hand in 2010, after a year of pain and medical consultations, I began once again looking for a local polio doctor—this time to address the pain in the top of my left (strong) foot.

By this point, that foot had been painful for more than a year. Anyone I spoke to in the medical profession now considered it chronic and not a result of injury, and the question kept coming up, whether stated aloud or implied: "Why did you wait to address this instead of coming in when it first hurt?"

At this I would retell the story of how the pain in my foot was not keeping me from performing daily functions as my thumb pain had been, so I had handled that first. I respect doctors, but sometimes they seem to regard problems as occurring one at a time. Perhaps geriatric doctors don't think in those terms.

Through a few polio organizations (Post-Polio Health International in St. Louis, Northern California Post-Polio Group, and San Francisco Bay Area Post-Polio), I learned that the best of two or three northern California doctors with knowledge of polio was Dr. Carol Vandenakker-Albanese in Sacramento, about two hours away.

Rough estimates from 2005 indicate that there are approximately 400,000 US polio survivors who experienced paralysis—maybe by now, only about 334,000 (based on a rough extrapolation I did from death rates in the US population of people 55–85 years of age). In 2006, there may have been about 700,000 total polio survivors with or without initial paralysis in the US, maybe more if you count the people who had it and don't know they did. Maybe as many as one million. So that would leave us with perhaps 630,000 survivors in 2016—maybe closer to 900,000. Sounds like a lot, but those figures, considered low for a medical population, put us in the "rare disease" category, and because we are still dealing with new after-effects, it's no wonder Post-Polio Health International does a "We're Still Here" campaign every fall.

Further extrapolating has led me to think there may be about 9,000 polio survivors in the San Francisco Bay Area who had paralytic polio, although it may be lower; we have a lot of hills around here and for polio folks, flat is beautiful. But you'd think that in a population center as sophisticated as this, with at least a few thousand polio patients, there would be a few polio specialists. I do understand the reason for this lack, however: we are almost all older and dying off at a rate of around 10 percent a year, so it's a niche clientele, and difficult to support from a cost standpoint. Plus there's really no drug to prescribe that will cure us, and surgery is usually not an option. There's no quick fix.

I did get an appointment with Dr. Vandenakker. She has her polio clinic only on Friday mornings, however, and it would be three or four months before I could get in to see her.

⌒

While I waited to see Dr. Vandenakker, I managed to get an appointment with the same orthopedic surgeon who had assisted me with my badly sprained knee prior to the Germany trip the year before.

Our meeting was genial but strange. I was glad to see him again, since he'd helped me before and I was now well aware how few orthopedists had any knowledge of polio.

"Hello!" he said when he walked into the examination room. "What have you done to yourself this time?"

"Well, it's not an injury," I said. "I'm having extreme pain in the top of my strong foot, right here at the apex of this tendon."

"Apex!" He laughed. "What are you, a math major?"

"No, an accountant," I said. "That's just the way I speak."

"Okay, well, let's take a look at it. Walk across the floor for me."

I took a few steps back and forth.

"You have a fallen arch in your left foot," he said. "And the tibialis anterior tendon, the one that attaches at the top inside bone of the foot, is swollen and irritated from working to support the arch. You are also pronating that ankle, and that exacerbates the foot problem."

All this made sense. I also knew that the strap on my Mary Jane was irritating the tendon—but Mary Janes are the primary shoes that will stay on my paralyzed foot, so my strong foot pays the price for that.

While I sat on the table, he pulled on my feet and looked to see that my hips were straight. "Wow, you've got quite a length difference," he said, eyebrows raised. "It looks like about two inches."

"Yes, that's right, exactly two inches. It's been that for all of my adult life."

"It's really a shame about the length difference," he said. "Perhaps the tibia in this leg"—he pointed to my polio leg —"could be cut and stretched to get some length out of it."

"But wouldn't it take an awfully long time to get even a small amount of length?" I asked, surprised at the suggestion.

He mused and nodded slowly. "Yes, it could take a while, at least months . . ."

"And wouldn't I have to be in bed the entire time?"

"Well, yes, most likely."

I was incredulous but kept calm. This was yet another example of how doctors sometimes assume disabled people are just sitting home not doing much anyway, though I doubt that he was thinking about the details. In his defense, he was looking for possibilities.

He lightly tapped the shin of my left, strong leg. "Or perhaps a piece of the bone in *this* leg could be taken out, to shorten it."

"And if it didn't work, then I'd lose the use of both legs . . . do you think that would be wise?" I was not taking this seriously, but felt I should still be respectful.

"Yes, yes . . . there could be risk of infection . . . and then possible amputation. It was just a thought."

And an alarming one, don't you think? At least as cavalier as my mom's amputation idea forty years before.

He finally said, "I think you should get an arch support." (This sounded reasonable, at last.) "Do you know John Allen, the orthotist?"

"Yes, I've worked with him," I said. John makes orthotic braces for patients who have lost the use of muscles or tendons in their ankles and have a drop foot like me—instrumental in helping to prevent trips and falls.

The orthopedist called John while I was still in the room.

"I have Francine Falk-Allen here in my office," he told him, "and she needs an arch support. You know, she has a *horrendous* limp . . ."

He went on to describe the type of support he thought I should have, but I got stuck on "*horrendous*," and basically couldn't concentrate on anything else he said. No one had ever called it that before. I kept thinking, *Uh, I'm right here; I can hear you. "Horrendous?" Really? Have you never seen another person who's had childhood polio paralysis?* I would have expected him to use a word like "severe" or "marked." But many doctors have a habit of discussing patients as if we are not humans with emotional responses to their comments. "Horrendous," after all, comes from "horror." And it's true, my walk could be compared to Frankenstein; children imitate me in that mode. Dogs sometimes bark at me because my sway from side to side frightens them. But they're to be excused for their poor manners.

❧

At John's orthotic office, he told me that instead of just diving into an arch support, I should see a podiatrist first. And I did, a few days later; I had already made an appointment with him prior to seeing the orthopedist, on the advice of another doctor.

"I think you might have arthritis in that foot, besides a fallen arch," the podiatrist said after examining me.

"I come down fairly hard on that foot," I said.

"You can never have more than 100 percent of your weight on either foot at once, so each foot has equal weight on it," he replied.

True; however, I do leave my weight on that strong foot for about twice as long as the other one when walking, since my weak leg cannot hold me up on its own for more than a second. (The sound of my walk is "*DUNT-duh, DUNT-duh.*") When I am walking quickly my pace is somewhat more even, but with a limp, you do work the stronger foot harder. I walk as if I were falling from the small foot to the strong one—and I've done that for sixty-plus years. If nothing else, my larger foot was and is stressed from compensating in gait or stance for the lack of strength on the other side.

I was surprised that this highly-recommended podiatrist couldn't see all this, but I didn't bother trying to explain it to him. Often, doctors are pressed for time, and they go with their own primary diagnosis and analysis regardless of patient input. I didn't feel like he wanted to hear my theories.

He did suggest an arch support (he sold me a temporary altered ready-made), a small elastic sleeve around the arch, and also said that I should stretch the calf in that leg, because the outside calf muscle supports the arch by wrapping around underneath it.

In the weeks that followed, I tried doing the stretches—leaning my arms or hands against a wall with my weak knee bent and the strong leg back straight with foot flat on floor—and very soon I began to have worsened back and hip pain every time I did the stretch. I found, however, that I could do the stretch comfortably in the pool on the ramp we installed.

☙

We all have to adapt to whatever turns up in life. On a daily basis we make constant decisions and adjust to changes we did not expect.

Your favorite radio station won't come in for some reason, so you turn it off or grab your iPod for some tunes. You realize that your old toothbrush is not presentable any longer and you throw it in the trash, thinking you have a new one in the drawer—but you don't. You break a shoelace. Your back hurts, must have slept on it wrong. You keep having to change lanes on the freeway, seemingly cursed by a parade of tortoise-like Priuses (Prii?) or Volkswagen buses in the fast lane.

Stuff happens.

All this stuff happens to me, too, and to all disabled, handicapped, and differently-able people. We have a lot of other limitations and changes we have to adapt to on top of the usual things, which can be really overwhelming. Over time, of course you get used to it, but honestly, part of why I am such a terrible "time debtor" (often late) is that I have convinced myself that I'm the same as everyone else and can throw on my shoes and dash out the door. If only.

As my current polio doctor tells her student interns, "Polio patients know a lot about their bodies and aren't afraid to tell you. They are pretty sure they know everything, in fact!" (Wink. Or I hope she's winking.)

Some of my doctors have been remarkable and some of them, as you can see, have been, well . . . less so. Luckily, I've always managed to find my way to the good ones eventually.

keep on truckin'

*B*y the time I arrived at Dr. Vandenakker's door in Sacramento, about a year-and-a-half after my initial foot pain had begun, I had also begun having pain in the top of my strong hip, radiating from my spine. Whenever I'd had back pain previously, it had generally been low-back. I had found that stretching, icing for twenty-minute sessions, and sometimes massage were the most effective in alleviating my back pain. But this time, none of that was really working.

Dr. Vandenakker and the internist she was training were both far more concerned about my back pain than the foot. This was reasonable, since a fallen arch is something a lot of older people get, but if your back is giving you daily trouble, you may have something going on that is more serious. I was not happy to hear this, since the foot pain was constant and the hip/back pain was intermittent. But I complied.

We did x-rays and later an MRI, which together indicated a multitude of interesting lower-back maladies: slight disc degeneration, slight arthritis in my back and hips, slight disc swelling, and two Tarlov's cysts the size of Jordan almonds.

After doing my own research on this (Tarlov's cysts, it turns out, are abnormal sacs filled with cerebrospinal fluid that can cause nerve pain), my concern heightened and I got in to see another UC Davis back doctor. I took the MRI report to the appointment.

At his office, the doctor said, "The Tarlov's cysts are inconsequential and benign. They rarely cause problems. But I'd like to take a moving x-ray of your back. You have such a length difference in your legs, and I see from your MRI that you have arthritis, disc degeneration, and canal stenosis [narrowing of the spinal canal] in your back."

In the x-ray process, the machinery moved me up and down from the waist and x-rayed my back at the same time.

At 7:00 p.m. the doctor called me at home, after reviewing the x-rays. He said, with some urgency, "You are *way* too flexible. I recommend that you have a spinal fusion right away—as soon as possible."

I was alarmed. I consulted my other doctors: Dr. Vandenakker, Dr. Byers (my new back doctor here in Marin), my physical therapist, and even my gynecologist, who'd had back trouble. All of them recommended against surgery, telling me there was about a 50 percent chance that after surgery, my back would be the same or worse.

⤚

Dr. Vandenakker had recommended physical therapy for my back, which was helping, but we weren't getting anywhere with my foot, even after trying TENS electrical stimulus and ultrasound. I saw another orthopedist and he too was more concerned about my hip and back. Finally, John Allen recommended the orthopedist I now see. "He does nothing but feet," John said, and assured me he was the best in Marin.

This doctor knew just from looking at my foot that I had an irritated tendon and tenosynovitis, irritation of the tendon sheath, which was causing severe electrical-feeling shocks, sometimes every thirty seconds, making it impossible for me to sleep. He recommended I try a new procedure that often assists

300 ᕙᕗ FRANCINE FALK-ALLEN

stubborn tendons to heal, called PRP. It involves drawing some of the patient's blood, putting it into a centrifuge, and condensing it into platelet rich plasma (PRP), which is then shot into the tendon. The procedure was incredibly painful, my foot did not recover as quickly as expected, and I had to wear a plastic cast, making my limp worse—plus my back pain then worsened in the following weeks. Another dead end.

I requested one more prescription for physical therapy. Another new therapist suggested, after a couple of sessions, that we try using Kenesio Tex Gold tape. This is a stretchy tape that pulls the skin away from the tendons and ligaments slightly, which seems to result in their having more space to get proper circulation—very helpful for tenosynovitis nerve pain. One can wear the tape while showering and swimming, and it stays on for up to five days. The therapist started the tape on the outside of my knee and ran it down the exterior of my shin bone, made a U-turn across my ankle, went over the sore point on top of my foot, and then under my arch, ending just at the outside of my foot.

A week or so later, I had less pain. I could then do the arch- and tendon-strengthening exercises she recommended, using rubber Thera Bands, which provide varying levels of resistance. Gradually, over a period of many months, having worked up to about twenty minutes a day of exercises, my foot healed. (This time was in addition to the average of an hour of yoga and other physical therapy I do daily.)

After this long ordeal, I felt like I deserved a medal for perseverance, for not giving up on myself. Then again, as one of Dr. Vandenakker's student assistants said to me, "Pain is a great motivator."

Later, my strong thigh was diagnosed with tendinosis at the top back, a permanent condition I needed to address with more targeted exercises for two years. I now baby this with a seat cushion and limited time spent gardening. At one point I realized my foot and thigh had caused no pain for a while. I have experienced months of relatively low pain. My thumb, back, foot, and thigh pain do flare, and I have consistent mild-to-sharp arthritis pain in my major joints and back. Yoga, core strengthening, specific stretches, frozen gel packs, taping, and rest help correct or alleviate these issues. I also use non-steroidal anti-inflammatory drugs, such as ibuprofen, in moderation. The persistence in self-care is necessary for me to keep functioning. But as my polio doctor told me early on, I will probably never be completely pain-free.

I used to be a meditator, and I think I need to resume that practice. My pool therapy is a form of meditation, but activity requires a certain amount of attention and thinking—not the same as sitting meditation. Several studies indicate that people who meditate, especially using the technique called mindfulness, report feeling significantly less pain than other people, and that meditation is particularly helpful for people who are trying to reduce pain medication. (Mindfulness is simply focusing on the present, and watching thoughts come and go with no emotional attachment.) This lower experience of pain is in spite of the meditators' MRIs showing slightly more activity in the area of the brain associated with pain. It seems—based on their having less activity in the regions involved in emotion and memory—that meditators experience the pain but not the unpleasantness of the sensation, because their brains avoid identifying the sensation as painful.

I gradually fell off of meditating because every time I sat quietly, though I experienced more peace of mind and quiet joy, I also was flooded with inspiration and felt overwhelmed by all I wanted to accomplish—more than was physically or energetically possible for me. I also felt less tired and needed a little less sleep. So I will need to re-learn ignoring the inspiration and letting those thoughts go when I start up again. One more thing to do, but worthwhile.

There's hope. As a friend said to me decades ago when I was complaining about a situation, "One thing you can count on is change. The seasons come and go, and if this one is not going well, there's another one coming along. Put one foot on the ground and then the other." I do this attitudinally, even when I can't do it physically.

As we age, there is always physical stuff to deal with. I've been physically handicapped most of my life, so my parts wear faster and get out of balance more easily. It takes constant vigilance to take care of my dear, hard-working body and to keep on truckin'.

ageism and reverse ageism

*O*ne day a few years ago, I went into a hair salon to buy several products. Parking is not good in that area, so I didn't go in very often, and when I did, I bought a lot. I had found a parking space just a couple of doors away so I was only using my cane and not a crutch (or two). It's also very difficult to carry a bag when using two crutches, even of the arm cuff variety.

A new clerk at the salon, who had not seen me before and who looked to be only about ten to fifteen years younger than me, was hovering to make sure I could find what I was looking for.

Okay, over-serving is all right, but then she said, "Are you still driving, dear?"

I was stunned. I looked at her and replied, "Yes . . . I had polio." By which I meant, but did not say, "I'm not *that* old, *dear.* I'm not a decrepit old lady who can't drive anymore. I'm only about ten years older than *you, dear.*"

After I made my purchases, she said, "Would you like help to your car?"

I was happy enough to let her carry the bag, only about five pounds. Then of course she saw me climb into my Lexus hybrid SUV. Not really a little old lady's car. But it did throw me to be treated as if I were ancient and decrepit. I told my close girl-friend about the incident and she also thought it was weird. I feel it was the cane that caused the woman to stereotype me.

One of the oddest things people seem to think, in my point of view, is that most handicapped people are old. This has been brought home to me numerous times, but there are two very different ways in which this manifests. It will be helpful for you to know that my sister, my mother, my nieces, and I have all generally looked younger than we really are, at least on most good days, by about five to fifteen years—a combination of genetics and our use of cosmetics.

I use a handicapped placard and have permanently disabled vehicle license plates, and what a difference those have made in my life. I am often able to park close enough to my destination so that I can make the distance to a front door without having to sit down and take a break on the way—or having to skip the venue entirely. (Sometimes, if there's no close parking, I do just turn around and go home.)

So many times, an older person, usually in their fifties, sixties, or seventies, has come up to my car window, angrily asked me to roll it down, and said, "You can't park here! This is for *handicapped* people!" To which I have answered, sometimes with a little impatience but in later years with almost no emotion, "I *am* handicapped. I had polio as a child and I have a paralyzed leg." To which the curmudgeonly old person has invariably responded, "Oh. Well, you don't look old enough to be handicapped."

Though I am rarely at a loss for words, this leaves me speechless. Sometimes, the crank will say, "Oh, I'm sorry," turn, and walk away in embarrassment, or, "How could you have had polio?"—possibly thinking I'm lying. I always want to say, "You don't have to be old and ugly to be handicapped," but instead I usually explain that I was born in 1947, to which they usually reiterate that I don't look that old. Nice, but it rankles to be interrogated in this way. (These are folks who had not seen me walk; they'd only seen me from the shoulder up, sitting in the driver's seat of my car.)

This age-related disability mindset is a sort of reverse ageism. Since when did disability affect only old people? It's a prevalent concept: you are (or look) young, you could not be disabled, or, you must be old if you are disabled. There are plenty of young people with Crohn's disease, heart trouble, and other ailments, however, so I never assume, when I see a young person using a DP placard, that they are an able person doing something unethical (and also illegal). I have, however, occasionally asked people whom I've seen sprint from a DP spot into a store if they are disabled; when they've answered yes, I've said, "Oh! What's your disability? I've had polio." I hope that if they are using the placard illegally they'll think twice about it the next time, and if they're legit, I might learn something.

∾

The other side of this coin is that frequently when young people see me walk into a room with a cane, they treat me like I'm a really old person—which was weird when it happened in my thirties and forties, when I looked like I was in my twenties and thirties. There is a difference between being treated like you are handicapped and being treated like you are old.

People treating you like you are handicapped can vary from the obsequious hand-wringing over whether you're going to trip, the "do you need someone to hold you up to get across the room," and the "let's put you in a wheelchair-accessible room" at hotels (even when you don't have a wheelchair) to the much-appreciated simple query regarding whether you need a little assistance, might want to use the elevator around the corner, and/or are capable of managing a few stairs.

But being treated like you are old also means that when you are out with someone, if the waitperson sees your cane, you are always handed the check. It means that *maître d*s speak to you as if you might not be able to understand or might be deaf, and say, apparently in the way they talk to Grandma on holidays, "Now, are you okay sitting here?"

The first time this happened to me, I went to the restroom a bit later and took a really good look at myself in the mirror. I thought I looked a little tired, perhaps, but I certainly did not look elderly; *it must be the cane*. Of course, one must remember that to teenagers and people in their twenties, it may be that *everyone* looks old . . . but the cane certainly adds to that. I limped worse without it, but was not assumed to be old, just deformed or in pain. When I picked up my first cane at a flea market, I thought it was so hip looking—a little old tree branch with an antler handle—that it might enhance my appearance more than it aged me. I don't know how long I was under that delusion, but it was pleasant while it lasted.

᷍

When I was in my forties, I saw that being handicapped means people consider you "less than." I had not fully realized before then that I was part of a minority group—one toward which there was a substantial amount of discrimination.

Not long ago, I attended a concert at a big arena—a big deal for me, as the steep, scary steps are always hard to manage with my crutches. Maneuvering into a row is yet another challenge. I usually need whomever goes with me to spot me in case I lose my balance.

The headliner that evening (The Dixie Chicks!) eventually came on, and when they did, about a quarter of the people in the arena stood up in excitement. I stood up for a minute as well, but even standing I couldn't see the stage and could barely even see the jumbo screen. It reminded me of the scene in *The Polar Express* where the kid who wants to but does not quite believe in Santa can't see him for the crowd of elves in front of him; he can only see St. Nick's shadow.

Well, surely they won't all stand for long, I thought, and sat down to wait.

But several minutes later, no one in front of us was beginning to sit down—so finally, in frustration, I tapped one of the two young women in front of me on the shoulder and said, "Would you please sit down?"

The two women were also short and couldn't see as much if they sat, but I anticipated a slow domino effect: they'd ask the people blocking the view in front of them to sit as well, and so on.

"Look behind you," one of them said. "Everyone is standing up; just stand up."

I shouted back over the high volume, "I can't; I have a paralyzed leg." It also wasn't true that everyone was standing; some people behind us were as irritated as I was that the throng had stayed up for so long.

The young woman and her friend did try to accommodate me briefly; they tried sitting down. But they didn't ask anyone else to sit down, so they, like me, could only see the jumbo screen in bits. For about a minute they sort of half-stood and crouched—but then they gave up and stood.

We'd paid a lot for these seats. *I could have stayed home and listened to the CD*, I thought. *Is this how this concert is going to play out, sitting here behind a wall of people?*

I found it incredible that people would block others' view for more than a moment. When I saw the Stones and all those hot groups in the sixties, maybe we'd stand up and dance for a minute when they played a song that was irresistible, but to stand and block others' view for a long period of time at a seated concert was rare. If we wanted to dance or stand, we got floor seats and danced in the aisle. Finally, after a couple of songs were sung, some people began to sit, and I could see the stage again.

After the concert, on our way to the car, my companion expressed irritation with me.

"You were being selfish and inappropriate," she said. "You should have apologized to those girls. You should have just lived with it. Did you see how they were trying to crouch and were so uncomfortable? You played the crip card! It was okay for you to ask, but when no one else sat down, it was inconsiderate and not compassionate for you to let them try to accommodate you. Especially without an apology!"

I heard that—but I'm not sure I would have done anything differently in that situation. What I'd do next time is get seats on the aisle nearest the stage or see if there were ADA seats available (although usually those are for a wheelchair with a companion, not a person who wants an actual seat), or just not go.

Internet research on my friend's part found that "concert etiquette" has people in 50/50 camps, the polite "you should sit" group and the (I'm guessing) libertarian "you should be able to do whatever you want" crowd. The point being that I can't expect people to accommodate me, that I have to deal with my condition on my own—something that is not news to me.

I felt that I had not been 100 percent honest with the two girls, because I can stand, I just can't stand there for fifteen minutes or more like most everyone else can, especially with nothing to hold on to, to steady myself. I actually would have liked to stand up once or twice and shake my booty around a bit later in the set, but I felt I couldn't do that after telling the girls I had a paralyzed leg. I didn't think they were going to want to have a long, shouted-over-the-loud-music conversation about it with this older woman. They were, appropriately, into the concert, and not interested in having a conversation with cranky old me.

On the other hand, if I looked to be in my eighties instead of my fifties, I suspect they might have been more accommodating. Poor old lady. But maybe not.

I wish it had turned out differently, and that all of us had gotten what we wanted, which was to see the whole concert.

So, there's another example of "you should not expect that you get to do everything everyone else does," and also one of assuming that disabled people should always be nice and concurrently not put anyone else out. Well, it's true, "Human life is conditioned and unfree," as the *I Ching* says. So, there you are, I have warts, as do those people who are view-blockers. But if we don't ask, we don't even have a shot at having our needs met; that, at least, is true for everyone.

occasional poster child

*T*he Sufi spiritual name I was given means "the one who has overcome." I thought when I was given it, *Wow, somebody sees that,* just like when my Grandma Allen gave me my world globe and atlas with a card that said, "Happy birthday, little soldier." When I read that, I knew she saw me—not just for being a polio survivor but for being a crippled kid with no daddy. A bit too much adulthood too soon, and not the aspect that gives you freedom but rather the one that imparts responsibility and a need for strength. So, I appreciate all that. Yes, polio survivors and other disabled people have a certain heroism, all of us. But I would have preferred to be one of the kids on the block.

When I was in my thirties, one friend said to me, "You aren't handicapped, Francine, you just limp."

I had then, and still have now, various thoughts about that comment. What she meant was that my disability doesn't keep me from functioning; I simply have a gimpy walk. I've had other close friends and new acquaintances tell me they do not think of me as handicapped as well. When I was discussing handicaps about forty-five years ago with a fellow I greatly respected and who knew me fairly well, he said, "You don't really notice the limp, Francine." I am guessing this is because people get used to how I walk, just like you get used to someone's lisp or droopy eyelid or whatever we may have going on. People who think this way are also generous about people's differences, and not everyone has that nature. These attitudes have helped me feel like a normie. And I have certainly worked hard over the years to be thought of as normal, at least in the range of activities in which I could participate.

Either I have put on a good show or my peeps just don't realize how weary a time I have had. Additionally, when I was younger, it was easier. I could climb stairs without holding on to banisters then, though it was difficult. Now I take them one at a time—one foot on the step, then the other, then on to the next step—and I need both the banister and my cane or crutch. Sixty-seven years of limping has worn many parts of me out, and I'm weaker now. Now I get the occasional comment, "You must really be hurtin' today, kid," when a friend sees me using my crutches. Sometimes I am in pain, but usually I'm "only" extremely fatigued and need some physical support.

Another friend said recently, when she helped me carry my stuff up a stairwell, "I'm so sorry it's so hard for you. It's not fair, especially since you're such a nice person."

I didn't debate the issue of how nice I may or may not be. I did tell her that some people think I am nice because all this happened to me.

"Those people are mean," she said.

I am moved when people acknowledge my struggle without dwelling on it. I also appreciate that people now see that I'm in physical difficulty—but it was always that way, just a little less so. Disability becomes more apparent to people when one uses an assistive device. This is part of why many aging adults resist using them, when in fact they improve function and help to keep our parts from incorrect use or from wearing out earlier.

One thing that happens to me from time to time is that when someone I know has had a leg or foot injury, they'll tell me, "I've been thinking of you since this happened." I'll say,

"Yes," and wait—and often what follows is something along the lines of, "Man, what you must have been through. What you must go through." To this I might say, "Yeah, it hasn't been easy," and ask how they've been doing with it all; sometimes I have tips for use of crutches, managing energy, icing, whatever. And I appreciate that they have "gotten" it. Sometimes they then want to know how old I was when I got polio, and I hear or see them silently doing the math. Thirty years of this. Forty years of this. Sixty-seven years of this.

I'm embarrassed to tell you that I also cannot help but think sometimes in those instances, since I am not a saintly person, *I'm surprised you didn't think of this before; you've seen me limping around for thirty years now, at least . . .*

I'd never say that, of course. I take no satisfaction in people feeling bad about not having thought of me in this light before. It just surprises me. It seems to take common experience for most of us to see others' difficulties.

I started grappling with physical hardship so early in life that there was hardly a time when I didn't immediately see it in others. I saw the girl with the deformed arm and knew her limitations, knew that her pretty face might not make up for that arm when the fellows were thinking of whom to date. I notice when people have a limp and can often guess what the problem is. But I probably did a little kicking-the-dog as a kid, too—making fun of the "queer" guy behind his back, for instance. I'm deeply ashamed of that now, and fortunately dropped that prejudice before I was twenty, but I lived in a small town with little diversity, and was raised to be prejudiced in many respects— something I now find ironic, given my own condition. My mother must have been so embarrassed by my crippled body and walk.

Often when I first meet someone, they will right-out-front say, "Oh, what happened to your hip?" As I mentioned earlier, my deformed hip and pelvis and short leg require me to roll my small hip up so that my foot clears the floor. As I've aged, it has become even more apparent that something's going on there.

When people find out my walk is a residual from polio, they seem to be sorry they asked. First there is that moment of silence for the polio epidemic, both of us thinking about that; then, sometimes, a naïve person will say, "Oh, well it will get better!" Sometimes I tell them it won't, and sometimes I just let it go. It makes people feel bad to learn that my condition is permanent.

Despite the occasional awkwardness, I appreciate when people want to talk about my disability, because I like to inform people about polio and its late effects. This can be a bit of a downer at a party, though, unless the person I'm talking to finds all kinds of life experiences fascinating and/or wants to get to know me. If someone is going to become depressed by discourse on disability, I'd rather we talk about our other interests.

⌐

You have probably determined by now that I am not one of those constantly optimistic people about whom it's said, "She never complains. I know she's having a hard time, but you never hear a negative word out of her." To me that sounds like, "She's such a sweet old grandma."

That's not me. I do know a few handicapped people like that, and I'll admit it, I have encouraged them to complain. Not because I want them in my rebellious camp, but because I believe it's healthy to tell the truth—that sometimes it is overwhelmingly difficult to be paralyzed, in pain, exhausted, nauseous, light-headed, dizzy, or whatever the condition is, especially when others your own age or who share your general fitness level are able to do much more. I wouldn't advise anyone to dwell on it and turn it into a litany, but some of the "ladies" I've known who are handicapped who seemingly do not complain do it in another way, which borders on being passive-aggressive. They say, for example, "Oh, no, I wouldn't want to bother anyone," if you ask if they tried to find a ride to an event they wanted to attend. Brings to mind the old, "I'll just sit here in the dark . . ."

Here's something you might not realize: some of the handicapped people that folks think are so nice and uncomplaining take opioid medication and are a little spacey, so they don't really care that much about their condition—which is not the same as real optimism, if you ask me. To those who really are in a hell of a lot of pain or exhaustion and truly are happy all the time, I say, accolades. Maybe they're saints, or maybe they were born insanely happy, or maybe they've found the secret to life. (The Dalai Lama says the purpose of life is happiness. And he says that question, "What is the purpose of life?" is easy. The hard question is, "How do you maintain happiness?")

I notice that some people aren't motivated to look at life circumstances deeply, or would prefer not to. Sometimes I think that must be nice; I have never felt I had the choice to Scarlett O'Hara my experience ("I'll think about that later"). I do practice focusing on the positive, but that's not the same as pretending the situation isn't difficult. And no disrespect to the Dalai Lama, whom I believe to be enlightened, but I'm not sure the purpose of life *is* happiness. I'm not sure life even has a purpose. But I think an aspiration in life can or should be learning how to attain or maintain peace in the face of adversity. And peace does seem to bring happiness!

Scientific studies have shown that happiness comes directly from low expectations. My husband and I looked at each other with amusement when I read this to him recently. Lowering my expectations has definitely been a challenge for me.

‿

A common thing I've seen in disabled or handicapped people is what lies at the other end of the spectrum from optimism: the resentment and anger that is natural to feel, whether occasionally or as something that comes up so much it wrecks your life. Watch *Coming Home, Forrest Gump,* or *The Sessions* for some contrast. Those were all quite believable anger scenarios, in my estimation. For some folks, the anger at being limited physically has become a *modus operandi.* And I agree with normies who think these folks should try to find *something* to be happy about.

I believe that it is more difficult, in some ways, to become handicapped as an adult—which almost everyone will eventually be in some way—than it is to live with it all of your life. We with lifelong disabilities have had year after tedious year to get used to it, whereas if it happens suddenly—if, for instance, a person is made paraplegic after a car accident, has a stroke or a botched operation, or loses a limb in a military injury—he or she has gone from probably being at the peak of physical ability to far less ability than they thought they might have at, say, eighty. It's almost too tough. And chronic pain makes it even worse. A lot of people who have had these unfortunate events become drug addicts or alcoholics, and honestly, I don't blame them. I am saddened when they are moved to the point of suicide, of course, but I would never blame them for this choice.

Disability wears on you, and not only emotionally; it causes your body to wear out faster or requires more maintenance to keep it in shape. It takes a lot of perseverance to keep addressing a handicapped condition. I do not advocate suffering. I only hope that those who are depressed, enraged, or deeply aggrieved by being disabled can pull some motivation out of it, use the minimum medical aids necessary to manage pain, and find some joy somehow. I want that for everyone and feel fortunate that I am nearly overwhelmed by all that beckons me to understanding and study. As Rudyard Kipling wrote, "The world is so full of a number of things, I'm sure we should all be as happy as kings."

Some people have used their anger energy well, by channeling it into things like advocating for DP (disabled person) rights or learning to play wheelchair basketball (although that's mostly for people who have major upper body strength to begin with, and no upper body fatigue issues). A lot of polio survivors have become doctors or lawyers and done great good not only for polio patients but for thousands of disabled and normal people. Me, I was just grousing, so I wrote this book.

aging well

*T*hese days, you will find me in a pool almost daily unless rain is pouring or the air or water's too cold. My pool therapy includes walking, yoga or stretches, arm exercises, core strengthening and stabilizing, kicks while standing and while floating on a "noodle," and swimming laps. Although water creates resistance and is harder for most people to walk in than on land, it is much easier for me to walk in waist- or midriff-deep water, since the water helps hold me up. This is the only way I can get the benefits of walking; otherwise, it's a detriment to me, because of the strain it causes in my body.

We use a solar heater for our pool in warmer months and gas in winter (yes, it's horribly expensive); polio patients are not supposed to remain in water under 86 degrees Fahrenheit for more than a few minutes due to our circulatory problems. I used to work out all winter, an average of about an hour, four days a week, in temps averaging 52–65 degrees. In the summer, I was doing about seven hours a week. And what with sweeping off the cover, opening it and closing it again, putting on sunscreen or three or four winter water jackets and a ski mask, it's quite a process. (Richard says I look like a ninja when I wear my mask with my black swim jacket, sunglasses, and a waterproof base-ball cap. I thought that when I got out and pulled my robe hood over my head I looked more like the Unabomber, so I'm happy to think I have some ninja in me.)

A year or two ago, all this exercise, in addition to my daily ten to twenty minutes of yoga, therapy stretches, and core strengthening, plus gardening, running errands, and cooking dinner almost every night, began to fatigue me even more than what is usual for me. I had to be prone at least once but prefera-bly twice each afternoon, for at least twenty minutes. Finally, my polio doctor diplomatically asked me if I didn't think I might be exercising a little *too* much. I smiled and said, "Uh, ya think?!!! Yes, I agree."

I've since cut back to three to five days a week of one hour of water therapy, often a little more in one session, and I'm slightly less tired now. This reduction in my exercise means I must limit my food intake, however—especially simple carbs—or I gain weight daily. Not that everyone doesn't have to do that, but for people who have little choice but to sit a lot, the danger is imminent. I don't want to trade fatigue for diabetes or a heart attack.

Having cut back on exercise a little, I'm less dependent on resting and can get by with lying down just once an afternoon (if I can fit it in). When polio, MS, cystic fibrosis, or chronic fatigue folks overdo it for some time, it's common for us to not get full strength back. Management of energy output is really important and not much fun. I feel I lost a little strength in the last five or ten years, but am now stable.

❦

And then there's Richard. We have some separate interests and are both pretty independent, but we agree on a lot and have similar, goofy senses of humor and a deep emotional bond. We worked through the child-bearing question early in our relationship, given that I was in my mid-forties when we met, and by the time we married I was approaching menopause, anyway.

Now we have been together for twenty-five years, and married for twenty. It has not been easy all the time, for either of us. I had been unmarried for eighteen years when I met Richard, and he was eleven years younger and had never lived with a woman. Our independence led us to some arguments, but also, more positively, to consenting that we each do what we wanted or needed to do much of the time.

My regret for him is that post-polio fatigue came much earlier than I expected—in my early fifties. Although we discussed what might happen as I aged before we married, neither of us thought that I would lose the ability to walk as far as I used to before I was in my seventies or later.

I'm sorry that my younger husband has had to share this disappointment with me. I know it scares him sometimes, especially when I'm in pain or cranky over fatigue or loss of function, whether it's temporary or something that threatens to be ongoing. This upsets me too—that he has fear or trepidation about my future condition—but I try to keep the perspective that it's a package deal. We have taken care of each other in different ways for over two decades now: I handle or manage much of the physicality of our life, and he provides nearly all the income and does do chores as well. I anticipate that there will be a good twenty years in front of us.

Aging is crummy for everyone at some point. He may get Alzheimer's. (We joke that if he does, I'll die first and he'll be alone, but he'll forget me anyhow.) I also think women deal with aging a little better than men. It may be in women's DNA to expect difficulty and plan for it, or perhaps it's a learned skill.

But we have a good life. Our relationship is normal and healthy, when I look around at what's going on with others.

We've been to counseling to work out difficulties, most of which have had more to do with concepts we grew up with than my being handicapped, though that has sometimes been a factor. No surprise, he's got his "stuff," too, and I've come to think that almost everyone has some handicap or another.

Luckily, Richard is a techno guy, not an outdoorsman. As long as he has a computer, an iPhone, a TV, and a stereo, he's happy. And there are many activities we can share: We enjoy swimming together in our pool. We make love as much as any other long-married couple I know (or so I assume!). We love to go to movies, concerts, occasional stage shows, and dinner with friends, and to have them over when I have the energy to put together a party, or a little meal for our best buddies.

We travel as much as we can now, too, partly because we see that the older I get, the more difficult it will be for me, and probably later on the same will be true for him. I've been using wheelchairs in airports for most of our relationship, but in some "walking cities" I find I usually need an electric scooter. I just purchased a small collapsible battery-powered travel tricycle, and that has broadened my horizons, but it's likely that someday there will be places I cannot visit. Amsterdam is particularly difficult for handicapped people; the transportation is awful. I will never see Positano, the beautiful Italian seaside cliff city with its thousands of steps. But will you go there before you die? Perhaps not.

The other reason we are traveling now instead of later is that Richard's parents planned to travel after his dad retired in his seventies, but he soon began having back trouble, which made it difficult for him to sit on airplanes for more than an hour. So saying "We'll do that when we retire," began to sound unrealistic.

Given that we both love to stay home, we will probably really enjoy that when neither of us are working. There is a great deal of natural beauty and culture in the San Francisco Bay Area, and we'll never run out of things to do and see here. But we're not yet done gadding about.

So for anyone who wonders how it is to live with or be married to a handicapped person, and is it not awfully hard, or could you do it, or is it worth it?—all I can say is that nearly everyone discovers the answer to those questions eventually. You or the person you choose as a spouse will one day have physical limitations (unless death comes early in a sudden tragedy, so let's hope you *do* get old and creaky), and there is always something bigger and more beautiful in our lives than our difficulties. Often, that something is love for at least one other person.

Love may not conquer all. But respect, affection, and humor go a long way toward making things right, no matter one's physical challenges.

On a rented scooter at Yosemite.

40

—

chop wood, carry water,
stir the oatmeal

The title of this chapter is a paraphrase from Ram Dass's book *Be Here Now*. It refers to minding what's in front of you and just keeping on with daily tasks and accepting them in a peaceful manner. I couldn't find the oatmeal part when I perused the book again recently, so maybe someone else said that. Stirring the oatmeal, in any case, can be a meditation. These things we do are sacred, the rituals of existence, if we can be present to them—if we can just *be here now* with a focused mind.

I'm seventy as I write this. I'm a little chubby but definitely not obese. I have never inhaled tobacco other than a couple cigarettes in high school, once or twice (I found it quite painful). I have exercised fairly regularly most of my life. Aside from childhood illnesses, the breast cancer bout thirteen years ago, occasional colds or flu, a couple of cases of pneumonia, and my shingles debacle, I have had no major health risks or organ issues. I'm mostly healthy.

But the stuff I go through with regard to my structure—the tendon, muscle, and bone effects rendered by polio, in tandem with spots of arthritis—has me walking and sometimes feeling like I am ten years older than I am. It's not constant, but it is frequent. I still accomplish more than many normies do in one day, but it's in spite of a lot of challenges.

It takes me longer than many people to get things done if walking or standing is involved. I'm perpetually late, partly due to all the stuff I have to do to get my body going for the day and partly from my mom demonstrating, unrelentingly, how to be tardy—my former shrink said it is in some people's neurological makeup, so maybe I'm slightly off the hook. I still chide myself, though, because I once attended a four-day conference with about two hundred polio survivors, and most of them did not seem to have the chronically late paradigm in their lives, even though some of the women were impeccably groomed. I think I stay up later than most older people and try to jam too much into too short a day. Oh well.

To give you a taste of what my daily life is like, let's talk about my routine.

❧

When I go to bed, I take 200 mg of Neurontin (Gabapentin), officially a nerve drug given to epileptics to help prevent seizures—but for me, it's partly for pain, partly to ward off muscle cramps or spasms; red yeast rice, for lowering cholesterol; melatonin, to help me stay asleep; and calcium, because I already have osteopenia moving toward osteoporosis (very common in polio bones; they don't pound the earth as hard as other human legs, and pounding makes bones stronger).

I occasionally awaken to sharp, stabbing pain in one place or another. It's usually the tendon in the top of my strong foot. Sometimes I get a cramp in that foot or leg while asleep. Massaging the calf or the arch until my strong foot no longer looks all crabbed up like it's the crippled one has always worked so far. Lately this problem has become rare, due to my perseverance in exercising and strengthening my foot tendons.

The other wake-up calls are aches in one of my hips, my

low back, my shoulder, or arthritis in my elbows or thumbs. It is hard for me to get comfortable in any position because, on my right side, the most comfortable position, my left leg is too heavy on top of my polio leg. I've tried pillows but they always seem to be the wrong size, fail to stay in place, or make me too hot. I have a mini-pillow that I put between my knees; it doesn't stay in place, of course, but it helps me get to sleep and I wake up with less or no knee pain. It's hard for me to roll over fully from one side to the other. Usually I sit up, turn, and lie down again. Conversely, sitting up sometimes wakes me up, and then I have difficulty getting back to sleep.

If it's not the pain that wakes me, it's the bathroom run a lot of older folks make in the middle of the night. We keep our bedroom virtually pitch black, since almost any light awakens me, so I have to wake up sufficiently so that I don't fall on my way, or slam my feet into a misplaced shoe or malevolent furniture, especially since I "list" from side to side. So, around 5:00 a.m., I stand up in the dark and wait a few seconds before I take off. Falling in the daytime is bad enough; falling in the dark is dangerous. Having a drop foot and no brace in the middle of the night also means that I'm safer if I do a Frankenstein walk—feet wide apart, arms out for balance—until I am more awake. I always hope Richard doesn't wake and see me as it's particularly unattractive, *Bride of Frankenstein* notwithstanding.

Sometimes I cannot get back to sleep afterward, and have to swallow some Chinese herbs, or, very rarely, something stronger, half or one-third of an Ambien. It's especially important that I get enough sleep, because when I'm tired, I am at higher risk for tripping, slipping, and falling, and I'm more prone to pain or having weak or inflexible parts. If I'm annoyed by all of that, I can also be bitchy. (*Moi?! Oui.*) Just like other tired people, but probably with more self-blame and wishing I were not handicapped.

ᴖ

Hopefully after seven hours of sleep, I awaken to a good morning. Some days I have very little difficulty walking; some days my leg and back are so weak that I have to hold on to furniture, counters, or walls to get from room to room, referred to as "traveling" by physical therapists, and not considered a good practice. I often need a cane for support if I'm having a weak day.

Every morning, I spend a few minutes sitting on a rug with our two cats, Leila and Lucy, and then I stay down there (it's a big deal to get up from the floor, so I don't get down *to* it more than once or twice a day) and do some physical therapy, core strengthening, and yoga for about fifteen minutes. A person who does not have a stand-up routine worked out after sitting on a rug may have difficulty getting to a telephone or chair after a fall, so I intend to keep doing floor exercises as long as possible.

After this, I have a normal day for a while. I am a black tea fiend, so I have to have that, and it does get my energy up (a good excuse for a habit beloved by those of us with British blood or cultural inclinations). I eat a high-protein breakfast, often an egg and some leftover sautéed veggies or some plain yogurt with berries and nuts. I never skip breakfast, because I have to take my supplements, a tiny amount of generic Mobic, plus Allegra for my tinnitus, and I can't take this stuff on an empty stomach.

Next, if I'm going to do my pool workout in the morning, there are the sunscreen and suit-up routines. I take a towel, maybe the pool jackets and a robe, plus my cap, goggles, ear plugs, a heavy clock (that the wind cannot blow over) with secondhand for timing my exercises, waterproof ball cap, sunglasses to ward off cataracts and macular degeneration, water shoes, maybe ankle weights, phone, and some other accoutrements. I practically need a Sherpa—the stuff is heavy—but I would never make two trips.

Before I get in the pool, I usually do at least a half hour of gardening. Next is sweeping leaves off the pool cover. We have an electric control for the pool cover; it's operated by holding a key, which taxes my funky arthritic thumbs, but it's necessary. Then the pool sweep has to be fished out of the pool.

Now I can finally get in the water! All this, from suiting up to entry, takes maybe fifteen minutes (plus the time spent gardening).

I do eight minutes of walking in the shallow end, then forty minutes spent in kicks, arm exercises with paddles, leg and arm stretches, yoga moves and isometric strengthening, squats, jumping, and sideways walking. Then, I take a noodle float down to the deep end, where I do various kicks and leg lifts for ten minutes. After all this, I do eight minutes of swimming. Then one last leg stretch and I'm done, an hour later. Some days I do abbreviated or longer sets, but include all of the above in proportion to the time I have available. And of course, after I swim, I put the sweep back in the pool and close the cover.

As to the gardening, we have a mow-and-blow guy who works here about three hours a month, and annual tree pruners, but otherwise I do most of the outdoor maintenance on our one-third acre—trimming, weeding, pruning the roses and shrubs, planting or harvesting my few veggies and herbs, feeding the roses and citrus, all that stuff. Richard feels about gardening as I feel about root canals, so I am looking to lower-maintenance replacement plants as things die off, and eventually hiring more help.

⤳

We've almost come to The Putting On of the Shoes. This is a big deal. I cannot throw on a pair of flats or sandals or any other slip-on shoe and do a quick trip to the store or anyplace else— never could and never will.

First off, as you may remember, I wear two drastically different sizes. Please pardon me if part of this section is a duplication, but it's a huge issue in my life. Not only are my feet four and one-half sizes apart, my polio foot is a seven-year-old girl's size and my other foot is in the women's range. The only way I can get shoes that match, even roughly, is to buy in the youth range—already a narrow selection, and made even narrower by my requirements (basically, a supportive Mary Jane with a strap, or an Oxford, a loafer, or, infrequently, a boot).

Depending on which shoes I'm wearing, I might first put a silicon bunion shield on the big toe of my polio foot. I pull on a knee-high stocking over that, and then I don my knee-ankle orthotic (AFO), the minimal brace that supports my ankle and my drop foot so I am less at risk of catching my toe on things. Another knee-high over the brace keeps it in place; otherwise it slaps up and down annoyingly with each step, and can cause a callus to form. I can only wear sandals if they have lots of straps, especially around the ankle. They aren't really safe for daily wear so I only wear them around a pool. Sometimes people suggest that I not wear "those hot stockings," but there's no choice if I want to wear my orthotic brace and be safe.

I also wear a silicon heel cup in the polio shoe because, for some reason no one can explain, that foot has started sliding from side to side in shoes. It may be because my ankle fusion is weakening and the ankle is starting to pronate a bit. In my left shoe, I place a custom-made arch support which has a heel cup to keep that foot from sliding side to side. The arch support assists the fallen arch and pronation issues I've had in my strong foot. Sometimes I need to wrap my strong foot with a little lightweight Coban tape if I'm having pain in that poor pesky tendon.

Now I can actually put my shoes on. But first, getting my foot into a pair of pants: I can't point my toes down on my polio foot, so I carefully wrangle my foot and leg down through the pant leg. Then, on go the shoes.

This whole shoe-donning process takes about five minutes. (I know, sounds minimal, but isn't the time to put on shoes usually seconds?) I do this at least once a day, often two or three times—it's not comfortable to wear the orthotic when I'm resting—and you might think I'd be used to it all by now, but the process always feels like a bother, especially if I'm late for an appointment.

Sometimes I put the whole set of gear on and take a few steps and something is painfully wrong, so I have to take it all off and start over. That seems to predictably happen on days when I am running late. I often swear prolifically and creatively on those occasions and damn the freaking polio virus. Again.

‿‿

Sometimes I'm too tired after the pool and shower to stand up and fix a meal, though I'm supposed to do this to recharge, so I lie down and read for a while and then am ready to get going again.

When I've done temp work for another accountant or a little bookkeeping, I have put in from three to six hours of work daily and then had to stop. It's become too hard on my back and lower-body tendons to sit for longer than that, especially when I add in the commute. I have only "done tax season" for at most three months a year recently, and have decided that now that I'm seventy, I'm going to quit. At home, I sometimes set a timer so I'm reminded to stand up for a minute. Both prolonged sitting and standing are really hell for me—something neither my mom nor I knew when we used to talk about which professions would allow me to sit all day. Getting up and moving around a little is even more essential for me than it is for normies because of the imbalance I have in my back.

On any given day I may pay bills, manage medical providers or health insurance, run errands, shop, manage repair people, go to doctor appointments or my writing group, and so on. I try to get out and have lunch with a girlfriend at least a couple of times a month. Since I can no longer do a lot of the things I used to do, like go for a hike, go to places that require a lot of walking, or go to a Sufi dance meeting, I make it a point to socialize when I can so I don't get too isolated. I love to be with my girlfriends, mostly one at a time, and am in several groups that meet regularly: a supportive monthly women's group, which has the purpose of listening with compassion; a Sufi women's group, which does spiritual practices and hangs out for a day together every two months; the polio support group I started, meeting once per quarter; a writers' Meetup group I founded, which I facilitate twice a week; and a tax professionals' group, which has a fun small lunch bunch that meets once a month. I have taken my new TravelScoot battery-powered trike to fairs and to malls, where a little shopping has become realistic for me again, though it's not a priority for me (I didn't get the shopping gene), and I look forward to going to parks again, where my friends can walk and I can tool alongside them.

The internet and email are a time sinkhole, but also a necessity for me. I have shopped online for twenty years for all our clothing and shoes, as well as many household items and gifts. It was a breakthrough for me to realize I could do this instead of foot shopping. At the same time, I can sit down intending to spend a half-hour on email plus its attendant responses or new tasks, and get up two hours later angry with myself.

Around 7:00 p.m., after resting, it's time to cook dinner. I like a freshly made meal, with a nice piece of fish or chicken and interesting veggies, with maybe a little brown rice, sweet potato, squash or quinoa, and Richard needs a healthy dinner because there is no telling what he's eaten during the day. Meal prep takes me forty-five to ninety minutes. After cooking, I'm sometimes in considerable pain, either in my back or strong foot, from standing for too long. I try to organize things in order to do part of the prep at the low counter we put in opposite our sink, and have been more committed to this of late. Otherwise I can barely make it to the dinner table or the couch when dinner's ready.

By later in the evening, I am ready to veg in front of a good movie, and I'm wiped out by about 11:00 p.m., though we're rarely asleep by then.

Weekends we finish what didn't get done during the week and sometimes get into the pool together, go out to dinner or get take-out (on weekends, I deserve a break), spend time with friends, go see a movie or hear some music. When we go out, Richard drops me off near the venue. If he can't, and it's more than a half-block walk, I use two crutches (instead of just one or a cane), or assemble the scooter.

This is how I live. I think it's similar to other older women, just with more limitations. Being handicapped (or aging) requires a lot of discipline, especially given I've been rather like an oldish person since I was three. No surprise that I like a glass of champagne now and then.

as good as it gets

If the world were merely seductive, that would be easy. If it were merely challenging, that would be no problem. But I arise in the morning torn between a desire to improve the world and a desire to enjoy the world. This makes it hard to plan the day."

—E. B. White

This quote describes how I feel almost every morning.

In the Jack Nicholson/Helen Hunt movie with the same title as this chapter, he plays a guy with a pretty advanced case of obsessive-compulsive disorder, OCD. She plays a waitress and dedicated mom with a kid who has a serious chronic illness. They are an unlikely romantic partnership, but they seem fated to have some kind of relationship. In one scene where he's in his psychiatrist's office (he's butted in to get a session, feeling that his issues are more pressing than other people's), he looks around the waiting room at the other patients and says, "What if this is as good as it gets?"

Indeed.

Living with a disability is limiting. There is no way around that. But we all have limitations of some type. My physical ones are just well above average—and perhaps way below that of an amputee or maybe a blind person, I don't know. I try to keep away from comparing handicaps, though it does come up, given the competition for handicapped parking and good seating. *How handicapped* are *you, anyway?* No one ever says this, but I'll bet I'm not the only one who's had the thought.

I once read an article by an eighty-nine-year-old polio survivor. He said that having had polio as an infant had left him with a debilitated upper thigh and he'd had one foot-tendon operation. He'd actually tried to join the army, perhaps for the Korean War, and been rejected. He found himself with a drop foot when he got into his seventies, which slowed him down a bit—but he said polio had basically not affected his life, except for his not being allowed to fight in a war.

I chuckled while reading his story, and said aloud, "Good for you, Friend. I wish I could say the same." Polio, as you now know, has affected my life every day since I contracted it. By the end of most weeks, I feel like I have climbed Mount Everest.

It's interesting to me that many people have accepted me as totally normal even though there have always been a lot of things I could not do or had difficulty doing. Either they could not see it was difficult, or they cared so to include me that they acted as if I were the same as anyone else. Then there are the folks who saw I was handicapped and would be a consideration and drawback for group activities (the ropes course). And there are my friends who don't know I have to rest after walking a short distance or cooking dinner, or who perhaps have silently thought, *Good for her that she keeps up despite her limitation.* People do like us best when we try not to let our disabilities limit us. I can tell you, though, that as a group, polio survivors almost always take on more than we should, and we'd do better to conserve our energy.

I have a friend who thinks I am a hero who takes on a lot of life experience and just gets on with it despite difficulty. I so appreciate that she sees that—and though at first it felt embarrassing to hear her praise, she has gotten through to me. I do find, however, that sometimes people who put us crips on a pedestal are then disappointed when we eventually display that we have the same warts as everybody else.

Like I said, not a poster child.

Occasionally I see myself as heroic, but usually I just see my condition as the hand I got dealt (and I'd as soon have had a royal flush). Everyone has something they have to face that they wish they didn't. Some folks have clearly had a difficult life, while others seem to have had it easier, but any unwanted problem seems tough to the one who's having it—and any choice is a problem, of sorts, anyway. There are lots of problems to answer daily, and it's possible to address them as curiosities! Experiences! I'm not saying I can always do this, but it is a muscle I had to develop relatively early. In every moment, we are choosing our actions and attitudes, whether automatically or with awareness.

The crux of the matter with problems is what we do with them, not that we get them in the first place. That we keep getting up and looking out the window and finding something to anticipate and to motivate us is the real stuff of life.

In the long run, people love us for what we bring to the party, not because we are heroes. There's a bit of star power in being a hero—some might want to be around that energy for the warmth, intensity or because the strength might rub off—but heroism can distance people a bit, too. Being strong and being tough are not the same, but from the outside, they may be misconstrued.

We can't much help what pops into our heads, but I like to be aware that what I think either limits or expands how I see myself and others. And I've found that appreciation and gratitude are the keys to happiness. It is not always easy to remind myself that I'm lucky I have not spent my life in a wheelchair. I do reflect on that sometimes; I actually say to myself, "I could have been dead by now from having even less physical activity." As difficult as it has been to move, to accomplish, the challenge is better than if it had all been impossible. But that's kind of abstract when I'm reaching for furniture and walls in order to walk to the kitchen in the morning. So I have to consciously move my thoughts toward whatever good there is, whatever I can love. A good laugh with a girlfriend. A cup of strong black Assam tea with a little milk and sugar. Popcorn. My affectionate cats. An engaging novel. A banner crop of roses. Being in a warm pool. Richard remembering that I'd like him to do some task (without being asked), or sharing some humor with me, and especially his tenderness.

Life turned out. I married a life partner, despite those who thought it was a long shot, or that I might not be equal and worthy. I have at least two dozen close friends, a few close relatives, and a couple hundred other friends with whom I have loving relationships. I have a beautiful home, set up to be accessible. I've written a book. I've worked really hard to have all of this, and much of it has been a joy. I still have probably twenty or more years left. Though everything physical is getting harder to do, and every step has been a challenge, I am still bound to have some fun.

I have not shied away from much of anything in my life, though I probably should have concentrated my efforts and not spread myself so thin. I could have had more perseverance about finding work in a creative field. I remember thinking in my twenties that I wanted to do everything, see everything, and go everywhere I could, have as many life experiences as I could find. Yet I wound up being an accountant, having started out determined to be an artist. However, I loved my clients, and along with Sufism, singing in many groups, and other artistic expressions, my social and spiritual sides were fed.

I was able to do a lot of volunteering for the Sufi and other organizations, attend many classes, and do self-study in a wide variety of subjects: art and accounting in college, spiritual studies, self-growth seminars, songwriting, poetry, more painting and drawing, genealogy, psychology, taxes, and more. My varied interests were also served by not having children, though there are days when I feel a little sad about this. I have traveled a great deal—not nearly as much as I would have liked, but I think sixteen countries and twenty-four US states is pretty good.

One could say that polio has not kept me back. But it did. I really would have liked to do a lot of mountain hiking, or to have languidly wandered for hours through gardens, art galleries, museums, and quaint little shopping streets with intriguing cafés. At this time in my life, walking for more than half a short block requires that I stop and rest due to my leg's weakness.

We have taken my new TravelScoot portable trike to Scotland, Ireland, England, Tennessee, Colorado, and Hawaii, and with it I felt liberated in the world of travel. It traversed flat cobblestones quite well, and although it has its limitations—some terrain is impossible—it's so lightweight that Richard can pick it up and roll it on the front wheel or even carry it up stairs for me. The trike allowed us to do far more together than we've ever experienced. We went on long "walks" through big gardens, museums, and castles where he did not have to push me in a borrowed wheelchair; I'd just hop off whenever I wanted to and have a look around. It saved me a huge amount of energy, and we enjoyed each other's company so much in our new mode. You may even see me soon at a mall, the kind of place to which I rarely ventured in the last decade. (Actually, you'll more likely see me on some paved pathway at a lagoon or park, but you get the point: I'm determined to have it work, despite the obstacles.)

I love my life. And I love my husband, who has become,

over time, my best friend. We have learned so much together. I accept (most of) his foibles and (I hope) he turns off his listening when I swear after tripping or dropping something. He has a great sense of humor. He's affectionate, smart, works hard, and is helpful around the house (except in the garden; he's forgiven for that).

Since children were not in the cards, I have loved having pets, who have been there for me through thick and thin. Now we have Leila and Lucy, two tortoiseshell cat sisters, one black and one grey, who are sweet and amusing. Evenings find us all gathered around the plasma TV, maybe with a fire and popcorn, Leila behind me on the back of the couch, Richard working and intermittently asking me what's just happened in the movie we're watching, Lucy actually watching with us (she loves *Ratatouille* and *Wall-E*), and me often falling asleep three-quarters through the film.

Our home is a haven for me, and it's been that for others as well. Assuming we never have to sell it, I will not have to move or change anything if I do end up using a wheelchair at home. We also have room for a live-in caregiver if we need one. We've tried to make the place lovely and welcoming, if a little full of the clutter that's sneaked in and settled into a few of the rooms.

We have a hard time finding places we want to go to when we need or want to get away because our home is so idyllic for us: warm pool, nice garden, great bed, kitties, almost no stairs, nice neighbors, liberal county with great scenery, and San Francisco culture nearby.

The pool is my lifesaver in many ways. I am fortunate that we were able to install it. I should be able to use it for years, given the ramp we put in. Someone could even wheel me in there later on if necessary, though I hope I will always be able to get in by myself. (My older polio friends are an inspiration to me; most who are in their eighties or nineties are using walkers, but they still manage to at least do chair yoga and keep their weight at healthy levels. So, fingers crossed.) It is so rejuvenating to walk in the pool with the water supporting me, rock and roll on our outdoor radio, and look out at the hills a few blocks away. I enjoy sighting the occasional red-tailed hawk as the crows chase her from their nests in our few local redwoods, and watching the clouds breezing in from the Pacific. The pool has reduced my back pain, helped me keep my weight down, and kept me flexible and my lungs (and probably everything else) strong. I get a lot of thinking and problem-solving done out there. I also manage to empty my mind and enjoy what my body *can* do: the power of the butterfly stroke, and the ease of lying on my back doing a frog stroke and viewing our jacaranda, sycamore, and oak trees through the seasons' changes.

I have good relationships with all my relatives, despite the anguish I went through with my mother, and despite many of my mom's siblings and children having radically different political and religious views from me. This has not destroyed our affection for each other. (The Allen side is a bit more liberal, though they are also spiritual. I have great friendships with Richard's family, too.) I have forgiven Mom and I hope that if she was disappointed in me, which I am fairly sure she was, that she forgave me too. Who knows what my dad would have thought of my somewhat unconventional choices and left-wing politics? Then again, he was kinda maverick-y, and given how much my internal makeup and genetics are like his, I like to think he would have eventually let me off the hook as well.

I am thankful for my phenomenal girlfriends—intelligent, funny, compassionate, open-minded people. Both my women's groups and individual friends have been so supportive, hearing my struggles, triumphs, and comedy for two or three decades. All the laughter, the tears, the insight, and the wisdom have made me feel so content, whole, complete, and truly known.

It is hard for me not to envy others' being able to walk for a half-mile without sitting down or leaning against a post every block. That "lazy" but hard-working leg is there every day, with every step I take, even with where and how I sit, since one of my hips is so much smaller than the other. I have to say no to things I'd like to do, and save my energy so I don't wear out what I have left, unlike others who may need to do more to keep their bodies in shape.

If I were to have a choice, I definitely would not be handicapped in my next life, nor would I have consciously wanted it in this life. If I did choose this condition in a spirit world in advance of coming here, I hope I learned whatever I needed to and can skip this type of lesson next time around, if there is another time around.

Meanwhile, I'm glad to be here, albeit not as fully functional as I was twenty or thirty years ago, and never in my life as able as most people, at least since I was three. That's getting to be longer and longer ago, so much so that I felt I needed to write this book before I forgot what it was like to run down the sidewalk.

Looking ahead, I have a quiet excitement about pruning my roses each winter and enjoying bouquets from March through October, though that might sound boring to some. There's more travel in my future, more live music, more great books and movies, occasional relaxing swims with girlfriends, and a lot of time laughing with friends and relatives. I am facilitating and creating beauty, and I take my small pleasures in life as they come. I am often filled with wonder and gratitude.

I'm looking forward to doing as much as I can for as long as I can without doing myself any damage.

And that's a good plan for anyone.

Richard and I on a recent wedding anniversary.

AFTERWORD

—

parting shots: about vaccines

*S*everal people who knew I was writing this book said to me, "Are you going to talk about vaccinations?"—and I realized I really wanted to address this topic. So please put on your best studently attentiveness for just a couple of minutes. It's interesting, I promise.

A disease like poliomyelitis is not something that just happens and then it's over, as in maladies where you get better and then life is about the same as it was before.

There are, of course, a number of other diseases that also leave people with diminished function. They may be just as dramatic, or they may be more subtle, leaving the patient with, for instance, lifetime diminished breathing capacity, which means they'll have to limit their activities and possibly be on a ventilator (like many polio survivors) later in life.

There are breakthroughs being made in the field of paralysis rehabilitation. Electrical signals are being used to rekindle connections between the brain and damaged nerves in spinal cord injury patients, with remarkable success in a very few experimental cases. (National Institute of Biomedical Imaging and Bioengineering and the Christopher & Dana Reeve Foundation funded the research on one program.) Stem cell research may bring other innovations. New bracing techniques are getting people who would have otherwise been doomed to wheelchairs up and walking. These miraculous improvements cannot come quickly enough, though we can all be happy they are at least on the way.

Many people who lived through the polio epidemic have since died. There are fewer and fewer of us who remember those days and the frightening specter it presented. The worry that one's child would possibly become gravely ill and subsequently be paralyzed and/or crippled for life, or even die before they passed third grade, is something most Western people no longer have to face, thanks to vaccines. But there are purportedly around 500,000 to one million polio survivors in the United States, and millions more worldwide. (This is the second-largest disabled group in the US, with stroke survivors being the most prolific of those of us who qualify as "disabled.") In terms of the entire world population, this is not a huge figure, but there was a time when nearly 1 percent of everyone in the United States had had polio, and if you lived in a large population center, it could be five or ten times that many (though not all with paralysis). Imagine if one in every ten to twenty people you knew had polio! In the short time frame between 1940 and 1952, more than 420,000 Americans were crippled by it, and many millions more contracted the virus. Most of them were children. 1952 was the worst year, with 58,000 diagnosed cases in the US. These are not just statistics; they are real people whose lives were damaged by this disease.

Whooping cough, polio, smallpox, measles, mumps, chicken pox—all of these are "childhood" diseases, and most of them are life-threatening. When I was little, parents went out of their way to expose their kids to chicken pox and "get it over with." Now we know that if you've had chicken pox, you have a 30 to 40 percent chance of getting shingles as an adult. From my experience, you don't want that, and no one wants their six-year-old to face that condition forty to sixty years from now.

Those are not low percentages. (The lifetime risk for breast cancer is 8 percent.) Shingles is maddeningly painful, and although some people find it just "uncomfortable," it is often described as nearly intolerable. A woman friend likened it to childbirth, except childbirth does not go on every night for weeks. A man I know said he lay in bed whimpering and wishing he were dead when he had the malady all down his leg. A friend of mine whose dad had it refers to shingles as "ghastly."

Mumps is another now-preventable disease that is dangerous for young men to contract, causing potential damage to the testicles. It can also lead to deafness and brain inflammation in anyone. This disease is at a ten-year high, with outbreaks in forty-six states in the US, having jumped from 226 cases in 2012 to more than 4,000 in 2016, with more than two hundred people diagnosed in Texas alone in the first four months of 2017. It is thought that this is only partly because of the anti-vaxxer movement; immunity to the disease seems to be fading, so it is possible that a third dose of the MMR (measles, mumps, and rubella) vaccine may now be necessary rather than just the two lifetime doses medicine has prescribed up to this point.

In Germany, the 2014–2015 emerging measles epidemic, with roughly thirty Berliners a day contracting the disease during some months, stoked a fire under those who have been hesitant to call for mandatory vaccinations. Now, journalists and parents there have started pushing for compulsory vaccinations. Measles, too, can cause brain and lung damage, and has seen a serious resurgence in the US, even though it was only eliminated as a threat here in 2000, quite recently. The first recent subsequent death from the disease occurred in Washington State in mid-2015. The patient had a compromised immune system, but infectious-disease specialists point to the movement among parents to abstain from vaccinating their children as the culprit in breaking down established "herd immunity," which is what is being blamed in Europe as well.

In 2016, there was a measles outbreak in Romania and Italy. As of this writing, the virus is now spreading across Europe. Diminutive Romania had 3,400 cases in fifteen months, resulting in seventeen deaths. This is partly due to scarcity of vaccines and cumbersome administration. In France, three medical appointments are necessary before inoculation actually happens.

There's no value in contracting any of these diseases. They are not like the common cold and exposure to minor bacteria, which help boost a young child's immune system.

All that stuff about vaccines causing autism is bunk. It's been disproved. The *one* study that claimed in 1998 that MMR vaccines cause autism was proven fraudulent; the author's medical license was even revoked. When researchers examined the eleven-year medical records of 96,000 children, the causes of autism were found to be either genetic or unidentified environmental factors. One portion of that study indicates that mothers who ran a fever in the first or second trimester of pregnancy had a 34 to 40 percent increase in incidence of autism. It seems a fever may cause inflammatory chemicals to cross the placenta. Pre-natal care, as ever, is the focus for fetal health.

There was that *one* batch of US polio vaccine in the early 1950s that was not stored correctly (at Cutter Laboratories) and contained live virus that was not the prescribed weakened, highly effective vaccine. A couple of hundred people were infected by that vaccine, but in all my reading about polio in the last fifteen years—far more than the average American—I have read of only one elderly man who got polio from that bad batch of polio vaccine. I have met hundreds of polio survivors in the last five years, and of those, only three have said they contracted the virus from live vaccine. One of them believes he may have contracted the virus after a live polio virus inoculation in the US in the 1950s, perhaps the Cutter batch, although it is also possible he was exposed to polio before he was vaccinated or was given the live oral vaccine. The other two people were from India and said they got polio from live oral vaccine, which had still been in use there when they were vaccinated.

In 2012, 144 countries still were administering the weakened live polio virus orally. This was discontinued before 2002 in the US; here, only killed, inoculated virus is used. As of 2017, the only remaining countries using live virus vaccines are Nigeria and Pakistan. (Live oral vaccine has historically been used primarily in impoverished countries, where syringes are not always available because they are expensive to obtain and require more training to administer.) The infection rate from oral vaccine (one child in one million) in these populations is much lower than the overall infection rate experienced from non-vaccination (in countries where less than 95 percent of people have been vaccinated).

Whooping cough has reached near-epidemic proportions in some parts of the United States, including free-thinking California, because many parents have made the independent decision that their kids don't need to be vaccinated and are more at risk if they are. This just is not true. If 95 percent of a population is vaccinated against a disease, that population rarely sees a case of that disease—so rarely that the disease is considered eradicated in that population. If the vaccination percentage is less than that, outbreaks are unpreventable. This happens with measles and is currently a problem with an enterovirus that has reared its ugly head in California, causing paralysis similar to polio symptoms. There is no vaccine for this virus yet.

I had whooping cough when I was thirty-five and was afraid I might die. I'd had the vaccination for it as a child, but it requires boosters, which I had not known. I had to sleep sitting up and there were long periods of at least thirty seconds when I could not get a breath in or out. Fortunately, my yoga and Sufi practices had trained me to relax in order to breathe deeply, and this helped me have faith that my breath would come. I had the thought that if I were a small child, I would have panicked—which, of course, would have made it even more difficult to resume breathing. Small children can die from this disease, and suffocation is an awful way to go.

Many people will never get one of these highly communicable diseases even if they don't get vaccinated, especially since most people in Western countries have been vaccinated. But if they do get sick or carry a microbe, even without symptoms, they are putting hundreds of other children (and adults) at risk—especially since people may not know they are contagious until days after they contract a virus, if ever.

With the help of the Bill and Melinda Gates Foundation and Rotary International, India was brought to the magic 95 percent vaccination rate in 2012. Bill Gates said in 2012 that he hopes polio will be eradicated worldwide by 2018, and that this will be a better economic deal for the world than continuing to treat the disease, which cost about $2 billion yearly in 2012—money that, by necessity, mostly comes from Western countries where the virus has already been defeated. In interviews, Melinda Gates has described vaccines as the most exciting of all health technology breakthroughs. She speaks of women she's met in the developing world who have walked ten kilometers in the heat to stand in line to get their children inoculated for various preventable diseases. They have told her that they know that a vaccine often means the difference between life and death for their children.

Polio was nearly eradicated. After 2011, when the last new case was reported in India, polio moved from Pakistan to Syria, where Pakistanis went to fight either against the Syrian rebels or Assad's regime. News bulletins from the World Health Organization (WHO) in May 2014 said that new cases had also been reported in Cameroon, Ethiopia, Somalia, Iraq, Equatorial New Guinea—and Israel. You will note that Israel is not a "third world" country; it's a Western nation in the Middle East. So, for a year we were back to nine countries (including Nigeria) where polio was not eradicated. The eradication victory is still tenuous when non-vaccinated people who have been in infected countries travel. The last countries where new cases have been identified in recent years were Nigeria in 2016, and Afghanistan, Pakistan, and Syria in 2017.

If you have ever known anyone who traveled to any of these countries (I've been to two of them myself), you may have been exposed to the polio virus, but your vaccinations have protected you from infection. Many disease carriers have no symptoms, and most people who come down with active polio illness do not experience paralysis (though they may have early fatigue and weakness as they age). But why take a chance? This world has become small in terms of moving populations, with air travel today nearly as common as bus travel was in the 1950s and 60s. All it would take for polio to make a comeback in the US is for a number of exposed or infected visitors or unvaccinated US tourists coming from these countries to enter the US— and if this were to happen, the most likely targets of infection would be children. (Because polio tends to attack primarily the youngest children, a frequent synonym for poliomyelitis is infantile paralysis.) That's how an epidemic starts.

The WHO declared India polio-free in March 2014. Many young people there are already suffering from the late effects of polio, however. They do not have the extensive access to bracing and therapy that we have had in the US, though government funding has been increasingly addressing this issue. In Pakistan, the vaccination program was damaged, according to *The New*

York Times and *The Nation*, by our CIA colluding with a Pakistani hepatitis vaccination doctor to obtain DNA information that led to the location and assassination of Osama bin Laden in 2011. When this happened, it was easy for the Taliban to start a rumor that this vaccination program was a method of sterilizing Muslim girls. As a result of that misconception, vaccine workers began being murdered, both in Pakistan and Nigeria. In 2014, Pakistan had fifty-nine cases of polio by mid-year, compared to only six cases in all of 2013. In January 2016, a suicide attack in southwestern Pakistan killed more than a dozen policemen gathered to escort health workers to and from a polio vaccination center, and wounded at least twenty-three civilians. I'm not sorry to see bin Laden gone, but it's really unfortunate that this violence was a byproduct of the CIA's methods.

Though we might not experience an epidemic, I am not *laissez-faire* about exposing anyone to the poliomyelitis microbe or any other deadly, paralytic, or disfiguring bug. You may be relieved to know that Pakistan, Cameroon, and Syria have been ordered by the World Health Organization (as of May 2014) to vaccinate all travelers leaving those countries (assuming they have control over this, given the massive numbers of refugees fleeing Syria). The spread of Ebola to Dallas, Texas, and New York City from Liberia was a surprise in 2014. Hopefully there will soon be a vaccine for that.

My opinion, and that of most well-informed medical people, is that it is foolish not to vaccinate children. It is socially irresponsible to expose kids and their families to diseases that are still all too common.

If my story is not enough to convince your loved ones of the danger of these viruses, please at least have them watch the short PBS film made by Nobel Prize Media, Ed Gray Films, and Kikim Media, "The War Against Microbes," which you can view at www.nobelprize.org. You'll also get to meet me there briefly (though a friend says I look ten years younger in person). But the real reasons to watch it are to get a quick education in the insidiousness of viruses and bacteria, the value of vaccines, how much life has improved for millions of people because of vaccinations, and, lastly, the new protein microbes recently found to be infecting football players and others with repeated concussions. (Research on this new area is taking place at University of California San Francisco Medical Center.)

Here's some unsolicited, unabashed advice: get your shots (or whatever form they are currently using), and most especially, encourage your children and grandchildren to be inoculated against anything that has a vaccine. They can always spread the shots out; I agree that sometimes it seems that too many of them are given at one time to infants, although recent research indicates multiple vaccinations are not harmful. Give this book to your children or grandchildren if they do not "believe" in vaccinations. Ask them if, after reading at least the chapters on my physical difficulties, they think that the nearly nonexistent risk of vaccine side effects is a good bet against the proven risks to their kids (who can't read up on this issue and make their own decisions) for these childhood diseases.

In 2015, an Ottawa, Canada, mom left the anti-vaxxer movement after all seven of her children contracted whooping cough. Her comments, as published, were, "Right now my family is living with the consequences of misinformation and fear. But we can learn from this."

Resources for Readers

My website and blog: www.FrancineFalk-Allen.com
Facebook: @FrancineFalk-Allen, Author

Polio and Other Disability Organizations

There are many polio organizations all over the United States and in other countries. PHI is the most extensive and has lists of all polio organizations worldwide; PSA is in California (where I live); and PSNUK is another English-speaking organization, representing Europe, so I chose to stop with these three:

- Post-Polio Health International (PHI), www.post-polio.org. This is *the* polio organization. They have a great website, including many articles written by polio survivors and polio doctors. There are stories about our polio experiences, great suggestions, articles on drugs, and many links to post-polio support groups, polio doctors, organizations nearest to you, and much more. They have a quarterly newsletter to which you can subscribe. 4207 Lindell Blvd., #110, St. Louis, MO 63108-2930, info@post-polio.org.

- Polio Survivors Association, http://polioassociation.org. 12720 La Reina Avenue, Downey, CA 90242, info@polioassociation.org.

- Polio Survivors Network of the United Kingdom, http://poliosurvivorsnetwork.org.uk. A good European site. Good suggestions for how to communicate with doctors so they understand that your current issues could be related to previously contracting polio and are not just "normal" symptoms of aging.

Abilities.com is an organization that holds multiple Abilities Expos—large indoor fairs where a variety of innovations (bracing, auto adaptations, scooters) can be seen and investigated—each year. They are held in at least the following cities, if not more: San Jose, Los Angeles, New York, Houston. Information about these expos and myriad other resources can be found at www.abilities.com.

About Disability, www.aboutdisability.com, is an organization started by Anthony Tusler, a lifelong disability advocate (and vibrant disabled person). A wealth of info is to be found here.

American Physical Therapy Association, www.apta.org, is an online directory that can help you find a physical therapist (association member) near you. They also have a consumer website, www.moveforwardpt.com. (Recommended by Cleveland Clinic's *Arthritis Advisor* newsletter.)

Books on Post-Polio Management

Handbook on the Late Effects of Poliomyelitis for Physicians and Survivors, edited by Frederick Maynard, MD, and Joan Headley, MS. Essential reading on polio effects.

Managing Post-Polio, by Lauro Halstead, MD. This is the authoritative book on post-polio, with explanations regarding what is happening to the polio patient thirty years or more after the initial onset, and how to make your life easier.

More Polio-Related Reading (plus a video)

My article "Conquering Mysterious Foot Pain," published in the PHI newsletter, can be found at: http://www.post-polio.org /edu/pphnews/PPH28-fall12p.1-5.pdf. It delineates the odyssey

I went through discovering that I had acute tendinitis and tenosynovitis in my strong foot, and how I eventually healed this condition. There are also links within the article to the exercises I learned that were essential to my healing. The link may say the article is in Japanese (the Japanese polio community was especially interested in the article), but it's not!

My article "The Wild Handicapper in Yosemite" (*Ability Magazine*, Feb/Mar 2016), can be found at: www.abilitymagazine. com/Ray-Romano/Yosemite.html. It is also mentioned in Post-Polio Health International Polio Place: www.polioplace.org /history/artifacts/accessible-yosemite

The War on Microbes, PBS/Nobel Media. This is a half-hour film on the eradication of diseases through immunizations, in which I appear as the polio representative, and also the only person in the film who talks about what it was like to have a communicable disease that has since been nearly eradicated through the use of vaccines. You can view it at: http://www.nobelprize.org /mediaplayer/index.php?id=1824.

"Sixtieth Anniversary for Polio Pioneers," by Karie Youngdahl, shares stories from people who participated in Jonas Salk's 1954 blinded polio vaccine trial. It can be found at: https://www. historyofvaccines.org/content/blog/sixtieth-anniversary-polio-pioneers.

"When Meeting Friends with Disabilities," thirteen general rules from Easter Seals on how to treat friends with disabilities: http:// es.easterseals.com/site/PageServer?pagename=ntl_friends_hint.

Pain-Free Living, a magazine with useful, researched articles and tips. www.painfreelivinglife.com

Helpful Technologies

Dynamic Bracing Solutions, www.DynamicBracingSolutions. net. Contact for an orthotist near you. Not for everyone, but those with less-severe polio effects may find very helpful. BracingSolutions@aol.com.

Human Gait Institute, www.humangaitinstitute.org. Training orthotists, research of orthoses for musculoskeletal deficits, some financial support for newer orthotic technology for those who need it. Closely connected with Dynamic Bracing. 9461 W. 37th Place, Wheat Ridge, CO 80031-5438, (303) 829-1538.

Lofstrand crutches: The best brand of these arm cuff crutches I know of is WalkEasy, based in Florida. They ship all over; the crutches are made in Germany and France, depending on size, so they are available in Europe as well, though probably under a different name. They come in lots of different colors, too! www.walkeasy.com, (800) 441-2904.

TravelScoot, www.travelscoot.com. These scooters are made in Germany. I love mine: it's lightweight, comes apart, and the heaviest part weighs only about twenty pounds. No lift is necessary for putting it into a trunk or the back of a car. You do not take it apart for plane travel; you just remove the lithium battery and take that into the cabin, and the scooter is taken to the hold, just like a baby stroller. It is not recommended for people who have severe mental difficulty or poor balance, since it is tricky on hills with slanted paths. (800) 342-2214 in the USA; website directs you to foreign availability.

Pride Go-Go scooters (www.pridemobility.com) are also an option, though these require either a van with a lift or a strong individual to lift the parts, the heaviest of which on the small model is about thirty-five pounds. These and heavier models are fine to rent, and may better serve on rougher grassy or graveled terrain.

Disabled or Handicapped Sports

Disabled Sports USA, www.disabledsportsusa.org. Snow and water sports for people with handicaps, including mental handicaps.

National Ability Center, www.discovernac.org. Programs for the differently abled in many sports.

Achieve Tahoe Adaptive Sports Center, https://achievetahoe.org, founding chapter of Disabled Sports USA, Alpine Meadows, Northstar, and Squaw Valley, South Lake Tahoe, CA. Snow and water ski instruction for ability-challenged.

Handicapped Travel

The Rough Guide (published New York, London, and Delhi) and *Lonely Planet* (published in Oakland, London, and Melbourne) are my overall favorite travel guides for just about any destination. While these are not specifically written for handicapped travel, they often describe the difficulty of a particular walk and, importantly, exactly how long it is, as well as whether there is an elevator where you want to go. They also sometimes indicate wheelchair accessibility. I have also used the AAA guides (Automobile Association of America). I use the Trip Advisor website frequently to search hotels, though once I find lodging that seems well located, has a pool, and doesn't require me to use stairs, I call to see if there is accessibility for the pool, the front door, and whatever else I need in order to be comfortable there. Trip Advisor reviews tend to be reliable and I have reviewed about one hundred hotels myself on that site. Rarely does anyone address handicapped issues, so I always note whether there are accessibility problems (even if I can manage, but a wheelchair user would have difficulty).

Accessible Cruise Planners—worldwide destinations. 800 801-9002. My info says, "ask for Steve."

Accessible Journeys, www.disabilitytravel.com, is dedicated to travel for people in wheelchairs and their companions.

Access Tours, www.accesstours.org, offers accessible package tours of National Parks and other areas in the western states. (800) 929-4811.

Angloinfo "People with Disabilities" page, www.angloinfo.com /how-to/france/healthcare/people-with-disabilities. Disability info for English-speaking travelers in Paris, France.

MyHandicap, www.myhandicap.com. A European site; not a lot of info, but a start.

National Park Service "Accessibility" page, www.nps.gov/ accessibility.htm. Here you can download the National Park Service's access guide for visitors and potential employees. I download this guide when I go to Yosemite to update myself on their latest wooden and paved pathways and options.

No Limits Foundation, www.nolimitsfoundation.org, provides a camping experience to children who have lost a limb. They also partner with Yosemite National Park to bring wheelchair access there.

Travelconsumer.com "Traveling with Disabilities" page, www. travelconsumer.com/disability.htm. Lots and lots of info! It even lists cruises that have dialysis available.

VacationsToGo "Travelers with Special Needs" page, www. vacationstogo.com/special_needs_cruises.cfm. Information about the special-needs facilities, amenities and services provided by a number of cruise companies.

Yosemite Conservancy "No Limits: Yosemite Adventures for Wheelchair Users—2017" page, www.yosemiteconservancy.org/ visitor-services/no-limits-yosemite-adventures-wheelchair-user s-2017. A program partnering with the No Limits Foundation to provide greater access to a wider range of Yosemite National Park for adult and youth wheelchair users, with adaptive outdoor recreation assistants.

Buying Mis-Mated Shoes

National Odd Shoe Exchange, www.oddshoe.org, accepts new mis-mated shoes as charitable donations and also matches people with mis-mated shoes, though I have not been successful in determining how to trade shoes in the last several decades. I just donate my mis-mates and take a tax deduction.

Nordstrom, www.nordstrom.com. You buy the two different-sized pairs and then ship back the mis-mates (with an explanatory letter and request for refund), and they give you a credit card refund for the price of the less expensive pair.

Zappos, www.zappos.com. They do not split pairs, but this is the easiest way I have found of buying shoes: just buy two pairs and donate the leftovers. They also provide free shipping coming and going.

Bibliography

Bernstein, Lenny. "Fever during pregnancy may increase autism risk in offspring." *The Washington Post*, June 13, 2017.

Bhandari, Neena. "India Needs to Focus on Its Polio Survivors." *Post-Polio Health* 31, no. 2 (2015).

Bishop, Jack. *Vegetables Every Day*. New York: HarperCollins, 2001.

Bogardus, Meghan. "You've Seen Them Care, Now Show You Care About Them." *AARP The Magazine*, October/November 2015.

Brookes, Linda, MSc. "Spotting the vaccine-preventable diseases that are in the back waiting room." *Medical News Today*, April 17, 2017. https://www.medicalnewstoday.com/articles/316824.php.

Cooper, Chet, and Lia Martirosyan. "Zach Anner." *Ability Magazine*, April/May 2016.

Coy, Lowe, et al., *Coping with Disaster: Voices from the 1955 Flood, Sutter County, California.* Community Memorial Museum of Sutter County, 1995.

Crocker, Ann. "What to Eat: Revisiting the Basics." *Post-Polio Health* 32, no. 2 (2016).

Daggett, Richard. "Polio Facts." *Sacramento Post-Polio Support Group Newsletter*, April 2009.

Debley, Tom. "Kaiser Permanente's Historical Role in Rehabilitation Medicine." Kaiser Foundation Health Plan, 2009.

Donahue, Deirdre. "A Conversation with Melinda Gates." *AARP Bulletin*, March 2015.

Doucleff, Michaeleen. "Why Bill Gates Thinks Ending Polio Is Worth It." *Post-Polio Health International Newsletter*, May 2013.

The Economist. "Democracy in America." October 29, 2009.

The Economist. "Pariah State—Polio in Pakistan." May 10, 2014. https://www.economist.com/news/asia/21601903-huge-vaccination-drive-taliban-still-hampers-eradication-efforts-pariah-state.

Goodacre, Mark, and Richard Neave. "Son of God." British Broadcasting Corporation, 2001.

Haiken, Melanie. "A New Leaf." *Marin Magazine*, April 2017.

Halstead, Lauro, MD. *Managing Post-Polio: A Guide to Living Well with Post-Polio Syndrome.* Arlington: ABI Professional Publications, 1998. Revised 2005.

Harvard Medical School. *Core Exercises.* Boston: Harvard Health Publications, 2013.

Harvard Women's Health Watch. "Treating pain with your brain." September 2016. https://www.health.harvard.edu/mind-and-mood/treating-pain-with-your-brain.

Hicks, Jesse. "The CIA's Fake Vaccine Drive to Find Osama Bin Laden Lowered Vaccination Rates in Pakistan." *Tonic*, September 15, 2017.

Holmes, Oliver. "One million people wounded, diseases spreading in Syria: WHO." *Reuters*, December 19, 2014. https://www.reuters.com/article/us-mideast-crisis-health/one-million-people-wounded-diseases-spreading-in-syria-who-idUSKBN0JX0V720141219.

Huckert, Greg. "Integral Orthotics and Prosthetics," talk given at Sacramento Post-Polio Support Group, May 3, 2014 (published as notes in their newsletter, September, 2014).

Hucklenbroich, Christina. "How to stop our measles outbreak." *The Week*, March 13, 2015.

Junger, Sebastian. "The Bonds of Battle—The Never-Ending War." *Vanity Fair,* June 2015.

Kabat, Herman, MD, and Miland E. Knapp, MD. "The Use of Prostigmine in the Treatment of Poliomyelitis." *Journal of the American Medical Association*, August 7, 1943.

Khan, Inayat. "Stages on the Path of Self-realization." *The Alchemy of Happiness—The Sufi Message*. United Kingdom: Sufi Order Publications, 1962.

King, Bryan H. "Promising Forecast for Autism Spectrum Disorders." *JAMA*, April 21, 2015. https://jamanetwork.com/journals/jama/fullarticle/2275426.

Li, Ying. *Mu Mengjie—The Power of a Teacher's Love*. Huntington Beach, CA: *Ability Magazine*, 2015.

Linden, David. "Fingertips To Hair Follicles: Why 'Touch' Triggers Pleasure And Pain." *Fresh Air*, February 3, 2015.

Lupkin, Sydney. "Measles Death Points to Need for Herd Immunity." *MedPage Today*, July 25, 2015. https://www.medpagetoday.com/infectiousdisease/generalinfectiousdisease/52473.

Machell, Stephanie T., PsyD. "Promoting Positive Solutions." *Post-Polio Health* (32), no. 2 (2016).

Maron, Dina Fine. "What's Behind the Mumps Spike in the U.S.?" *Scientific American*, December 16, 2016. https://www.scientificamerican.com/article/whats-behind-the-2016-mumps-spike-in-the-u-s.

Maynard, Frederick, MD, and Joan Headley, MS. *Handbook on the Late Effects of Poliomyelitis for Physicians and Survivors*. St. Louis: Gazette International Networking Institute, 1999.

McNeil Jr., Donald G. "Polio's Return After Near Eradication Prompts a Global Health Warning." *The New York Times*, May 5, 2014. https://www.nytimes.com/2014/05/06/health/world-health-organization-polio-health-emergency.html?_r=0.

Mitchell, Paulette. *The 15-Minute Gourmet: Chicken.* Foster City, CA: IDG Books Worldwide, Inc., 1999.

Oshinsky, David M. *Polio: An American Story.* New York: Oxford University Press, 2005.

Parker, Amy. "Growing Up Unvaccinated." *Slate*, January 6, 2014. http://www.slate.com/articles/life/family/2014/01/growing_up_unvaccinated_a_healthy_lifestyle_couldn_t_prevent_many_childhood.html.

Presley, Gary. "You Can't Always Blame Other People." *Gary Presley.* May 29, 2013. http://www.garypresley.com/2013/05.

Roth, Philip. *Nemesis.* New York: Houghton Mifflin Harcourt, 2010.

Sattar, Abdul. "Suicide Attack on Pakistan Polio Vaccination Center Kills 15." Associated Press, January 13, 2016. https://apnews.com/41793b4af3db46dfac083f624dbb2d9c

Schmitt, Rick. "The Stranger in Your Home." *AARP Bulletin*, March, 2015.

Scrase, Richard. "Sixty years of the polio 'miracle' vaccine." *Understanding Animal Research*, April 13, 2015. http://www.understandinganimalresearch.org.uk/news/video-of-the-week/sixty-years-of-the-polio-miracle-vaccine.

Schroeder, Stephen M., DPM. "Triple Arthrodesis." *Medscape*, August 16, 2011. https://emedicine.medscape.com/article/1234042-overview.

Sedaker, Cheryl. *365 Ways to Cook Chicken.* New York: Harper & Row, 1986.

Seltzer, Beverly. *The Lady and the Lingcod.* Canada: Trafford Publishing, 2003.

Shapiro, Joseph P. *No Pity: People with Disabilities Forging a New Civil Rights Movement.* New York: Random House, 1993.

Shreve, Susan Richards. *Warm Springs: Traces of a Childhood at FDR's Polio Haven.* New York: Mariner Books, 2007.

The Week. "Bionic breakthrough." March 13, 2015. http://theweek.com/print/710/32676.

The Week. "Boring but important—The globe goes gray." April 8, 2016. https://archive.org/stream/The_Week_April_8_2016_USA /The_Week_April_8_2016_USA_djvu.txt.

The Week. "Good week/bad week." April 16, 2015. http://theweek.com/login?issueId=716&printArticleId=33663.

The Week. "The future of artificial limbs." March 22, 2014. http://theweek.com/articles/448972/future-artificial-limbs.

The Week. "Why we are as backward as Nigeria." May 15, 2014. http://theweek.com/login?issueId=669&printArticleId=25082.

Thompson, Dennis. "The Salk Polio Vaccine: A Medical Miracle Turns 60." *HealthDay*, December 1, 2014. https://consumer. healthday.com/infectious-disease-information-21/misc-infections-news-411/the-salk-polio-vaccine-a-medical-miracle-turns-60-6 91863.html.

Verville, Richard. *War, Politics, and Philanthropy: The History of Rehabilitation Medicine.* Lanham, MD: University Press of America, 2009.

Wilson, Daniel J. *Polio (Biographies of Disease).* Santa Barbara, CA: Greenwood Press, 2009.

Winters, Catherine. "When Words Hurt." *Arthritis Today*, March/April, 2016.

Weisberg, Joseph, PT, PhD, and Heidi Shink. *Three Minutes to a Pain-Free Life*. New York: Atria Books, 2005.

World Health Organization. "Measles continues to spread and take lives in Europe." Press release, July 11, 2017. http://www.euro.who.int/en/media-centre/sections/press-releases/2017/measles-continues-to-spread-and-take-lives-in-europe.

Acknowledgments

Thank you to everyone who has hung in with me during this project, listening to both my perhaps self-absorbed excitement and my occasional discouragement. But in particular, thank you to my writing group, Just Write Marin County, and within that group, especially Aline O'Brien, Lori Samuels Amada, Maryan Karwan, Johanna Kee, Steve Shoen, and Sandy Handsher, who have either read parts of the book or listened to me read, and most importantly, provided unlimited encouragement and camaraderie. Thanks of the bow-down-and-grovel type to Gillian Glover, Shirley Klock, David Wagner, Sharon Skolnick-Bagnoli, and Steve Bratman, who read *entire*, early, partly-crummy, mind-dump drafts and gave me valuable feedback on potential refinements. Thanks to Leslie Davenport (also for your feedback), Katherine Falk, Nancy Falk, Farida Fox (who knew the brand was "Taylor Tot," not "Trailer Tot"), Tom Paratore, Alan Rinzler, David Roche, and anyone else I've neglected to include who also read beta versions, even partially. Special thanks to Ed Gray, Susan Richards Shreve (whose memoir inspired me to write mine), Brian Tiburzi, and Anthony Tusler for reading the whole nearly-final draft and "getting" the book, and for your feedback. Thanks to Brooke Warner, Lauren Wise, Julie Metz (who expertly made the cover I imagined better than I dreamed it would be), and the staff at She Writes Press for believing in this book. Deep appreciation to Krissa Lagos, my kind and intelligent editor, who listened to my revision anguish through email and knew which rambling side trips to cut and what needed magnifying; and thanks to Chris Dumas for his eagle proofreading eye. Kudos to Maggie Ruf of SparkPoint Studio, who apparently did a mind/heart meld with me to create my website; I stand amazed. Thanks to Dave Eggers for your generous encouragement and advice. Thanks to Daralyn Hansen for nearly seventy years (and counting) of friendship. Thanks to Krysten Elbers for your surprise contribution and for always knowing what is important to me. Thanks to Mom for not giving up on my little leg and loving me as best you could. (Next lifetime, if there is one, more fun, OK?) And a constant thanks to Richard Falk, who supports me in all ways and without whom I would not have had the time or financial wherewithal to write and publish a book.

About the Author

Photo credit: Patty Spinks

FRANCINE FALK-ALLEN was born in Los Angeles and has lived nearly all of her life in northern California. As a former art major who got a BA in managerial accounting and ran her own business for thirty-three years, she has always craved creative outlets. Over the years, this has taken the form of singing and recording with various groups, painting, and writing songs, poetry, and essays, some of which have been published. Falk-Allen facilitates a support group, Polio Survivors of Marin County, and also a Meetup writing group, Just Write Marin County. She was the polio representative interviewed in a PBS/Nobel Prize Media film, *The War Against Microbes.*